Israel & the Arabs:
PRELUDE TO
THE JEWISH STATE

Israel & the Arabs:
PRELUDE TO
THE JEWISH STATE

Edited by Anne Sinai and I. Robert Sinai

FACTS ON FILE, INC.   NEW YORK

Israel & the Arabs:
PRELUDE TO
THE JEWISH STATE

Library of Congress Catalog Card No. 78-161364

ISBN 0-87196-169-5

9 8 7 6 5 4 3 2 1

PRINTED IN THE UNITED STATES OF AMERICA

CONTENTS

N 106

i

INTRODUCTION

THE STATE OF ISRAEL AROSE OUT OF a conflict between 2 peoples occupying the same general territory and unable to settle their differences within it. The UN decision to partition Palestine in 1948 was intended to pave the way for a sovereign Palestinian Arab state in that territory alongside the sovereign state of Israel. The proposed new Arab state never came into existence, because of the historical events that preceded Israel's War of Independence and out of which the state of Israel arose.

The 2 peoples—Arab and Jewish—began their political struggle in the area of Palestine after the Balfour Declaration of 1917. It was a struggle between 2 rights; it found expression in the 2 movements of Zionism and Arab nationalism, both of which movements antedated that struggle.

The existence of a substantial and active Jewish community in Palestine grew out of the Zionist movement, which developed a program for settling Jews in that area of the Middle East. This movement began near the end of the 19th century, when a new wave of nationalism in Europe gave rise to the creation of most of the modern independent nations. Political Zionism was initiated by an Austrian Jewish journalist, Theodor Herzl, who saw an immediate need to find a haven for the Jews of tsarist Russia and Eastern Europe, who were enduring severe oppression and constant harassment. The Zionist aim was to obtain national sovereignty for a people who had been deprived of national roots for 2,000 years and had not been absorbed in any of the countries in which they had settled. Mobilizing support from the Jews in every land, the leading figures of Zionism focused on Palestine, which historically and by religion and tradition was considered the original Jewish homeland. The Jewish return to Palestine was thus triggered by necessity as well as by an ideology of national renaissance.

1

Jewish settlement in Palestine meant, in the Zionist philosophy, the normalization of national life. It was a social revolution, making Jews a landed people, changing the Jewish occupational structure, creating towns and villages, reviving the Hebrew language and starting a new national culture, history and mystique. Jewish national aspirations took many forms but mainly resulted in the establishment of economic enterprises, agricultural and religious schools, farms and settlements, cities, the Hebrew University and other similar undertakings. In all, these created an organic Jewish national strength in Palestine that in due time reinforced the Zionists' political goals.

While the Zionist ideology and its active program provided the leadership and served to mobilize the resources for the Jewish endeavor in Palestine, it was felt that the actual creation of a Jewish state in the country would not have been realizable without British approval. Great Britain gave the Jewish community of Palestine the opportunity to establish a secure base through the promise of the Balfour Declaration. This declaration was contained in an official letter dated Nov. 2, 1917 and sent by British Foreign Secy. Lord Arthur James Balfour to Lord Rothschild, a British Zionist leader.

The text of the Balfour Declaration: "His majesty's government view with favor the establishment in Palestine of a national home for the Jewish people, and will use their best endeavors to facilitate the achievement of this object, it being clearly understood that nothing shall be done which may prejudice the civil and religious rights of existing non-Jewish communities in Palestine, or the rights and political status enjoyed by Jews in any other country."

It was generally understood that the British government had issued the Balfour Declaration primarily in its own interest. The British felt that large-scale Jewish settlement in Palestine might be a stabilizing force in this area where important British interests were at stake and might contribute to the revival of the Middle East as a whole. The British also hoped to use Zionist aspirations as a buffer against French influence in the Middle East, in pursuit of the British aim of bringing the whole area under British sponsorship.

After World War I, the Balfour Declaration was approved by the chief Allied powers, including the U.S. The League of Nations July 24, 1922 gave a mandate incorporating the declaration's principles to Britain with which to govern Palestine. The mandatory power was directed to encourage the immigration and settlement of Jews on the land. The League permitting, the mandatory government made Hebrew—with Arabic and English—one of the country's 3 official languages. At the behest of the League Council, it also initiated the formal establishment in 1929 of a Jewish Agency to represent the Jewish community in Palestine, to advise and cooperate with the British mandatory administration in economic, social and other matters that might affect the establishment of the Jewish national home and to assist in the country's development.

The history of the *yishuv* (the settled Jewish community in Palestine) under the British mandate can be divided into 3   X periods. In the first period—between 1922 and 1932—there was a slow evolution of growth. The basic Jewish institutions were established and consolidated. These included communal self-government, the founding of the Jewish Agency, the *Vaad Leumi* (an elected assembly and executive, which handled domestic matters), the labor movement, the *kibbutz* (roughly, collective farm) and *moshav* (cooperative farm) as forms of agricultural settlement, the political parties, the Hebrew educational system, the Hebrew press and the establishment of self-defense organizations. Jewish immigration flowed slowly during this period. Immigration from Russia, Zionism's most lively source, was frozen by the new Soviet government. The British built roads, developed the harbor at Haifa and improved sanitation and water supplies. The Arab population also increased, as Arabs in neighboring countries were attracted by the new Jewish enterprises.

With the rise of Hitler in Germany in 1933, a great stirring of conscience mobilized the *yishuv* and Jews everywhere. The Zionist movement became the most powerful and widely recognized spokesman of the collective voice of the Jewish people. It pressed for the rescue of Jews trapped in Europe under the Nazi yoke, and Palestine became, in the 2d period of the *yishuv*'s development, the only country to which the Jews of Europe could turn with any hope since the gates of all other countries were closed to them. Palestine was the only country that, in Churchill's words, Jews could enter "by right, not on sufferance." Therefore, Jewish opinion of all political colorations flowed to the support of Zionism to keep the gates of Palestine open.

Tens of thousands of Jews, fleeing from the Nazis, began to pour into Palestine from Germany, Austria, Czechoslovakia and Central Europe. Highly skilled and qualified, large numbers passed the mandatory government's tests devised to restrict immigration in line with the economic absorptive capacity of the country. Those able to settle created further absorptive capacity for more Jews to enter the country. Thus, from 1934 to 1939, more than twice as many Jews went to Palestine as in the previous 12 years. By the outbreak of World War II, the *yishuv* numbered 500,000 people and appeared to have an over-all potential to absorb hundreds of thousands more.

The 3d decisive period—from 1940 to 1948—covered the Jewish community's development in technical efficiency and economic strength, and, beginning in 1945, the national struggle that it waged against the mandatory government for immigration. It was also the period during which the *yishuv* was able to merge all its waves of immigration into a cohesive and determined national community.

It was at this stage, also, that American concern about Palestine began to be expressed. U.S. interest in the Middle East as a whole and in Palestine in particular dates back to the late 19th century, with the advent of private missionary activity and the setting up of educational and philanthropic institutions.

A section in Pres. Woodrow Wilson's "14 Points" program of 1918 had asserted the right of the non-Turkish areas of the Ottoman Empire to be free, and this touched on Arab nationalist feelings. The King-Crane Commission on Syria & Palestine, dispatched as a purely American venture, had been an effort to consult the wishes of the peoples of the area on their future political development. Its report of Aug. 28, 1919 advised against the establishment of a Jewish state in Palestine and created a widespread popular impression among the Arab peoples that the U.S. was a friendly and disinterested power that would aid them in their strivings for independence.

Yet some Americans were deeply concerned with the success of the "Jewish national home," as embodied in the Palestine mandate. And Congress, in a joint resolution Sept. 21, 1922, had formally indorsed the Balfour Declaration. By the 1930s the pressure of American Zionists to induce the U.S. government to persuade Britain to alter its immigration policy in Palestine, though it met with little success on the governmental and State Department levels, had influenced Congress, which was sensitive to the thinking of its electorate and had already established a tradition of sympathy with Zionist aspirations. Thus it happened that an outspoken segment of American public opinion criticized British policy stringently, and this policy had an increasing impact on the Palestine problem.

At the time of the Balfour Declaration neither the British nor the Zionists, however, had fully taken into account the existence of an Arab community in Palestine, nor did they fully anticipate the fears aroused among the Arabs by Jewish settlement.

Even before the mandate was confirmed, the Palestinian Arabs expressed their antagonism to Zionist aspirations in the riots of 1920 and 1921. In 1929 Arab hostility burst out in a series of murderous attacks on the Jewish population, triggered by a conflict involving the Western (Wailing) Wall of the Temple courtyard in the Old City of Jerusalem. In Apr. 1936 the British-appointed grand mufti, Haj Amin el-Husseini, called a general strike of Arabs that lasted for 6 months. For the next 3 years Arab terrorist bands were active in much of Palestine, Jewish settlements were attacked, roads mined and crops burnt. By ambushes and murders, the terrorists forced public transport to travel in convoys, escorted by armed vehicles.

The step-by-step growth of the Jewish community thus generated the simultaneous growth of Arab hostility and stimulated the emergence of a Palestinian nationalism in opposition to Jewish nationalism. Caught in these crosscurrents, the British government continually narrowed the intent and purport of its original commitment and finally reached the conclusion that the mandate itself was "unworkable."

Dr. Chaim Weizmann

In 1922 the British government issued the Churchill White Paper, designed to assuage Arab fears and check Zionist hopes. In the White Paper, the government stated that a "Jewish national home" did not imply that all inhabitants of Palestine would be forced to accept Jewish nationality, although the existing Jewish community could develop into a center in which the Jewish people could take pride.

The Peel Commission of 1937 concluded that the mandate was not workable and that no unity was possible between the Arab and Jewish populations without betraying the national aspirations of both sides. In its report, the Peel Commission proposed the partition of the country into a Jewish state, an Arab state and a British zone. This was accepted by the Jews but rejected outright by the Arabs, and a commission appointed to work out the details of the partition submitted a report in which it was concluded that partition was impracticable. Anxious to win Arab goodwill in order to secure Arab oil and to protect its communications link in the Middle East, Britain in May 1939 issued what became known as the White Paper of 1939.

In the 1939 White Paper it was proposed that Britain give up the mandate in favor of an independent, predominantly Arab Palestine, to be established within 10 years, if a constitution protecting Jewish rights could be secured. Meanwhile, Jewish immigration was to be fixed at a maximum of 75,000 in the first 5-year period. Thereafter the number of Jewish immigrants would depend on Arab consent. The Jews were to be allowed to acquire land from the Arabs in only a small portion of Palestine. As the Zionists saw it, the "Jewish national home," which had been promised by the British, assured by the League of Nations in 1923 and upheld by the mandate commissions during the 1930s, was to be nullified. Those in direct need were to be excluded from their only haven.

The 1939 White Paper policy was considered inhumane in many circles in the U.S. and was regarded as illegal by the Zionists. It came up for discussion in June 1939 by the Permanent Mandates Commission of the League of Nations but was never debated because of the outbreak of war. Hence, it could not be regarded as having been legitimately approved, since Article 26 of the mandate required the consent of the League of Nations for any modifications introduced in the mandate.

When World War II began, the British decreed that people from Germany or German-occupied Polish territory were not to be admitted into Palestine. This decree was, in effect, a rejection of a Jewish Agency request for the immediate admission of 20,000 children from Poland and of 10,000 young men from the Balkans, which had been made just before war broke out. Denied exit from Europe, the children and young adults were sent to Nazi concentration camps, where virtually all of them died or were killed. Even before the White Paper had been promulgated, in March and April 1939, 3 refugee ships, the *Assunda, Assimi* and *Panagia Konstario,* packed with Jews trying to escape from Germany, had been refused admission to land in Palestine and had been sent back to Europe. Another incident that seared *yishuv* minds was the blowing up of the *Patria* Nov. 25, 1940 with 1,400 persons aboard in a scene witnessed by their relatives in Haifa. The immigrants had been deported by the British authorities for illegal entry and opted for death rather than a return to Europe.

World War II brought to a halt the political conflict in Palestine. The majority of the *yishuv* turned to the support of the British war effort against Hitler, their common enemy. In the Zionist view, however, experience had taught the *yishuv* to distrust British intentions. As the war ended, Chairman Chaim Weizmann of the Jewish Agency for Palestine submitted the Agency's next petition—for the immediate granting of 100,000 immigration visas to Europe's Jewish survivors.

It had been at the Biltmore Hotel in New York early in May 1942 that the official Zionist position on Palestine had taken the form of a definite, concrete program. That program, relying heavily on the support of Jews in the West, had envisaged the organization of a *yishuv* army to implement the conversion of Palestine into a Jewish commonwealth and had laid plans for the conduct of unrestricted immigration into Palestine under Jewish Agency control. Dr. Weizmann, a Russian-born, noted European chemist and the acknowledged leading statesman of world Zionism, had addressed the conference May 9, 1942. He had asserted that Palestine was the only possible postwar home for the "2 million to 4 million" Jews then mingled among the uprooted peoples of Europe. Weizmann also said that, according to a "calm, statistical estimate" made by informed observers, "25% of central European

Jewry will be 'liquidated'" by Hitler's forces before the end of World War II. This figure proved to be a great underestimate.

In Britain, the postwar general election brought the Labor Party to power. Labor's preelection conference had indorsed a Jewish state in Palestine and free immigration and land sales, but Ernest Bevin, the new Labor foreign secretary, refused to grant a single visa above the 2,000 still available under the 1939 White Paper and continued the British restrictions on land purchases. U.S. Pres. Harry S. Truman, on his own initiative, advanced a plan to open Palestine's doors to 100,000 survivors of Hitler's death camps; he thus involved the U.S. in the Palestine issue.

The Zionists identified the British mandatory administration as the immediate enemy and proceeded to defy it actively. Under Jewish Agency auspices, war-trained commandos of *Haganah Le-Yisrael* ("Defense of Israel"—the *yishuv*'s underground army) built an illegal organization to rescue Jewish survivors in Europe and to smuggle them past the British blockade into Palestine. Outside Palestine, Jewish organizations collected funds and found means of transporting the refugees in leased ships.

The Zionist movement and the Jewish Agency felt that if the 1939 White Paper's provisions were carried out, the *yishuv* would be at the mercy of the Arabs and that the result would be another Nazi-style holocaust. The Arabs argued that allowing more Jewish immigration into Palestine was tantamount to making the Arabs there pay for the crimes of the Nazis.

Haganah and 2 dissident, independent paramilitary groups began training their members to sabotage British installations and for defense against Arab attack. Haganah functioned under the Jewish Agency, while the other 2 groups—the Irgun Zvai Leumi (the "National Military Organization") under the command of Menahem Beigin and the Stern Group—refused to place themselves under Agency directions, but all these groups by definition reflected the growing despair and militancy of increasing numbers of Palestinian Jews.

The militant activities of the Jewish paramilitary forces dimmed the terrorist activities of the Arabs to the world's view, although Arab terrorism continued unabated. The new drama in Palestine was played out by Haganah under *yishuv* and Jewish Agency authority, the dissident groups engaging in acts of sabotage and terror, and the mandatory authority, which responded with hangings, martial law, curfews, arrests of Jewish leaders and the deportation of illegal immigrants to Cyprus and even back to Germany.

The denouement of Jewish, Arab (the Arab side by the postwar period comprising not only the local Palestinian community but also the states belonging to the Arab League) and British actions and counteractions forms the substance of this book. The end result was the UN's partition resolution (supported by both the USSR and the U.S.), the creation of the state of Israel and the Israeli War of Independence. As with most INTERIM HISTORY books, much of the material in this volume is based on the record compiled in FACTS ON FILE. This material was supplemented by the records of various Jewish, Israeli, Arab, British and other government institutions as well as press sources. Despite the often highly controversial nature of the subject, a conscientious effort was made to present this narrative without bias.

PALESTINE AT THE END OF WORLD WAR II

The Ethnic Face of Palestine

Palestine had an area of little more than 9,000 square miles when the British mandate came into operation in 1923, 3 years after the separation of the 35,135-square-mile Hashemite Kingdom of Jordan from the jurisdiction of Palestine (but not from the total British mandate).

A census of Palestine in 1940 put the total of its inhabitants at 1,544,530 people, of whom 947,846 were Moslem Arabs, 120,587 were Christian Arabs or Europeans, 12,562 others were Arab Druses or Samaritans, Metawilehs (Shiite Moslems, dwelling near Lebanon), Baha'is, Indians of such ethnic and religious distinctions as Sikhs and Hindus, or others of no professed religion—while 463,535 were Jews.

By the end of 1946, the total population of Palestine had grown to 1,912,110, the main divisions consisting of 1,143,330 Moslem Arabs and 607,230 Jews.

One can obtain a good picture of the extent and pattern of real property holdings by Jews in Palestine in 1946 by recourse to supplementary information submitted Mar. 27, 1946 by Eliezar Kaplan, treasurer of the Jewish Agency Executive, in response to questions raised by members of the Anglo-American Committee of Inquiry on Palestine during the committee's hearings in Jerusalem Mar. 6-28. Kaplan, noting that "Jewish land holdings and the density of [Jewish] population [had] formed the subject of many questions," said:

"According to the statement of [the Palestinian Arab leader] Mr. Jamal Husseini, the Jews have acquired, since the Balfour Declaration, $\frac{1}{3}$ of the cultivable land of Palestine. This statement calls for a close scrutiny. Jewish land holdings cover an area of 1,775,000 dunums [17,750 hectares, or approximately 68½ square miles] out of 26,400,000 dunums [264,000 hectares, or approximately 1,019 square miles], *i.e.,* about 7% of the total area. This land is divided among the various regions as follows: 165,000 dunums [1,650 hectares, or approximately 6⅓ square miles] in the Negev; 475,000 [4,750 hectares, or approximately 18⅓ square miles] in the hill country; 702,000 [7,020 hectares, or approximately 27¹⁄₁₀ square miles] in the Maritime Plain; and 415,000 [4,150 hectares, or about 14¹⁄₁₀ square miles] in the valleys."

11

"175,000 dunums [1,750 hectares, or about 6¾ square miles] of the total Jewish land area consist of state domain, such as the land around the Dead Sea, the Hula concession, etc., which are not cultivable at present. The remaining 1,600,000 dunums [16,000 hectares, or 61¾ square miles] are subdivided approximately as follows:

	Dunums
Urban areas and reserves	250,000
Forest and forest reserves	100,000
Scattered areas and land partly still in Arab occupation	100,000
Uncultivable land	200,000
Communal areas, roads, farmyards, etc.	90,000
Land under cultivation	750,000
Cultivable land not yet allocated	100,000
Total	1,600,000

"The total area of both cultivable and cultivated land aggregates accordingly 850,000 [8,500 hectares, or 32⅘ square miles] out of about 8 million dunums [80,000 hectares, or 308⁹⁄₁₀ square miles] cultivated in Palestine in 1936, according to government data ... and more than 9 million dunums [90,000 hectares, or approximately 347⅓ square miles] according to our own estimates.

"The split-up of the land of the Jewish National Fund according to its use can be given more accurately. At the end of 1945, the Jewish National Fund had in its possession 813,000 dunums [8,130 hectares, or about 31⅜ square miles] of land. This area was divided into 3 categories: 669,000 dunums [6,690 hectares, or something in the vicinity of 25⁹⁄₁₀ square miles] of agricultural land; 75,000 [750 hectares, or 2⅞ square miles] of urban land; and 69,000 dunums [690 hectares, or 2⅔ square miles] of forest and forest reserves. Of the agricultural land, 591,000 dunums [5,910 hectares, or 22⅘ square miles] was allocated and leased to settlements and settlers, and about 78,000 dunums [780 hectares, or a little more than 3 square miles] is still reserve. Of these 78,000 dunums, 32,000 dunums [320 hectares, or about 1¼ square miles] is reserved for ex-servicemen, and the balance of 46,000 dunums [460 hectares, or a little more than 1¾ square miles] is not yet suitable for colonization, being scattered in small parcels or still in *musha'* with Arabs. About 10% of the total area of agricultural land still requires substantial improvement. It should be stressed that, of the one million dunums [10,000 hectares, or about 38⅗ square miles] of land acquired during the past 25 years, more than half was thought uncultivable and unhealthy waste land. The Jewish institutions drained about 40,000 dunums [400 hectares, or more than 1½ square miles] of swamps, which affected a much wider area. The total area reclaimed is about 660,000 dunums [6,600 hectares, or just under 25½ square miles]. Wadi Hawareth, now called Emek Hefer, is a striking example of such land reclamation. Out of an area of 30,000 dunums [300 hectares, or more than 1³⁄₂₀ square miles] infected with malaria, only 5,000 [50 hectares, or just over ¹⁹⁄₁₀₀ square miles] were cultivated, and the population consisted of 200 Bedu families. Now the land is drained; 28,000 dunums [280 hectares, or 1²⁄₂₅ square miles] are cultivated, of which 12,000 dunums [120 hectares, or approximately ¹¹⁄₂₅ square mile] are irrigated; the former occupants are all there, and much better off. The population is 5,000.

"The following statement of the Royal Commission is relevant: ... 'Some of the colonies were in the hills of Galilee, but the great majority were in the Maritime Plain and the Plain of Esdraelon. The conversion of the latter from a swampy and thinly-peopled area into healthy and highly cultivated farmland, at the cost of much suffering and mortality from malaria, had been a particularly notable achievement from the Jewish point of view.' *

"In this connection the problem crops up of the so-called dispossessed Arabs and destroyed villages. ...

"Our policy was to acquire land, not by violence or force but by agreement with the owners of the land as well as the tenants. We paid exorbitant prices, and we always saw to it that the people involved were provided for. But for instigation from outside, sometimes developing into a 'racket,' we could have reached, and in the majority of cases we did reach an agreement to the benefit of all parties interested. May I put before you a few additional figures. If we take the Northern Region of Palestine, add only the northern part of the Negev and exclude the Judean Desert, we find that the inhabited part of Palestine covers about 17 million dunums [170,000 hectares, or 812⅓ square miles]. The Jews constitute about 1/3 of the total population and possess about 10% of the inhabited land. If we take only the northern part of Palestine and the whole of the Negev, and exclude the Judean Desert, the remaining area will be 12,700,000 dunums [127,000 hectares, or a little more than 490 square miles]. Jews possess less than ⅛. The density in this area per square kilometer is 100 for the Arabs and 375 for the Jews. If we take only the rural population of Palestine, we have a figure of about 725,000 non-Jews and about 150,000 Jews, making the ratio as between Jews and Arabs about 1:5, as compared with the ratio of cultivated land of Jews and Arabs of 1:10, in accordance with government data. ...

"According to government data, in the season 1944 the Jews cultivated an area of about 560,000 dunums [5,600 hectares, or nearly 22⅞ square miles] and the Arabs an area of about 5,650,000 dunums [56,500 hectares, or about 218 square miles]. If these figures are correct, then there are about 8 dunums [.08 hectare, or .1976 acre] of cultivated land per head of the Arab rural population and less than 4 dunums [.04 hectare, or .0988 acre] per head of the Jewish. We challenge the total figures. In our estimate, there are now about 850,000 dunums [8,500 hectares, or 32⅘ square miles] of cultivated land in the possession of the Jews and more than 8 million cultivated dunums [80,000 hectares, or approximately 308¾ square miles] in the possession of the Arabs. The ratio per head does not change substantially."

Britain's Labor Party Wins Power

✕ 3 new factors that emerged at the end of World War II greatly affected the Palestine situation. One was the existence of what came to be termed a "displaced nation," *i.e.,* hundreds of thousands of Jews who had no roots left in their European countries of birth and who wanted to go to Palestine. The 2d

* Palestine Royal Commission Report, 1937, Chapter III, page 47, paragraph 10.

factor was the forging of a new national consciousness and unity of purpose in the *yishuv,* overriding internal conflicts. The 3d new factor was the polarization of the globe into an Eastern and a Western bloc, with Palestine as one of the points in the middle.

Germany had capitulated May 8, 1945. In July, the British general election brought the Labor Party to power, and Ernest Bevin was named to the office of foreign minister. British wartime policy in the Middle East had been determined by considerations of preventing the Axis powers from getting a hold over the Arabs. After the war, Britain was determined for similar considerations to prevent Soviet Russia from getting a foothold in the Arab states of the Middle East. This policy was handed over to the newly elected Labor government in Britain.

⅄ Of Europe's estimated prewar Jewish population of 7 million, only one million Jews had survived. Of these, 300,000 had some kind of foothold in western Europe, the bulk of the rest were trapped in eastern Europe, while some 100,000 others were living in the so-called displaced persons (DP) camps. The condition of this latter group took on the proportions of a massive dilemma. It was felt that the "DPs" had no way of rebuilding their lives unless they left Europe. The *yishuv* and the Zionist movement, and the vast majority of the displaced Jews themselves, expressed the belief that their only relief would be emigration to a new start in Palestine. They expected that the Labor government in Britain would also see this as the only feasible solution. But Britain appeared to the Jews to have become more interested in holding on to a Middle East position that involved keeping the good will of the Arab majority at the expense of the *yishuv* in Palestine.

Exponents of such a British policy had found more justification for a pro-Arab course after a serious—although isolated—act of terrorism that revolted the British public: the assassination of Lord Moyne, British resident minister in the Middle East. Lord Moyne, 64, was slain together with his chauffeur Nov. 6, 1944 in Cairo by 2 young Sephardic Jews. It was brought out at the 7-day trial of the 2 confessed gunmen, Eliahu Hakim and Eliahu Beth-Tsouri, which ended in Cairo in mid-Jan. 1945, that the main motive for Lord Moyne's slaying was political and was inspired by the so-called Stern Group of

Jewish extremists. The 2 assassins were hanged Mar. 22, 1945 at the British military jail in Cairo.

Britain Ends Pro-Zionist Stand

The British Labor Party, prior to its electoral victory, had been explicitly dedicated to a pro-Zionist view. Support for the "Jewish national home" had been embodied in Labor's war aims in 1917 and was repeated at successive party conferences. Labor had condemned the 1939 White Paper. In 1944 the annual Labor Party conference had resolved that: "There is surely neither hope nor meaning in a 'Jewish national home' unless we are prepared to let the Jews ... enter this tiny land in such numbers as to become a majority...." Several weeks before the Labor victory, Hugh Dalton, the future chancellor of the exchequer, had said: "It is morally wrong and politically indefensible to impose obstacles to the entry into Palestine now of any Jews who desire to go there. We consider Jewish immigration into Palestine should be permitted without the present limitations which obstruct it...."

Just prior to the elections, the Jewish Agency June 18, 1945 applied to the Palestine government for the allocation of 100,000 immigration permits "in order to meet the most urgent claims and in view of the untenable position of the surviving Jews in Europe." The application elicited no answer. In September, Pres. Truman, on receipt of a report from the Pennsylvania University law school dean, Earl Grant Harrison, U.S. representative on the Intergovernmental Committee on Refugees, about the plight of the Jewish DPs, wrote to British Prime Min. Clement R. Attlee, urging the immediate admission of 100,000 Jews into Palestine. This action too drew no reply. There was a sharp increase of articles in the British press making the points that the admission of Jewish displaced persons into Palestine would "set the Middle East aflame" and that if the Americans made proposals for British Palestine policy they should be prepared "to take their share of responsibility in carrying them out."

This apparent British repudiation of the pledge to allow DPs into Palestine dismayed many American Jews. While the British were asserting that the Jewish displaced persons issue, and the need to rescue the 100,000, had been artificially raised by Zionist propaganda, the first pictures of Dachau and Bergen-Belsen were flooding into world consciousness and mankind's conscience.

The Jewish Agency disclosed Sept. 4 that it had no Palestine immigration certificates left. Chaim Weizmann revealed Sept. 4 that instead of 100,000 certificates, the British Colonial Office had issued 1,500, with the comment that these "were the last available under the [1939] White Paper." Indignation and tension mounted inside Palestine, with repercussions on the political front in the U.S. In Palestine, 60,000 Jews, headed by survivors of Bergen-Belsen and Buchenwald, dressed in concentration-camp striped pajamas, marched Oct. 8 through the streets of every city. Palestinian Jews were enraged after Foreign Min. Ernest Bevin in London at the end of September received the secretary general of the Arab League.*

In this climate, Haganah, with the consent of the Jewish Agency, began to turn to terrorist tactics. Armed Haganah men Oct. 10 raided a camp holding illegal immigrants awaiting deportation at the Athlit detention camp and freed them, killing a British constable in the process. 10 days later, the night of Oct. 31, 1945, Haganah staged its first countrywide sabotage action, blowing up railway bridges at more than 100 points, while police patrol ships were exploded in Jaffa and Haifa and bombs went off in the Haifa oil refineries.

---

* The League of Arab States is an international organization of sovereign Arab states founded in Mar. 1945 to promote their union and common good. Its charter members were Egypt, Iraq, Lebanon, Saudi Arabia, Syria and Trans-Jordania—all but the former French mandates of Syria and Lebanon being kingdoms at the time. The kingdom of Yemen, invited to adhere to the League's pact, did so later in 1945. The pact, signed Mar. 22, 1945 by the first 6 states mentioned above, contained 20 articles and 2 special appendices, the first one relating to Palestine. It read in part:

"At the end of the last Great War [World War I], Palestine together with the other Arab States, was separated from the Ottoman Empire and became independent....

"Although the visible signs of this independence have remained hidden as a result of *force majeure,* it is not fitting that this should be an obstacle to the participation of Palestine in the League.

"Therefore, the states signatory to the pact of the Arab League consider that in view of Palestine's special circumstances, the Council of the League should designate an Arab delegate from Palestine to participate in its work until this country enjoys actual independence."

Bevin Nov. 13 made his first official statement on Palestine. He told the Jews not to "push to the head of the queue" in the general context of the DP problem in Europe. He refused admission into Palestine to the 100,000 and made a quota of 1,500 immigrants a month dependent on the "generosity of our Arab friends."

The essential point of Bevin's statement, however, was the announcement that Britain and the U.S. had appointed a joint fact-finding commission to make recommendations on Palestine's future. This Anglo-American Committee of Inquiry was formally appointed Dec. 31, 1945 and began its investigations in Jan. 1946, but its appointment had little effect on the troubled situation inside Palestine.

Bevin's general statement was regarded by the *yishuv* as an insult. The Jewish National Council called for a protest strike, and the Chief Rabbinate initiated a day of prayer and fasting Nov. 15, 1945 marked by the blowing of the ram's horn in the synagogues. An outbreak of heavy rioting late Nov. 14 in Tel Aviv preceded violent outbreaks all over Palestine, with 9 Jews killed, 37 British soldiers injured and a number of government offices demolished.

Jewish underground units struck at the Palestine coast guard Nov. 25 and destroyed 2 stations serving to bar the unauthorized admission of Jewish immigrants. The mandatory government retaliated Nov. 26 by deploying 15,000 troops of the 6th Airborne Division, the Brigade of Guards and other units to carry out arms searches in 3 Jewish settlements in the plain of Sharon and in Samaria, where 8 settlers were killed in the course of a search for illegal immigrants. The British that evening reported that Jewish underground units had taken arms and ammunition in broad daylight Nov. 22 from an RAF installation at Ras el Ain. Jewish underground units Nov. 26 blew up a police headquarters and several electric power stations throughout Palestine.

Jewish terrorists had created the increase in tension Nov. 25 by blowing up 2 coast guard stations at Givat Olga and Sidna Ali, north of Tel Aviv, wounding 14 guards, in retaliation for the capture 2 days earlier of the Greek motor schooner *Demetrios*. (The *Demetrios* Nov. 23 had brought in 200 illegal Jewish immigrants, 20 of whom—along with the crew—were taken by the British.) At least 9 Jews were killed and 75 injured Nov. 26 in clashes with 10,000 British troops and police scouring the Sharon Valley for terrorists. A terrorist leader proclaimed in Haifa that "the battle has begun." However, British airborne troops were withdrawn after confiscating explosives and making several arrests.

In Rome, spokesmen for 15,000 Polish Jews stranded in Italy told the British authorities Nov. 26 that they intended to proceed to Palestine "by all ways and means" despite the immigration curbs.

The Soviets too expressed their views at this juncture, as did the displaced Jews of Europe. A Paris diplomatic report Nov. 26 said that the USSR proposed submitting the Arab-Jewish problem to a Big 5* conference, a suggestion by no means pleasing to Britain and the U.S., which wanted no Soviet interference in the Middle East.

U.S. Zionists Demand a Jewish State

Zionists in the U.S. reacted with anger to the announcement of the Anglo-American decision to appoint a committee to make yet another investigation of the Palestinian problem. They pressed all the more urgently for a Jewish state. In Nov. 1945 an Elmo Roper poll of 3,330 U.S. Jews showed 80.1% in favor of a Jewish national state in Palestine.

The Zionist Organization of America, meeting in Atlantic City, N.J. in mid-Nov. 1945, elected Rabbi Abba Hillel Silver of Cleveland as its new president and indorsed a proposal that the Jewish National Fund‡ purchase an additional 500,000 acres of land in Palestine in defiance of British land transfer regulations. The organization also approved a $51.7 million budget for 1946 to be used for immigration, land acquisition and settlement programs supported by the United Palestine Appeal.†

---

* The Big 5 powers were the U.S., Great Britain, the USSR, France and China, then under Nationalist (Kuomintang) control.

‡ The Jewish National Fund *(Keren Kayemeth Le-Yisrael),* still in existence, is the Zionist agency for "redeeming," by purchase on behalf of the Jewish people, land in Israel (then Palestine) for colonization purposes or afforestation.

† The United Palestine Appeal, which in 1939 merged with other American Jewish institutions to form the United Jewish Appeal for the aid of refugees, needy Jewry overseas and Jews in Palestine, was the official fund-raising agency in the U.S. for the Jewish National Fund and the Palestine Foundation Fund *(Keren Hayesod),* which had pooled their fund-raising activities in 1925.

According to Rabbi James G. Heller, chairman of the United Palestine Appeal, the Jewish National Fund, the Jewish Agency for Palestine and the Palestine Foundation Fund had spent $31,104,146 in Palestine in the fiscal year ending Sept. 30, 1945, or 4 times the amount spent in 1940-1. A new fund-raising campaign was launched for 1946. Those at the meeting applauded Dr. Chaim Weizmann, president of the Jewish Agency and also of the World Zionist Organization, when he declared Nov. 19 that British Foreign Secy. Ernest Bevin's attempts "to drive a wedge between the Zionist movement and the Jewish people are doomed to failure."

On the whole, most Americans appeared to be sympathetic to the Zionist cause. The Senate Foreign Relations Committee Dec. 12, 1945 approved by 17-to-1 vote a resolution urging U.S. aid in opening Palestine to the Jews and in the building of a "democratic commonwealth" in Palestine. The Senate Dec. 17 voted overwhelmingly for a Wagner-Taft resolution urging the unrestricted entry of Jews into Palestine and the establishment of a Jewish commonwealth, and the House of Representatives Dec. 19 adopted the Senate-approved Palestine resolution.

Summing up the widespread U.S. sympathies, ex-State Undersecy. Sumner Welles, in accepting the chairmanship of the American Christian Palestine Committee in Baltimore, said Dec. 23 that the new UN International Trusteeship Council "should be charged with the obligation" of establishing a Jewish commonwealth in Palestine, with enough "armed force ... to give assurance of security."

THE ANGLO-AMERICAN COMMITTEE OF INQUIRY

"The Anglo-American Committee of Inquiry Regarding the Problems of European Jewry & Palestine" came into being under an agreement between the U.S. and Great Britain to investigate jointly conditions in Europe and in Palestine, confer with Jewish and Arab leaders and make recommendations on their findings to the British mandatory administration. British Foreign Secy. Ernest Bevin and U.S. Pres. Harry S. Truman announced the agreement Nov. 13, 1945 from London and Washington to their countrymen.

The joint committee issued its report Apr. 20, 1946; in it the committee urged that the mandatory administration immediately admit 100,000 European Jews to Palestine and annul restrictions against the purchase by Jews of land in certain areas there. The committee also recommended that Palestine become "neither a Jewish nor an Arab state" and called on the Jewish Agency to cooperate with the mandatory authorities in suppressing terrorism.

Committee Is Formed

Pres. Truman named the 6 U.S. members of the Anglo-American Committee of Inquiry on Palestine Dec. 10, 1945, and London nominated the 6 British members.

The U.S. members were Judge Joseph C. Hutcheson, of the 5th Circuit Court of Houston, Tex., as chairman; Frank W. Buxton, editor of the *Boston Herald;* O. Max Gardner*, a Washington attorney; James G. McDonald, ex-chairman of the American Foreign Policy Association; Frank Aydelotte, ex-president of Swarthmore College; and William Philips, ex-Undersecretary of State. The British members were Sir John E. Singleton, High Court justice, as chairman; Wilfred P. Crick, Midland Bank economic adviser; Richard S. Crossman, Labor

---

* Gardner was later replaced by Bartley C. Crum, a prominent Washington attorney.

member of Parliament; Sir Frederick Leggett, ex-deputy secre-
tary of the Ministry of Labor & National Services; Maj.
Reginald E. Manningham-Buller, Conservative member of
Parliament; and Lord Robert Craigmyle Morrison.

Washington and London jointly announced that the
Anglo-American Committee of Inquiry would open hearings in
Washington in Jan. 1946.

Arab & Yishuv Reactions

Arab feelings over the appointment of the Committee of
Inquiry were mixed. The Higher Committee of the Palestine
Arab Council* announced its flat opposition in Cairo, but the
Arab League offered to cooperate by giving testimony at committee sessions. About the same time, Jamal el-Husseini, exiled
leader of the Palestine Arab Party and cousin of the ex-grand
mufti of Jerusalem, warned in Beirut Dec. 30, 1945 that the
Arabs would revolt if they lost hope of defeating Zionism
politically.

The Zionist movement, while distrustful of this new committee, offered its full cooperation in giving evidence. Inside
Palestine, *yishuv* attitudes were concentrated against the
mandatory government. Jewish terrorist activities continued,
sometimes initiated and carried out by Haganah itself, abetted
by a sympathetic *yishuv*—so that the British faced the prospect of warring against a whole nation.

When bombs exploded Dec. 27 in the district police headquarters in Jaffa after an attack on the building, and a British
corporal was slain in an attack by 50 men on an arms depot in
Tel Aviv, the British responded with strong measures. British
forces Dec. 28 arrested between 1,500 and 2,000 persons, among
them Moshe Shertok†, a leading Jewish Agency official, and
deported 52 Jews, detained at Latrun on suspicion of being

* The Palestine Arab Council was founded after the 3d Palestinian Arab Congress (or Haifa Congress) in 1920. The Higher Committee of the Palestine Arab
Council—or Arab Higher Committee, for short—was founded Apr. 25, 1936
after the Palestinian Arab revolt of that year in order to coordinate the nationalist activities of the Palestinian Arabs' various factions.

† Shertok, seized for allegedly breaking the Nov. 27 curfew, was detained
several hours in a cell in Jerusalem's military barracks before being released.
Shertok later hebraicized his name to Sharett.

terrorists, to Eritrea. (More than 300 had already been sent there.) The Jewish Agency charged that the Palestine mandatory government had stopped issuing immigration certificates despite Bevin's declaration that a monthly quota would be permitted.

It had become impossible to fix the blame for the worsening situation on any single group. When 8 persons were killed in Jerusalem, Jaffa and Tel Aviv Dec. 27 in bomb blasts and gun battles, the British police accused Haganah of responsibility for the action. British 6th Airborne Division troops Dec. 29 surrounded the Tel Aviv suburb of Ramat Gan and arrested 800 men aged between 16 and 40, holding them for questioning in the bombings. The authorities said that any of the 3 underground organizations—Haganah, the Irgun Zvai Leumi or the Stern Group—could have been responsible for the bombings.

In a determined effort to clamp down on terrorism, the mandatory authority had augmented its police and army with the crack division of airborne troops that had participated in the invasion of Normandy during World War II. In addition, 4 destroyers and 2 cruisers lay in Palestine waters, while coastal and frontier patrols were constantly on the lookout to block illegal immigration. Tighter security measures were introduced on highways and in government buildings.

Outside Palestine, the measures were indorsed with an outburst of anti-Semitic expression by an influential British official. In a press interview that had wide repercussions, Lt. Gen. Sir Frederick E. Morgan, chief of the United Nations Relief & Rehabilitation Administration (UNRRA) in Germany, told reporters Jan. 2, 1946 that thousands of Polish Jews were coming into the U.S. zone from the east, appearing "well-dressed, well-fed, rosy-cheeked and with plenty of money," in a "well-organized, positive plan to get out of Europe." An unknown secret Jewish organization was behind this infiltration, he said. "I believe we are about to see a 2d exodus of Jews—this time from Europe." He declared that he was not convinced "by all the talk about pogroms within Poland" and that the persons coming in all had the "same monotonous story about pogroms." The Jews in Europe were "growing into a world force ... which is generating power for getting what they want," Morgan added. He urged that UNRRA and the

UN draw up a long-term program to settle the problem or "the seeds of World War III" would take root.

Morgan's comments brought immediate protests from leaders of the World Jewish Congress, the World Zionist Organization, the American World Jewish Congress and the American Zionist Emergency Council. Spokesmen called his statements false, "savoring of Nazism at its worst," "palpably anti-Semitic" and "vicious," and they reiterated that anti-Semitism was driving Jews from Poland. In an immediate denial that any conspiracy existed, U.S. District Court Judge Simon H. Rifkind, adviser on Jewish affairs to Gen. Joseph T. McNarney, commander of U.S. forces in Europe, stated Jan. 3 in Frankfort-on-Main that the Jews were leaving Poland "under a sense of compulsion."

Oscar Lange, the Polish ambassador, asserted in Washington Jan. 3 that Poland had become "a kind of cemetery" to the Jews because so many had been killed in the war and that they wanted to leave because living there was "torture." He said that there had only been one pogrom, at Cracow, and that "the persons who instigated it are being tried." He also linked Gen. Wladislaw Anders, a Polish Corps commander in Italy, with an underground movement in Poland that he called reactionary and anti-Semitic.

Gen. Morgan, summoned to New York to confer with UNRRA's director general, Herbert H. Lehman, insisted Jan. 3 in the Frankfort suburb of Hoechst that his purpose had been "to bring to the attention of the world the need for a solution more permanent than the ... [UNRRA] can possibly furnish." The UNRRA Jan. 4 ordered Morgan dismissed for his Jan. 2 statement on Jews. It took the position that his words had made it impossible for him "to serve the administration effectively in the future." Morgan replied that "I have not resigned because I see no reason why I should."

Meanwhile, Sir John V. W. Shaw, the Palestine mandatory administration's chief secretary, had disclosed in Jerusalem Jan. 2 that all the 75,000 immigration certificates granted under the 1939 White Paper "are now exhausted" and that he could issue no more.

The Zionist Federation of Great Britain & Ireland, meeting in London, demanded Jan. 27 that Palestine be opened to all Jews. He called reputed British plans for Transjordan independence a "unilateral partition" of Palestine.

In Munich Jan. 27 representatives of 60,000 displaced Jews in the U.S. zone heard David Ben-Gurion, head of the Jewish Agency in Palestine, charge that Britain was establishing a ghetto there and sending armed forces "to hunt Jews." Those at this meeting demanded that the UN declare a free Jewish state in Palestine.

The Arab League had announced Jan. 25 that each of its 7 member governments would support the Arab Higher Committee in rejecting the British proposal for Jewish immigration into Palestine at the rate of 1,500 monthly. (The statement came as the League prepared for the forthcoming meeting of the Trusteeship Committee of the UN General Assembly. The League wanted the Assembly to define the term in the UN Charter directing that "states directly concerned" should negotiate trust agreements with mandatory powers.)

The immigration proposal had been made by Britain Nov. 13, 1945 pending the results of the Anglo-American Inquiry Committee's findings. The Jewish Agency had accepted the proposal, albeit reluctantly. Yet terrorist attacks on British installations and personnel continued—in defiance of the High Commissioner's new decree Jan. 28, 1946 that the death penalty would be enforced for terrorists violating defense regulations and placing the burden of proof of innocence on the suspects.

Haganah & Militant Groups Unite

Continued British restrictions on all but a minimum of immigration prompted further terrorism while the new repressive measures taken in turn against the *yishuv* drove moderate Jews into militants' arms and gave increasing impetus to terrorist reprisals. While the Anglo-American Committee of Inquiry was conducting its sessions in Feb. 1946, Jewish terrorists attacked police headquarters in Haifa and Tel Aviv Feb. 21 after blowing up an RAF radar station Feb. 20 on Mount Carmel. 50,000 Jews attended the funeral in Tel Aviv Feb. 24 of 4 terrorists killed Feb. 22 during an attack on a British patrol at Sarona.

When British troops rounded up 5,000 Jews Feb. 26 in a search for terrorists who had attacked 22 RAF planes at Qastina, Petah Tiqva and Lydda Feb. 25, the clandestine newspaper *Herut (Freedom)* announced that Haganah, the Irgun Zvai Leumi and the Stern Group had united into one large organization. Made desperate by the state of their compatriots in Europe, whose plight was being publicly revealed by members of the Anglo-American Committee of Inquiry in the course of their investigations, and incensed by what they denounced as Britain's repressive measures, moderate and extremist Jews in Palestine united to become Britain's active and violent opponents.

7 British soldiers were slain Apr. 25 when a small Stern band including girls raided a British camp near Tel Aviv for the purpose of seizing arms. British forces rounded up 1,200 suspects during the night. The British High Commissioner for Palestine termed the raid "premeditated murder with no military motive whatsoever" and "gangsterism in its worst form." The military commander of the Lydda District imposed a strict curfew on Tel Aviv. Dr. Chaim Weizmann, the Jewish Agency, the Palestinian Jewish General Labor Confederation and the city of Tel Aviv all publicly deplored the raid.

Committee Opens Hearings

The Anglo-American Committee of Inquiry began its hearings in Washington Jan. 4, 1946. It conducted sessions with leading U.S. Zionist spokesmen and with politicians, experts and various public figures, both Christian and Jewish. Their testimony was predominantly in favor of a Jewish state.

Criticizing the British administration, Robert Nathan, a Washington economist, maintained Jan. 7 that Palestine could absorb 615,000 to 1,125,000 displaced Jews within 10 years. Highlighting the plight of Europe's Jews, Dr. Joseph J. Schwartz, the European director of the American Jewish Joint Distribution Committee, estimated that 600,000 of the 1,250,000 surviving Jews in Europe wanted to go to Palestine. Earl G. Harrison, who had surveyed the problem in Europe for Pres. Truman the previous summer, urged that 100,000 Jews be admitted to Palestine immediately. It was reported that about 2,000 Polish Jews, whom the Russians were planning to remove from Berlin to a camp in Prenzlau, Brandenburg, to ease the housing and food problems, somehow were found to have "disappear[ed]" during the night. Conditions in the Russian camps were denounced. The committee Jan. 8 heard testimony by Dr. Emanuel Neumann, Dr. Stephen S. Wise and Henry Monsky, who criticized the British administration. "The Christian world owes the Jews some reparation," Wise asserted.

Earl Harrison, appointed in 1945 to investigate the conditions of displaced persons in Europe, had said Jan. 7, 1946 that Palestine should be the chief source of a home for stateless Jews. Harrison, speaking as the representative of the Christian Council on Palestine (an organization of some 3,000 Protestant ministers), urged the creation in Palestine of a Jewish state supported by Britain and the U.S.

Joseph M. Proskauer, the American Jewish Committee president, urged Jan. 9, however, that Palestine be placed under a UN trusteeship. So did Prof. Albert Einstein, who told the committee Jan. 11 that he preferred UN trusteeship to British colonial policy, that the majority of Jewish refugees in Europe should be settled in Palestine and that he saw no need for the Jewish commonwealth advocated by the Zionist organizations. Einstein said he felt that the difficulties in Palestine existed because "first, I believe they are artificially created by the English. I believe if there would be a really honest government for the people there, which would get the Arabs and Jews together, there would be nothing to fear."

In a dissenting view, Lessing J. Rosenwald, president of the American Council for Judaism, testified Jan. 10 that his group's 11,000 members "reject the Hitlerian concept that the Jews are a race or nation." He held that the Zionists were arousing false hopes of Palestine as a solution to European Jews' problems. Rosenwald urged a UN conference to deal with the refugee problem.

Testifying before the commission in Washington Jan. 11, Dr. Philip K. Hitti, noted Arabist scholar, head of the Institute of Arab-American Affairs and himself a Lebanese-born Christian Arab, criticized the historical argument presented by the Zionists. It involved 3 factors, he said: "The occupation of the land by Moses and Joshua; the establishment of the kingdom under Saul, David and Solomon; [and] the continued settlement after the destruction of Jerusalem." To this the Arab rebuttal was: "You came from outside and occupied a land which was already occupied by peoples, Semitic peoples, called Amorites and Canaanites and by other Semites from whom we are descended." The very name Palestine "is not Hebrew; it isn't Semitic. It perpetuates the name of those Indo-Europeans who came from the Aegean Sea and occupied the coast about 1225 BC, which is about the time when the Jews came from Egypt under the leadership of Moses and then Joshua."

Hitti traced the history of the Jewish kingdom to its destruction in 586 BC by Nebuchadnezzar: "Since that time ... there has been no Jewish kingdom in Palestine in the full sense of the term.... Therefore, the Arabs maintain that for the last 2,000 years ... there has not been a Jewish state in Palestine, and there has not even been a Jewish majority in Palestine.... In the last analysis, the Arab claim rests on a very simple fact: It is the continued and uninterrupted physical and cultural association between land and people. No better claim can any people present to any land—continued uninterrupted physical and cultural association between land and people."

In response to the Zionist religious argument, Hitti countered: "First, many Jews do not interpret Zion in a physical or geographic sense.... We usually ignore the fact that this land called Palestine is equally holy to the Christians and to the Jews.... To the Moslem, Jerusalem is the first *qiblah* [direction]. It is a place toward which Muhammed and the early Moslems turned and faced to pray.... Today it is to them the 3d holy city after Mecca and Medina. Palestine was conquered by *jihad*—holy war. And any such territory, according to the Moslem theory of *jihad,* has been given to them by Allah, and to relinquish their claim upon it is tantamount to a betrayal of their faith."

Modern Jewish immigration was composed of non-religious Jews, Hitti declared. "Viewed from the historical standpoint, political Zionism is the rankest kind of imperialism." He called "a Jewish state ... impracticable and indefensible," declaring: "It is an anachronism. Even if it is established, it cannot be maintained. It is impracticable; it is indefensible, not only on historical and geographical grounds, but also from the military point of view. It is impracticable from the economic point of view."

"There is no such thing as Palestine in history, absolutely not," Hitti asserted. "I wish we had maps here to show you what I mean by an anachronism, but you can imagine ... a very small tiny spot there on the southern part of the eastern shore of the Mediterranean Sea, surrounded by a vast territory of Arab Moslem lands, beginning with Morocco, continuing through Tunis[ia], Tripoli [Libya] and Egypt, and going down to Arabia proper, then going up to Transjordan, Syria, Lebanon and Iraq—one solid Arabic-speaking bloc—50 million people—with this tiny little spot which has been chosen as the place of an exotic state, built up by international machinery, drawing support from all over the world, artificially stimulated. How can a state like that maintain itself?"

Hitti concluded his testimony by quoting from 2 works in support of his arguments. The first was *The Heritage of Soloman* by John Garstang, professor of archaeology in Liverpool (and later director of Palestinian antiquities for the mandatory government), published in London in 1938. In it, Prof. Garstang—as quoted by Hitti—maintained on page 115: "Since Palestine on 3 sides has no definite boundaries, it is not well adapted to become the cradle of one particular race, nor can it claim for its population a continuous national history. Indeed, only at long intervals and for relatively short periods has it ever been ruled from within.... It is essentially a part of Syria, with which it shares a common seaboard and a parallel range of mountains."

Hitti then cited "an expert on population" who knew "nothing first-hand about Palestine—never went there." "He, Frank W. Notestein, and another, Ernest Jurkat, wrote 'Population Problems of Palestine,' published in the *Milbank Memorial Fund Quarterly* Oct. 1945." Hitti quoted from page 350 of the periodical: "On the other hand, on the basis of the growth prospect, it appears that a catastrophe of major proportions is not outside the bounds of possibility if enthusiasm for a Jewish state would result in the really heavy immigration sometimes talked of." He then quoted from page 352: "Should the Jews achieve a national state, it is unlikely that in the long run it could be maintained, either as part of the region, whose only hope for economic development is as the center of a substantial hinterland, or as a minority ruling group supported by an outside power."

Hitti said: "This authority on population ... reaches the same conclusion. It is a conclusion that any serious student of history, geography and demography ... must reach—that a Zionist state in Palestine is impracticable and indefensible."

The Committee of Inquiry ended its hearings in Washington Jan. 14 and proceeded to sessions in London, beginning Jan. 23.

Testimony in London Jan. 23-Feb. 4 afforded a greater diversity of opinion. Prof. Selig Brodetsky, president of the (British) Jewish Board of Deputies, called Jan. 25 for the admission to Palestine of one million Jews to establish a numerical majority. He said that a Jewish state under the British flag would guard the Arabs' rights and give them a "full share" in the government. Sir Simon Marks, vice president of the Zionist Federation of Great Britain, also called for the establishment of a Jewish state. Representatives of the chief rabbi of Britain and the Federation of Synagogues described the historical and religious nature of the Jewish claim to Palestine.

Lord Samuel* proposed that Palestine be placed under some form of trusteeship for several years and that the Jewish, Arab and Christian communities receive the power to govern their own institutions. Mixed communities should have their own (mixed) governing councils with a central control, presided over by a British chairman, Lord Samuel suggested. He also proposed that an annual quota be fixed for Jewish immigration and recommended 50,000 as a figure.

Leopold S. Amery, former British colonial secretary and secretary of state for India, advocated the partition of Palestine as the only solution. He said there should be separate Jewish and Arab states, and Jerusalem should be placed under international protection. The historian Dr. James Parkes advocated an independent Jewish state in Palestine.

Expressing the views of Syria, Lebanon, Egypt, Iraq and Saudi Arabia, Faris el-Khoury of Syria, serving as the spokesman for these 5 Arab nations, said that the Jewish problem should be solved by the UN and outside Palestine. He declared that the Arab states strongly opposed partition. He denied that Jews had ever been persecuted in Arab countries but warned

---

* Viscount Herbert Samuel was the first high commissioner for Palestine and one of the principal figures behind the Balfour Declaration.

that continued Jewish immigration into Palestine would be greatly resented and universally opposed by all Arabs.

Other prominent British Jews, among them Maj. Sir Brunel Cohen, Basil Henriques and Col. Louis Gluckstein, described Jewry as a religious rather than a politico-national group. They asserted that Jews had no exclusive entry rights to Palestine by virtue of their religion and said that the problems of emigration from Europe and settlement in Palestine or elsewhere should be left to the UN.

Maj. Gen. Sir Edward Spears, former minister to the Levant States—Syria and Lebanon—and Dr. Maude Royden* opposed a Jewish state. Spears said that "Zionist policy" had "many of the earmarks of Nazism," and he accused the Zionists of a "Herrenvolk philosophy," adding, "They seek to impose their rule on weaker peoples." He called the Jews of Palestine "unloyal" to the British Empire and warned that a Jewish state in the Middle East would be a source of conflict, since large-scale Jewish immigration would be unfair to the Arabs, who would have to react.

Ending their session in London Feb. 4, the committee members broke up into groups that visited, among other places, refugee centers in Paris, Poland, Czechoslovakia and the U.S., French and British zones in Germany and Austria.

Before the committee's next full session Feb. 17-25 in Vienna, it was announced in the Austrian capital Feb. 13 that, according to an official census taken under foreign auspices by the Vienna Jewish Community Organization, 3,028 of the city's 4,418 surviving Jews intended to leave Europe. More than ½ of these were willing to go anywhere, but 1,065 wanted to go to Palestine. (Austrian Chancellor Leopold Figl announced Feb. 20 that Austria would restore full rights and privileges to Austrian Jews and that their property stolen by the Nazis would be returned.)

---

* Miss Royden, a widely known British preacher and social worker of anti-Zionist views, said that she sympathized with the tragedy of European Jewry but that the Arabs in Palestine had accepted a sufficient number of Jewish immigrants already and that therefore the 1939 White Paper was just. She warned that anti-Semitism would increase if the Zionists did not withdraw their demands.

The committee's session in Vienna brought to light a greater sense of urgency than before in the situation of those Jews remaining in central and eastern Europe. Bartley E. Crum, a U.S. member of the committee, asserted Feb. 17 that the plight of the 55,000 Jews housed in American-run camps in Germany seemed to him so desperate that he feared that they either might begin to fight their way toward Palestine or start a wave of suicides if left much longer in suspense over their fate. Committee members disclosed Feb. 19 that Hungary and Rumania had refused the committee permission to enter those countries and that Bulgaria had not replied to the committee's request for admission. After adjourning hearings in Vienna, the committee members visited refugee centers in Italy and Athens.

(While the hearings in Vienna were going on, terrorists Feb. 20 blew up a Royal Air Force radar station on Mount Carmel. Terrorists Feb. 21 attacked police headquarters in Haifa and Tel Aviv; 4 of them were killed in these attacks. Rep. Augustus W. Bennet [R., N.Y.] introduced in the U.S. House of Representatives in Washington Feb. 21 a resolution calling for a Congressional investigation of the situation in Palestine.)

The full committee reassembled in Cairo and conducted hearings there from Feb. 28 to Mar. 5. While there, the committee received a memo in which Secy. Gen. Abdul Rahman Azzam Pasha of the Arab League asserted that a Jewish state in Palestine would constitute "a center of conflicts, international intrigue and religious strife." Azzam declared that the League's 7 Arab member-states—Egypt, Syria, Iraq, Saudi Arabia, Lebanon, Yemen and Transjordan—had vowed together to fight to prevent the establishment of such a Jewish state. He demanded that the British mandate be ended and that an independent Arab state in Palestine be created instead.

The committee moved next to Jerusalem for a session that lasted from Mar. 6 to Mar. 28. Even before the committee's Vienna hearings, it had been announced in Jerusalem Feb. 11 that the Arab Higher Committee of Arab parties in Palestine had resolved to send Palestinian Arabs before the committee of inquiry when it reached Jerusalem.

Chaim Weizmann, chairman of the Jewish Agency for Palestine and the World Zionist Organization, presented Zionism's case. He proposed Mar. 8 the creation of a Jewish state in Palestine by the immigration of one million more Jews and the guarantee of equal rights for the Arabs living there. David Ben-Gurion, chairman of the Jewish Agency for Palestine, told the committee Mar. 11 that Palestine's Jews could and would defend themselves if British troops were withdrawn.

The Palestinian Arab leader Jamal el-Husseini testified Mar. 12. He reiterated the demands of Secy. Gen. Azzam Pasha of the Arab League for an independent Palestinian Arab state. Husseini, who had returned to Jerusalem Feb. 7 after 9 years in exile, was a cousin of and an aide to the exiled grand mufti of Jerusalem. He opened the Arab case with a flat rejection of Weizmann's earlier offer of friendship and repeated the Arab demands for an end to the British mandate, a halt to Jewish immigration and the creation of an independent Palestinian Arab state.

Husseini warned that if Jews continued to enter Palestine a state of war would arise and seriously harm the interests of Jews in Arab countries. The current situation, he said, was not a matter of "least injustice" but of "maintaining Arab interests." "Britain did not accept the proffered hands of its enemies in wartime because she knew what that would mean," he said. The Arabs regarded the Jewish offer in the same light, he added. Speaking on behalf of the (Palestinian) Arab Higher Committee and the Palestinian Arab Party, Husseini contended that, even if all displaced Jews entered Palestine, the Jewish problem would not be solved—but an Arab problem would be created. "The Arabs cannot take in even a few thousand refugees," he said. He suggested that the Jews accept the offer of the Dominican Republic to accept 100,000 refugees.

Husseini maintained that Palestine was overpopulated already and that the Jews' entrance had effected an ouster of Arab inhabitants. He called for "an end, once and for all," to all conditions that had caused the tragic state of affairs in Palestine. Referring to the earlier testimony of Ben-Gurion, Husseini said that he thought "Hitler was speaking from the grave." (At this point there was loud laughter in the hearing room.) He asserted that the committee had no right to examine or question the Arabs' natural rights and deplored the absence of his cousin the mufti, then under indictment as an Axis war criminal.

Under questioning by Committee Chairman Sir John Singleton about what would happen if the British left Palestine, Husseini replied that 30% of the Jews who had entered Palestine in the hope of building a Jewish state would withdraw, and the remainder would resume friendly relations with the Arabs. "We were always friendly with Oriental Jews," he said. Husseini concluded: "We are ready to shed our own blood once more.... This is invasion." He listed the Arab demands as: (a) "abandonment of the Zionist political aims"; (b) an immediate end to all Jewish immigration; (c) recognition of the right of the Palestinian Arabs to "complete independence in their own country"; (d) the end of the mandate and the establishment of Arab independence.

Dr. Weston H. Stewart, the Anglican bishop of Jerusalem, called both Arab and Jewish youth organizations in Palestine "pernicious influences" that only aroused violent political passions. Speaking for Arab Catholics, Archbishop George Hakim of Jerusalem opposed the Jewish positions and called Zionism "a menace" to Christian and Moslem Arabs alike.

The final Arab witnesses declared Mar. 26 that an independent Arab government of Palestine would crush immediately every vestige of Jewish immigration into the country. "We are against all Jews—Palestine is no asylum," Emile el-Khoury, the first Arab spokesman of the day, replied to questioning by Maj. Reginald Manningham-Buller. Khoury, secretary of the mufti's Palestinian Arab Party, demanded the return to Palestine of "our first leader, the mufti, and all exiled political leaders." He charged that the Jews wanted an empire "from the Tigris to the Nile" and declared his party against parity or partition. The Palestinian Arabs, he said, "shall not permit any slicing away of Palestine, even the city of Tel Aviv."

Sami Effendi Taha, general secretary of the Palestinian Arab Trade Union Society, said that "stories of Jewish historical bonds with this country and persecution in Europe are no more than imperialist strategy." (This evoked laughter from the audience.)

Threats of violence were voiced against the Jews of Palestine and the entire Middle East in the event of a decision against Arab demands. These threats came from 2 spokesmen for the Arab propaganda offices in Jerusalem and London, respectively, Ahmed Shukeiri and Albert Hourani, a British-born Christian Arab.

Shukeiri warned that any violation of Arab rights would result in violence in Palestine and throughout the whole Middle East dwarfing the Palestinian Arab riots of 1936. He added: "In time not far off, some sort of inquiry committee would have to be set up to deal with the problem of Jewish homelessness in the Arab world."

Hourani reviewed Arab attitudes toward binationalism and parity. "Dr. [Judah] Magnes [rector of the Hebrew University in Jerusalem and an advocate of binationalism and parity for Jews and Arabs in Palestine] might be the first victim of political Zionism" if binationalism were imposed, Hourani warned. Continuation of the *status quo* or the imposition of any policy contrary to the Arabs' basic interests would lead "very soon [to] some sort of violence and reaction in every part of the Arab world." "Either the Jews are bluffing about their military strength and their bluff would be called," he said, "or—if they are not bluffing—their strength must be curbed." Hourani saw the Jewish Agency as a "monster preparing to seize power" and said that "its teeth must be pulled." "It is unlikely that the Jews who gave rise to their own troubles will disappear with the establishment of a state. It is more likely that they will assume a new, more dangerous form," he said. In reply to questions, Hourani asserted that the Arab state in Palestine could withstand the resistance of the Jewish minority "with the help of the Arab League," and that any solution "would require some degree of violence."

The Zionist Case

Dr. Chaim Weizmann introduced the *yishuv's* case to the Committee of Inquiry Mar. 8, 1946. He proposed the creation of a Jewish state with equal rights for the Arabs there and the freedom of immigration for Jews. Speaking of the homelessness of the Jews in the modern world, Weizmann said:

> As a people, as a race, as a collectivity, the Jews are homeless, and this homelessness and the unchanging attachment of the Jews to Palestine did not begin with Hitler. It existed many, many years, many centuries before Hitler was ever thought of, and long before this hideous tragedy was enacted, the tragedy which would have seemed utterly incredible 15 or 20 years ago.

The developments of the last few years have produced a very considerable change in the distribution of the masses of the Jewish people. Taking first, let me say, the year 1880, you would find that at that time 75% of them inhabited the vast pale of settlement which was then Russia, which included the Czarist Russian province of Poland, and on the fringes of this vast pale were the communities of the Baltic provinces, Rumania, and some minor groups as in Northern Hungary....

Then a great change took place. Between 1880 and 1914, almost up to the very beginning of World War No. 1, mass emigration to the Western Hemisphere took place under the pressure of persecution in Czarist Russia. About 2 million Jews migrated in this relatively short period. 2 million Jews migrated to the [United] States, and some 300,000 migrated to Great Britain, to South Africa, to Canada. In other words, there was an emigration of almost 2½ million people between 1880 and 1914. So the numerical balance began to shift, and has continued to do so up to the present date.

In 1930 only half of world Jewry was to be found in east Europe. The rest, the other half, was across the Vistula, across the Rhine, across the Channel and across the Atlantic.

The first World War and the social and economic changes produced by it again brought a shifting of the balance in the Jewish masses. Russian Jewry was isolated. An iron curtain separated the great Russian Jewish communities from the rest of the Jewish world....

The statesmen responsible for the mandate and the Balfour Declaration were not dreamers.... They reckoned with this peculiar position of the Jews that I have tried to paint for you.... They realized that the Jews have a right to collective self-expression, like everybody else—that the existence of a "national home," if and when it is established and well-founded, would give poise and satisfaction and would render the Jew less unstable, even in the countries where he enjoys equality of treatment. He would feel that he had found collective self-expression in Palestine. They also realized that Palestine appeals powerfully to the Jews because there has been a connection between them and Palestine unbroken for thousands of years—not only in the moral and religious sense, but literally. With the exception of one or 2 periods—the period of the Crusades, when the Jews were more or less wiped out, and the subsequent Mongol invasion—there were always Jewish communities in Palestine and a certain amount of Jewish agriculture in Galilee. These communities were not sterile; they showed very considerable intellectual activity, spreading far beyond the confines of Palestine. And whenever there was the faintest possibility of going back, there was a movement, a literal, physical movement for return, even in the face of great difficulties.

There was a movement from Spain, a movement from Turkey, a movement from Germany, from Poland, from England—ships were always carrying pilgrims to Palestine to settle there, to live there, sometimes to die there, and to teach the word of God, which spread far beyond the frontiers of Palestine.

This was realized and taken into account, and embodied in the mandate....

I am reliably informed by men in whom I have absolute confidence—some of them trusted colleagues who have seen our country and studied it, who I think are unbiased and honest observers who would not mislead us—and they tell us that if the country is developed to the utmost, and the rain waters and the rivers utilized to the fullest extent, there would be room for many hundreds of thousands more. Some of them have named a figure of something like 900,000. As Lord Samuel pointed out, there would seem to be room for double or treble the present population of Palestine without—and I would like to emphasize it—without harm to the present population, Jews or Arabs, and without thinking of displacing anybody....

... We are sometimes accused by our Arab friends of having got hold of the best land in Palestine; that you can go round the coast and see the flourishing villages of the Jews, leaving only the poor lands and the hills to the Arabs. There is nothing more false than that accusation. It has become the best of land, but it has been marsh, it has been sand, it has been covered with rocks and with stones, and we have had to clean, to drain, to nurture and to build it up. Along with that, we have had to do the building up of the Jew to the soil, changing him from an urban inhabitant into a man who is attached to the soil. We had to build up the soil at the same time, and in this process we are all regenerated. The land which we have now was derelict, it is true, 25 or 30 years ago.... To us it is not merely an agricultural or industrial enterprise. To us it is a question of life and death. Only we could ever have achieved this progress in face of the heavy cost of material and moral effort....

I have witnessed the gradual whittling down of our rights in Palestine, and this culminated in the White Paper, which really, with the exception of 75,000 immigrants, put a stop to the "national home."...

The British government, in the White Paper of 1939, laid down once and for all that the Jews were to remain a minority of $\frac{1}{3}$ until the end of time.... This ... placed urgent problems of survival before us; not merely of salvage but of survival. My brain reels when I think of 6 million people being killed off in a comparatively short time, and if nothing is done of what can humanly be done to prevent a repetition of such a tragedy, then I fear for the survival of the Jews....

I recognize fully that what I ask for will meet with considerable opposition on the part of the Arabs, and I know there may be Arabs present, opponents or friends or whatever they are—I think probably opponents. But there is no counsel of perfection in this world, and there is no absolute justice in this world. What you are trying to perform, and what we are all trying to do in our small way, is just rough human justice. I think the decision which I should like this committee to take, if I dare to say this, would be to move on the line of least injustice. Injustice there is going to be, but if you weigh up, on the one hand how the Arabs have emerged out of this war—I do not begrudge it them—they have emerged with so many kingdoms, at any rate 2 kingdoms, 4 republics; they will have 6 seats in the UNO, one seat in the Security Council. To speak quite frankly, which may be forgiven—for at my age it may be permitted to be frank—I do not know if it is commensurate, what the Arabs have gained during this war. What is the number of their casualties? Have they suffered so much? If you compare it with our suffer-ings, with our casualties, with our contribution.... I say there may be some slight injustice politically if Palestine is made a Jewish state, but individually the Arabs will not suffer. They have not suffered hitherto. On the contrary, economically, culturally, religiously, the Arabs will not be affected. Not because we are so good—though perhaps something may be said for the character of the Jew who has gone through hell for thousands of years, and it would stultify his own history if, when he gets his slight chance, he started persecuting the Arabs. We know what it is to be a minority, we know it only too well, but there are quite different reasons. The Arabs have a perfect guarantee: whatever Palestine may be, it will only be an island in an Arab sea, and the Arabs will not need to appeal or to have separate guarantees inserted in the treaties; the mere weight of their existence in organized states would prevent any Jew from doing them injustice even if he wanted to, and I am sure he does not want to. The position of the Arabs as a people is secure. Their national sentiments can find full expression in Damascus and in Cairo and in Baghdad and in all the great countries which will, I hope, some day build up an Arab civilization which will equal the ancient glories of their people. Palestine is to the Jews what Baghdad, Cairo and Damascus all rolled together are to the Arabs, and I think the line of least injustice demands that we should be given our chance. When carried out, that will, I am sure, eventually lead to understanding and harmony between our 2 races, which are, after all, akin.

Ben-Gurion, in his testimony Mar. 11, made his case for a Jewish state. Outlining the reasons why Jews had come to Palestine, he concluded:

We came here with an urge for Jewish independence, what you call a Jewish state. I want to explain to you, since this is the center of the entire program, what is meant by that. When some people abroad talk about the state, it means power, it means domination. I want to tell you what it means to us when we speak of the Jewish state.

We came here to be free Jews. I mean free Jews in the full sense of these 2 words, 100% free and 100% Jews, which we couldn't be anywhere else. We couldn't be Jews in the full sense, we couldn't be free, in any country in the world; and we believe we are entitled to be Jews, to live a full Jewish life as an Englishman lives an English life and an American lives an American life; to be free from fear and dependence, not to be objects of pity and sympathy, of philanthropy and justice, at the mercy of others. We believe we are entitled to that as human beings and as a people.

We here are the freest Jews in the world. Not in a legal sense. On the contrary, here we are deprived even of equality before the law. We are living under a most arbitrary regime. I know no other regime in the entire world as arbitrary as the regime of the White Paper administration. The White Paper discriminates against us in land legislation and denies us the elementary right to the soil and freedom to settle in all parts of the country. In spite of all that, we here are the freest Jews in the world. Freedom begins at home, it begins in the human mind and the human spirit, and we are free men, and here we are building our Jewish freedom, more so than all the other Jews in the entire world. Why? Why do we feel freer than any other Jews? Because we are self-made Jews, made by our country, making our country. We are a Jewish community, which is, in fact, a Jewish commonwealth in the making.

I will tell you in a few words how we are making it. When we say "Jewish independence" or a "Jewish state" we mean Jewish country, Jewish soil; we mean Jewish labor, we mean Jewish economy, Jewish agriculture, Jewish industry, Jewish sea. We mean Jewish language, schools, culture. We mean Jewish safety, security, independence, complete independence, as for any other free people.

I will begin from the foundation. You heard already from Dr. Hitti that there is no such thing as Palestine, absolutely not. We are not coming to Palestine; we are coming to a country which we are re-creating. Building a state means for us in the first place a return to the soil. We found hundreds of Arab villages, Moslem and Christian. We didn't take them away; we didn't settle there. Not a single Jew settled in all these villages. We established hundreds of new Jewish villages on new soil. We didn't produce soil, it is made by God, but what nature left to people is not enough, they must work. We didn't merely buy the land, we re-created the land. We did that in rocky hills like Motza, of which you will find a description in the Royal Commission's report. In the swamps of Hadera, hundreds of Jews died of malaria, and they refused to leave that place until it was made healthy, because of love of Zion, because of the need to create their own soil. We did it on the sand dunes of Rishon le-Zion. With our toil, our sweat, and with our love and devotion, we are re-making the soil to enable us to settle there, not at the expense of anybody else.

The head of the Agency's political department, Moshe Shertok, concentrated in his testimony Mar. 27 on Jewish-Arab relations and asserted that the drive towards future cooperation was stronger than the difficulties of the current divisions. He said:

They [Arabs and Jews] can and they do [mix]. It is not a case of oil and water, which will not mix. They do mix. They mix in day-to-day life and get along well as neighbors. Nothing inherent in the nature of either prevents fellowship and good neighborliness.

The 2d question is—does the fact of the Jewish increase in numbers and expansion in area militate against peaceful relations in day-to-day life? The answer is no, they do not. Go to any settlement newly established by the Jewish Agency in the wilds, where no Jew was seen before but only heard of, and see how relations shape. They seldom sit apart and glower at each other. Generally there is much spontaneous, natural friendliness. Sometimes there are disputes as to land boundaries. So there are between the Arabs themselves. As a rule, peaceful counsels prevail. It is noteworthy that in the last disturbances very few of our settlements were attacked by their close neighbors. Mostly the evil-doers were brought from afar, while neighbors often warned the Jews against impending danger. Of course, the fear of armed reaction on the part of the Jews worked as a salutary deterrent. Defense, readiness for it, a capacity for it, breeds respect, and respect is the only sure basis for true friendship.

The 3d question is—is the Jewish influx, on balance, detrimental or beneficial to Arabs as individuals and to the Arab community as a social, as distinct from a political, unit? On this point objective evidence is overwhelmingly to the credit of Jewish development.

The last question is: Are the political interests of the Jew in Palestine and of the Arabs throughout the Middle East, broadly conceived, contradictory, or capable of being harmonized?

Our answer is, there is no inherent contradiction between their respective interests. On the contrary, they are basically in line with one another. . . .

The crux of the problem is the political conflict between the Jews and the Arabs of Palestine.

Jewish-Arab relations in this country proceed on 2 different planes: the first is the plane of day-to-day life, of economic and social affairs; the 2d is the political plane, that of the country's ultimate future.

On the first plane there is a great deal of peaceful collaboration. Jewish and Arab orange-growers are pulling together in forms more or less organized, more or less publicly expressed, according to political circumstances, but always on the basis of complete solidarity and with active interest in the same results. Jewish and Arab organizations of trade and commerce likewise often act in common. There is satisfactory collaboration on a number of government boards and committees. The committee has already heard here of the expressions of solidarity between Jewish and Arab wage-earners and of joint trade union activities. Jewish settlers give various forms of assistance to the *fellahin,* agricultural and medical.

In the mixed cities, when no political conflicts supervene, cooperation is smooth and effective....

Cooperation in all these fields of every-day life is restricted and hampered by the overshadowing political conflict. Yet, if it is so much in evidence while the conflict is raging—and, admittedly, it is hampered by the fact that the conflict is raging—how much fuller and more effective will it become once the conflict has been resolved.

This is true not only within Palestine. It holds good for the relations between Jewish Palestine and the neighboring Arab countries. On the surface the position in this regard is characterized today by the Arab boycott, but beneath the political surface there is a broad undercurrent of economic and scientific give-and-take, often with the initiative exercised on the other side.

In a memo submitted to the committee Mar. 27, Shertok elaborated on the Jewish Agency's preparedness to set up a government if necessary. He said: "With regard to the question put to me by Mr. [Bartley] Crum as to whether the Jewish Agency considers itself competent to form the provisional government, I beg to state that if, following a decision to establish the Jewish state, the arrangements for the transitional period are such as to require the setting up of a provisional government, the Jewish Agency will certainly be ready to set up such a government and seek the participation therein of such Arabs as may be prepared for it."

Finally, the Jewish Agency submitted to the committee a memo summarizing the *yishuv*'s objectives, reasserting its claim that one million more Jews could be absorbed in a relatively short period and tracing the history of Britain's mandatory policy as one of deliberate subversion of its original purpose— from its exclusion of Transjordan from the scope of the "Jewish national home" to its limitations on immigration and its hampering of Jewish settlement. The memo also provided this sidelight on Palestine's Oriental Jewish immigration:

The emigration of oriental Jews to Palestine has been continuous. In fact, a larger proportion of oriental Jewry migrated to Palestine in the prewar period than of the Jewish communities in the West. Within the last few decades, Palestine has absorbed about ½ of Syrian Jewry and nearly 40% of the Jews of the Yemen. During the war, immigration from Turkey has assumed considerable proportions,* and as soon as North Africa was liberated, immigration from those countries was resumed. Jews from Iraq and Persia have trekked on foot and used all sorts of devious ways in order to reach Palestine. In Egypt, serious organization and training work for Palestine among the Jewish youth is in progress, and throughout the Orient—from Morocco to Teheran, and from Istanbul to the Yemen—the urge to settle in Palestine and the practical preparations towards that end are growing. The only alternative focus of hope and devotion for the oriental Jewish youth is the Communist movement. If the writing on the wall is to be heeded, then the needs of oriental Jewry, as regards both magnitude and urgency, must be assigned their due place in the present consideration of the problem of Jewish immigration into Palestine.

Papers were also presented to the committee by the Jewish communities of Iraq, Rumania and Bulgaria and a cable was sent from the Jewish refugees in Shanghai.

In Palestine, there was, however, at least one major dissenting Jewish voice. Dr. Judah Magnes, rector of the Hebrew University in Jerusalem, advocated a union of Jews and Arabs in a "binational Palestine based on the parity of the 2 peoples." This union, he held, should be constituted as a regional association sponsored by the UN. Magnes, however, did not think that Jewish immigration should be stopped. He said that he himself would go down to the beaches to assist Jews in entering Palestine. He advocated the admission of the 100,000 Jews into Palestine "as an historical act of great mercy." This, he said, would not radically reduce the Arab majority in the country. He called for mutual tolerance, not

---

* Turkey Nov. 1, 1948 stopped issuing permits for Turkish Jews to emigrate to Israel. The exodus, however, continued, with Jews leaving Turkey on passports validated to Italy and then going to Israel instead. Jews from Yemen also continued to reach Israel. "From Dec. 1948 to Feb. 1949, 33,750 Yemeni Jews were flown to Israel and another 15,000 followed in 1950," the American correspondent Dana Adams Schmidt reported in his 1968 book *YEMEN: The Unknown War.* (Schmidt wrote that, to leave Yemen, each Jew had to travel to the capital, Sana, there pay a head tax of 3 Maria Theresa thalers and go east to the British protectorate of Aden, whence the American Joint Distribution Committee had arranged to fly Yemeni Jews to Israel. Large numbers of Jews had dwelt in Yemen since the destruction of Solomon's Temple in 586 BC.)

domination by either people, since Jews and Arabs together could "make their holy land a thriving, peaceful Switzerland of the Middle East." "The plain Jew and the plain Arab do not want war," he said.

Ending its sessions in the Middle East, the committee emplaned for Switzerland, arriving at Lausanne Mar. 29.

The Committee's Report

The Anglo-American Committee of Inquiry Regarding the Problems of European Jewry & Palestine was the 18th committee to study Palestine* but the first that linked European Jewry with that country. The committee's report was issued from Lausanne and was published simultaneously in Washington and London Apr. 20, 1946. Agreement on the findings was unanimous. The report was divided into short-term

---

* Palestine commissions of note among the previous 17 were: (1) the Palin Commission, 1920, to investigate the Jerusalem Riots under the British military occupation (its report was never published); (2) a commission led by Sir Herbert Samuel as financial and administrative adviser to Gen. Allenby, 1920 (its report was submitted to the cabinet of Lloyd George and resulted in Samuel's appointment as first high commissioner for Palestine); (3) the Haycraft Commission, to investigate the Jaffa riots, May 1921 (it blamed the Jews for creating conditions causing fear in the Arab community and disturbing the Arab way of life through Socialist ideas); (4) the Shaw Commission, to investigate the Wailing (Western) Wall Riots of 1929 (it cleared the grand mufti and the Palestine administration and blamed the Zionists, claiming that Jewish purchase of land caused Arab landlessness; a Minority Report by Harry Snell, however, rejected practically all these points); (5) the Hope-Simpson Commission, to investigate the Palestine Land Question, 1930 (it claimed that there was no more room in Palestine); (6) the Johnson-Crosby Commission to investigate the question of landless Arabs, 1931; (7) the French Commission to find land for landless Arabs, 1931 (its report concluded that no more land was available to Jewish settlement except for waterless desert and estimated the number of Arabs deprived of land by Jewish purchases as 1,000 to 2,000, but only 347 valid cases were found, including Bedouin); (8) the Strickland Commission, to form Arab cooperatives; (9) the Peel Royal Commission, to investigate the causes of the 1937 riots; (10) the Woodhead Commission, to delimit the boundaries of Jewish and Arab states in a partitioned Palestine, 1938.

As a result of the Shaw, Hope-Simpson and French reports, the Passfield White Paper to the Jews in 1931 was issued. The Woodhead Commission, set up to implement the Peel Commission's recommendations, found that these recommendations were unworkable. Malcolm MacDonald then called a round-table conference of Jews and Arabs and issued the White Paper of 1939, which fixed the Jewish community as a permanent minority in Palestine. Other commissions were mainly concerned with refugee problems.

and long-term recommendations. The main points of the short-term recommendations were that 100,000 immigration permits be granted immediately to displaced Jews in Europe and that the land-sale regulations of 1940 be rescinded. The long-term recommendations were that the British mandate be extended under UN trusteeship with the gradual development of self-governing institutions and that Jewish immigration be continued temporarily according to Article 6 of the mandate, pending the new trusteeship agreement under the UN.

The Committee of Inquiry, in its report, made 10 recommendations, with accompanying comments. It described the condition of Jews in Europe, analyzed the Jewish and Arab attitudes towards the problem of Palestine, sketched a review of the political background and traced the mandate's geographical and economic dimensions. In a detailed appendix it delineated the condition of Jews in the various European countries. *Its recommendations were:*

(1) *The Jews in Europe* —"We have to report that such information as we received about countries other than Palestine gave no hope of substantial assistance in finding homes for Jews wishing or impelled to leave Europe. But Palestine alone cannot meet the emigration needs of the Jewish victims of Nazi and fascist persecution. The whole world shares responsibility for them and indeed for the resettlement of all displaced persons. We therefore recommend that our governments together, and in association with other countries, should endeavor immediately to find new homes for all such displaced persons, irrespective of creed or nationality, whose ties with their former communities have been irreparably broken. Though emigration will solve the problems of some victims of persecution, the overwhelming majority, including a considerable number of Jews, will continue to live in Europe. We recommend therefore that our governments endeavor to secure that immediate effect is given to the provision of the United Nations Charter calling for 'universal respect for, and observance of, human rights and fundamental freedoms for all without distinction as to race, sex, language, or religion.'"

(2) *Immigration of Jewish refugees into Palestine* —"We recommend (a) that 100,000 certificates be authorized immediately for the admission into Palestine of Jews who have been the victims of Nazi and fascist persecution; (b) that these certif-

icates be awarded as far as possible in 1946 and that actual immigration be pushed forward as rapidly as conditions will permit."

(3) *Political principles of Palestine's government* —"In order to dispose, once and for all, of the exclusive claims of Jews and Arabs to Palestine, we regard it as essential that a clear statement of the following principles should be made: (i) that Jew shall not dominate Arab and Arab shall not dominate Jew in Palestine; (ii) that Palestine shall be neither a Jewish state nor an Arab state; (iii) that the form of government ultimately to be established shall, under international guarantees, fully protect and preserve the interests in the holy land of Christendom and of the Moslem and Jewish faiths. Thus Palestine must ultimately become a state which guards the rights and interests of Moslems, Jews and Christians alike and accords to the inhabitants as a whole the fullest measure of self-government, consistent with the 3 paramount principles set forth above."

(4) *Continuation of mandate under UN trusteeship* —"We have reached the conclusion that the hostility between Jews and Arabs and, in particular, the determination of each to achieve domination, if necessary by violence, make it almost certain that, now and for some time to come, any attempt to establish either an independent Palestinian state or independent Palestinian states would result in civil strife such as might threaten the peace of the world. We therefore recommend that, until this hostility disappears, the government of Palestine be continued as at present under mandate pending the execution of a trusteeship agreement under the United Nations."

(5) *Equalization of living standards* —"Looking towards a form of ultimate self-government consistent with the principles laid down in Recommendation 3, we recommend that the mandatory or trustee should proclaim the principle that Arab economic, educational, and political advancement in Palestine is of equal importance with that of the Jews; and should at once prepare measures designed to bridge the gap which now exists and raise the Arab standard of living to that of the Jews, and so bring the 2 peoples to a full appreciation of their common interest and common destiny in the land where both belong."

(6) *Policy on future immigration of Jews* —"We recommend that, pending the early reference to the United Nations and the execution of a trusteeship agreement, the mandatory should administer Palestine according to the mandate which declares with regard to immigration that 'the administration of Palestine, while ensuring that the rights and position of other sections of the population are not prejudiced, shall facilitate Jewish immigration under suitable conditions.' "

(7) *Land ownership policy* —"(a) We recommend that the land transfer regulations of 1940 be rescinded and replaced by regulations based on a policy of freedom in the sale, lease, or use of land, irrespective of race, community, or creed, and providing adequate protection for the interests of small owners and tenant cultivators. (b) We further recommend that steps be taken to render nugatory and to prohibit provisions in conveyances, leases, and agreements relating to land which stipulate that only members of one race, community, or creed may be employed on, about, or in connection therewith. (c) We recommend that the government should exercise such close supervision over the holy places and localities, such as the Sea of Galilee and its vicinity, as will protect them from desecration and from uses which offend the conscience of religious people; and that such laws as are required for this purpose be enacted forthwith."

(8) *Economic development* —"Various plans for large-scale agricultural and industrial development in Palestine have been presented for our consideration; these projects, if successfully carried into effect, could not only greatly enlarge the capacity of the country to support an increasing population but also raise the living standards of Jew and Arab alike. We are not in a position to assess the soundness of these specific plans, but we cannot state too strongly that, however technically feasible they may be, they will fail unless there is peace in Palestine. Moreover, their full success requires the willing cooperation of adjacent Arab states, since they are not merely Palestinian projects. We recommend, therefore, that the examination, discussion, and execution of these plans be conducted, from the start and throughout, in full consultation and cooperation not only with the Jewish Agency but also with the governments of the neighboring Arab states directly affected."

(9) *Educational reforms* —"We recommend that, in the interests of the conciliation of the 2 peoples and of the general improvement of the Arab standard of living, the educational system of both Jews and Arabs be reformed, including the introduction of compulsory education within a reasonable time."

(10) *Requirements for peace in Palestine* —"We recommend that, if this report is adopted, it should be made clear beyond all doubt to both Jews and Arabs that any attempt from either side by threats of violence, by terrorism, or by the organization or use of illegal armies to prevent its execution will be resolutely suppressed. Furthermore, we express the view that the Jewish Agency should at once resume active cooperation with the mandatory in the suppression of terrorism and of illegal immigration and in the maintenance of that law and order throughout Palestine which is essential for the good of all, including the new immigrants."

Position of Jews in Europe

The committee described in its report the plight of the 98,000 Jews categorized as DPs living in Germany, Austria and Italy and a small additional number scattered throughout other countries of Europe. According to the committee, the majority of these Jews were to be found in the U.S. and British zones of Germany and Austria, living in assembly centers once known as "camps," where accommodation was provided by military authorities. An estimated 30,000 of them had come from Poland, and there was an increasing movement from Rumania and Hungary. *Describing their condition, the committee said:*

In the cold print of a report it is not possible accurately to portray our feelings with regard to the suffering deliberately inflicted by the Germans on those Jews who fell into their hands. The visit of our subcommittee to the Warsaw ghetto has left on their minds an impression which will forever remain. Areas of that city on which formerly stood large buildings are now a mass of rubble, covering the bodies of numberless Jews. Adjoining the ghetto there still stands an old barracks used as a place for killing Jews. In the courtyards of the barracks were pits containing human ash and human bones. The effect of that place on Jews who came searching, so often in vain, for any trace of their dear ones, can be left to the imagination. When we remember that at Maidanek, Oswiecim and many other centers a deliberate policy of extermination, coupled with indescribable suffering, was inflicted upon the Jews, of whom it is estimated that certainly not less than 5 million perished, we can well understand and sympathize with the intense desire of the surviving Jews to depart from localities so full of such poignant memories. It must also be understood that this happened in what were regarded as civilized communities. There can scarcely be a Jew in Europe who has not suffered in greater or less degree either himself or herself or by the loss of relatives.... We could harrow the feelings of those who read this report by repetition of accounts we received of German frightfulness. We do not propose to do so. We wish to present a picture of the general situation as we saw it. Few of the older people survived; not many children, for special efforts seem to have been made to destroy them. The majority of the children who survived are orphans. The majority of the remaining survivors are young and middle-aged people, who escaped death only by their strong physique enabling them to sustain either the ordeals of forced labor in concentration camps or the privations accompanying hiding. The young people have had little or no education save that of cruelty. It is not too much to say that they all owe their lives to liberation by the United Nations.

It is rare indeed to find a complete Jewish family. Those who return to their old homes find them destroyed or occupied by others, their businesses gone or else in other hands. They search for relatives, frequently undertaking long journeys on hearing a rumor that one has been seen in another part of the country or in another center. Such was the system of the Germans that it is difficult for them ever to establish the death of their dear ones. They are faced also with very great difficulties in securing the restitution of their property. In Germany and Poland, which was often described to us as "the cemetery of European Jewry," a Jew may see in the face of any man he looks upon the murderer of his family. It is understandable that few find themselves able to face such conditions....

Whatever the previous position in life of those in the centers, from a judge in Memel to a young man who by reason of years of persecution has never been able to earn his livelihood, there is the widespread feeling that they have been brought to the same level of mere existence and homelessness. The first sense of happiness following release from the concentration camps and slave labor has passed. Now they are conscious only of the constraint of their camp life, even though it is under new and more favorable conditions.... We were deeply impressed by the tragedy of the situation of the Jewish survivors in the centers and by the tragedy of their purposeless existence. Many months have passed since they were freed from Nazi brutality, but they themselves feel as far as ever from restoration to normal life.

These men, women and children have a moral claim on the civilized world. Their pitiable condition has evoked worldwide sympathy, but sympathy has so far taken the form only of providing them with the bare essentials of food, clothing and shelter. It seems to them that the only real chance of rebuilding their shattered lives and of becoming normal men and women again is that offered in Palestine. Even though many might be glad to join relatives and friends in other countries, the doors of those countries at present appear closed to them.

If, as we hope, our recommendation for the authorization of immigration certificates is accepted, the great majority of Jewish DPs whose situation requires urgent action will be provided for, and it will be possible to achieve the desirable end of closing the Jewish DPs' centers and thereby discourage the further migration of Jews in Europe from center to center, zone to zone and country to country.

Jewish Attitudes

The committee said that it had found most Zionists in agreement on 3 main points: (a) that the mandatory power should transfer its control of immigration to the Jewish Agency; (b) that restrictions on the sale of land should be abolished; (c) that the ultimate aim of establishing a Jewish state as soon as a Jewish majority was achieved should be proclaimed.

Most of the Jewish opponents of Zionism, however, advocated assimilation as an alternative to Jewish nationalism, the committee found. The orthodox Agudath Yisrael Organization* supported Jewish immigration into Palestine but opposed the secular tendencies of Zionism. The committee also said that important sections of Middle Eastern Jewry were afraid that their good relations with the Arabs were being endangered by political Zionism.

The committee, in its report, also said:

The position in Palestine is somewhat different. Here the issue is regarded as a matter of life and death for the Jewish nation.... The Jew who lives and works in the "national home" is deeply aware both of his achievements and of how much more he could have achieved with wholehearted support by the mandatory power. His political outlook is thus a mixture of pride and frustration. Pride that he has turned the desert and swamp into a land flowing with milk and honey; frustration because he is denied opportunity of settlement in %10 of that *Eretz Israel* [land of Israel], which he considers his own by right; pride because he has disproved the theory that the Jews cannot build a healthy community based on the tilling of the soil; frustration that the Jew is barred entry to the "national home" where that community is now in being; pride because in Palestine he finds himself at last a member of a free community; frustration because he lives, not under a freely elected government, but under an autocratic if humane regime.... The sudden rise of immigration after the Nazi seizure of power had as its direct result the 3½ years of Arab revolt, during which the Jew had to train himself for self-defense and

---

* The Agudath Yisrael Organization is a political and religious movement that views the Torah, as interpreted by traditional commentators, as the only religious code of laws binding on the Jew as an individual and on the Jewish people as a whole. Adherents of this philosophy split off from the general Zionist movement in 1911, maintaining that the return to Zion could not be separated from the Messianic redemption, the time for which had not yet come. In Israel, the *Agudath Yisrael* Organization agreed to support the state and the government after the state was established.

to accustom himself to the life of a pioneer in an armed stockade. The barbed wire and watchtowers manned by the settlement police night and day strike the eye of the visitor as he approaches every collective colony. They are an outward symbol of the new attitude to life and politics which developed among the Palestinian Jews between 1936-39. The Jews in Palestine are convinced that Arab violence paid. Throughout the Arab rising, the Jews, despite every provocation, obeyed the orders of their leaders and exercised a remarkable self-discipline. They shot only in self-defense; they rarely took reprisals on the Arab population. They state bitterly that the reward for this restraint was the White Paper of 1939.

The mandatory power, they argue, yielded to force, cut down immigration, and thus caused the death of thousands of Jews in Hitler's gas chambers. The Arabs, who had recourse to violence, received substantial concessions, while the Jews, who had put their faith in the mandatory, were compelled to accept what they regard as a violation of the spirit and letter of the mandate. An immediate result of the success of Arab terrorism was the beginning of Jewish terrorism and a general militarization of Jewish life in Palestine. Deprived, as he believed, both of his natural and legal rights, the Palestinian Jew began to lose faith in the mandatory power. The dangerous belief was spread that not patience but violence was needed to achieve justice. The position of the moderates who urged self-restraint and reliance on Britain's pledged word was progressively undermined; the position of the extremists, eager to borrow a leaf from the Arab book, was progressively strengthened. ... During the war, tens of thousands of Jews learned to fight, either in the British Army or the Palestine Home Guard. They were with Britain in the fight against fascism; they were against Britain in the struggle against the White Paper, which they felt was not only unjust but totally inhuman as preventing the escape to Palestine of men, women and children in imminent danger of death in Nazi-controlled Europe. When the war ended and the Labor government came to power, the White Paper still remained in force. The Jews, who had expected an immediate fulfillment by a Labor government of the Labor program with regard to Zionism, felt a sense of outrage when no change of policy occurred. The bitterness reached a new peak of intensity, and the position of the moderates became almost impossible.

Arab Attitude

The committee described Arab tensions regarding the *yishuv*. It said, *inter alia:*

Stripped to bare essentials, the Arab case is based upon the fact that Palestine is a country which the Arabs have occupied for over 1,000 years, and [on] a denial of the Jewish historical claim to Palestine. In issuing the Balfour Declaration, the Arabs maintain, the British government ... [was] giving away something that did not belong to Britain.... The Arabs deny that the part played by the British in freeing them from the Turks gave Britain a right to dispose of their country. Indeed, they assert that Turkish was preferable to British rule if the latter involves their eventual subjection to the Jews. The Palestinian Arabs point out that all the surrounding Arab states have been granted independence, argue that they are as advanced as the citizens of nearby states, and demand independence for Palestine now.... They would like Palestine, as a self-governing country, to join the Arab League.

The Arabs maintain that they have never been anti-Semitic; indeed, they are Semites themselves. Arab spokesmen profess the greatest sympathy for the persecuted Jews of Europe, but point out that they have not been responsible for this persecution and that it is not just that they should be compelled to atone for the sins of Western peoples by accepting into their country hundreds of thousands of victims of European anti-Semitism. Some Arabs even declare that they might be willing to do their share in providing for refugees on a quota basis if the U.S.A., the British Commonwealth, and other Western countries would do the same.... In exasperation at the disregard of their objection to Jewish immigration, the Arabs of Palestine have repeatedly risen in revolt. A substantial number of them still declare their allegiance to the exiled mufti of Jerusalem and are satisfied with his policies. In the 2d World War Palestinian Arabs were on the whole spiritually neutral. As Jamal Effendi el-Husseini stated before the committee: "The grand mufti in Germany was working for the interests not of the English who were warring with the Germans, but for the interests of his people who had no direct interest in the controversy." They felt that it was not their war.

One witnesses in Palestine not merely the impact of European culture upon the East, but also the impact of Western science and technology upon a semifeudal civilization. It is not surprising that the Arabs have bitterly resented this invasion and have resisted it by force of arms. The Arab civilization of Palestine is based on the clan; leadership resides in a small group of influential families, and it is almost impossible for the son of an Arab *fellah* to rise to a position of wealth and political influence. Arab agriculture in Palestine is traditional, and improvement is hampered by an antiquated system of land tenure. The Arab adheres to a strict social code far removed from the customs of the modern world and is shocked by innovations of dress and manners which seem completely natural to the Jewish immigrant. Thus, the sight of a Jewish woman in shorts offends the Arab concept of propriety.... The Arabs of Palestine are overwhelmed by a vague sense of the power of Western capital represented by the Jewish population. The influx of Western capital and the purchase of modern equipment for agriculture and industry excite in the minds of the Arabs a sense of inferiority and the feeling that they are contending against an imponderable force which is difficult to resist. This feeling is accentuated by the fact that they realize that the Jewish case is well understood and portrayed in Washington and London, and that they have no means comparable of stating their side of the controversy to the Western world. They have particularly resented the resolutions in favor of Zionist aspirations, adopted by the U.S. Congress and the British Labor Party. Although the Arab States have diplomatic representation and 5 of them are members of the United Nations, the Arabs of Palestine feel nevertheless that they have not succeeded in making their case heard. The Western countries have many Jewish but few Arab citizens, and Arabs are less familiar with modern methods of propaganda. They feel that their case is being judged and their fate decided by mysterious forces in the Western world, which they do not understand and which do not understand them.

The period since the First World War has been marked by a rising wave of nationalism in all Arab countries. Palestinian Arabs share this sentiment and are strongly supported in their demand for independence by the states of the Arab League. Those members of the committee who travelled in the neighboring Arab countries found that hostility to Zionism was as strong and widespread there as in Palestine itself.

Geographical & Economic Considerations

The report showed Palestine as about the size of Vermont and divided into (a) a fertile coastal plain and the Plain of Esdraelon, with industrial towns and ports such as Haifa, Tel Aviv, Jaffa, Gaza and Acre and (b) the mountainous areas of the east and the desert in the south. Most of the Jews of Palestine and about ½ the Arabs lived in the coastal plain, although it comprised only ⅐ of the total area of Palestine. The mountain and desert areas were inhabited, with the exception of scattered Jewish colonies, by Arabs. According to official estimates, the population of Palestine had increased from 750,000 in 1922 to 1,765,000 in 1944. The Jewish increase (mainly through immigration) was from 84,000 to 554,000. The Moslem Arab population had grown from 589,000 to 1,061,000. There were 136,000 Christian Arabs. (Only 19,000 Arabs had come as immigrants.)

According to the committee, "the expansion of the Arab community by natural increase has been one of the most striking features of Palestine's social history under the mandate." The average annual rate of natural increase per 1,000 for the Moslem, Jewish and Christian communities were:

Years	Moslems	Jews	Christians
1922— 5	23.27	20.44	20.16
1926—30	25.19	22.70	20.60
1931— 5	24.97	20.91	20.85
1936—40	27.68	17.75	20.77
1941— 4	30.71	17.83	18.89

In the light of these statistics, the Jewish community would form a steadily decreasing portion of the population unless immigration were permitted. The high Arab rate of natural increase was attributed to "a fertility which is among the highest in the world" and the disappearance under the mandate of such counterbalancing factors as conscription for the Ottoman army and the former high incidence of malaria.

"On the economic side," the report continued, "Palestine is a country of marked contrasts. While the Arabs have remained preponderantly rural, in the Jewish sector there has been a remarkable industrial development. The passage of years has sharpened the contrast between the 2 economies. On the Arab side individualism is still characteristic, and small-scale peasant farming, still largely on the subsistence principle, remains predominant. In the Jewish economy, on the other hand, is to be found a nexus of centralized control. Thus the Jewish Agency, besides being a landowner on a large scale, is a promoter of agricultural settlement and has large participations in industrial and other enterprises... There can be few instances of so small a country being so sharply divided on the economic, let alone social and political, basis. Only in citriculture do we find close association between the 2 sectors.... Everywhere is to be seen a marked disparity between the standards of living of the Arab and Jewish communities. Jewish wage rates are consistently higher than Arab, those for unskilled labor being over twice as high. There is only a limited range of competition between them, and therefore a minimum of natural pressure towards equalization.... The war has done little, if anything, to weaken the division."

Public Security

The committee described Palestine as an "armed camp." It discussed the acts of terrorism in the country and warned of the "sinister aspect of illegal armed forces" growing in recent years.

The report cited 3 such illegal Jewish organizations: (1) Haganah, which it termed an illegal development of the former organization of armed watchmen set up under Turkish rule to protect the Jewish settlements and which then numbered some 60,000 persons under a central authority with large supplies of arms and ammunition concealed in caches; (2) the Irgun Zvai Leumi, which numbered 3,000 to 5,000 and which had split off from Haganah in 1935; and (3), the Stern Group, 200 to 300 strong, which had broken away from the Irgun Zvai Leumi. The 2 latter groups had been responsible for the most recent acts of sabotage and terrorism.

The committee stressed that the Jewish community as a whole and the Jewish Agency were opposed to the acts of sabotage and terrorism carried out from time to time by these organizations and strongly deprecated and condemned them. Nevertheless, the Jewish Agency, according to the report, had stopped cooperating with the mandatory government since the end of the war, and until it changed this policy the committee felt there was little chance of achieving more settled conditions.

Jewish & Arab War Efforts

Comparing the Jewish and Arab war effort, the committee said:

"With the outbreak of the 2d World War, the Jewish Agency and the Jewish community in Palestine offered their support to the war effort and agreed to lay aside their differences with the mandatory [government]. According to official figures, Jewish recruitment in Palestine for all types of military service between 1939 and 1945 reached a total of 27,028. The Arab community in Palestine showed itself largely indifferent to the outcome of the war. Out of a population twice as large as the Jewish only 12,445 persons were recruited for military service, less than half the Jewish total. The flight of the mutfi, Haj Amin el-Husseini, to Italy and Germany, and his active support of the Axis, did not lose for him his following, and he is probably the most popular Arab leader in Palestine today."

European Jewry

Statistics and descriptions of the condition of European Jewry were provided in an appendix to the report. Each country was dealt with individually:

Germany—Germany had about 74,000 Jewish displaced persons (54,000 in the U.S. Zone, 15,000 in the British Zone, 1,600 in the French Zone and 3,000 in Berlin—85% of the total being Poles). Only some 20,000 of the total number were the survivors of German Jewry, which, in 1933 had numbered 499,682. Since anti-Semitism was traditional in Germany, the committee pointed out that this remnant of German Jews was apprehensive about the future, after the Allied military governments would have left. There was "much shame and desire to make recompense" in some German circles, but in others there was a feeling that "now all traces of Jewish life had been destroyed no attempt should be made to recreate it and so give rise to the possibility of repetition of past events." Some of the more highly educated German Jews seemed willing to remain in Germany to rebuild Jewish life, but "a few unfortunate incidents might produce something of a panic and induce a change of attitude." The German Jews had great difficulty in finding a place again in the life of the country and unless greater opportunities of employment were afforded, it was not likely that many would wish to remain in Germany.

Austria —The number of Austrian Jews had dropped from 190,000 in 1938 to 7,000 in 1946 (with 4,500 of them in Vienna). Anti-Semitism still existed, and a high proportion of Jews were

---

Authoritative final figures for the destruction of European Jewry in World War II were collated by Jacob Lestschinsky and given on p. 60 of his book *Crisis, Catastrophe* and *Survival: A Jewish Balance Sheet—1914-1948* (1948, New York, Jewish World Congress Institute of Jewish Affairs):

Physical Losses in Nazi-Occupied & Nazi-Dominated Lands

Country	Number of Jews at the end of 1939	Those who perished Number	Percent of 1939 Jewish Population
Poland	3,300,000	2,900,000	87.9
Soviet Russia	2,100,000	1,500,000	71.4
Rumania	850,000	425,000	50.0
Hungary	403,000	200,000	49.6
France	300,000	90,000	30.0
Czechoslovakia	315,000	260,000	82.5
Germany	210,000	170,000	91.0
Austria	60,000	40,000	66.6
Lithuania	150,000	135,000	90.0
Latvia	95,000	85,000	89.5
Holland	145,000	105,000	72.4
Belgium	90,000	40,000	44.4
Yugoslavia	75,000	55,000	73.3
Greece	75,000	60,000	80.0
Italy	57,000	15,000	26.3
Bulgaria	50,000	7,000	14.0
Miscellaneous	20,000	6,000	30.0
Total	8,295,000	6,093,000	73.4

on relief, particularly in Vienna. As of Apr. 1, 1946, non-Austrian Jewish displaced persons totaled 7,000 in the U.S. zone and 1,019 in the British zone. About 73% of these were Polish Jews. Streams of migrants from Poland, Hungary and Rumania converged in Vienna. Many of them continued westward to the U.S. zone of Germany, but this movement was no longer being facilitated by U.S. and British authorities. The newcomers received humanitarian treatment on arrival.

Poland—In 1939 Polish Jews had numbered 3,351,000 (9.7% of the total population), and the best postwar estimates placed the number of survivors at about 80,000.

According to the committee: "There seems to be a very considerable measure of hostility among the population towards the Jews. In a country ravaged by war, perhaps more so than any other, with its economy disrupted, Jews and Poles are competitors for a meager livelihood. The laws give Jews the right to claim property that once belonged to them or to deceased relatives, but the exercise of that right against the Polish possessor is in itself a cause of hostility. Indeed, stories were told of Jews being deterred from claiming what was lawfully theirs by threats to their personal safety. Throughout the country there is a high degree of lawlessness. The government is doing what it can by legislation to destroy anti-Semitism, but until the rule of law is restored the enforcement of its mandates must be both spasmodic and ineffective."

The committee pointed out that political Zionism, always strong in Poland before the war, had become still stronger among the survivors of Polish Jewry, most of whom regarded Palestine as their only hope for rehabilitation. The committee expressed its opinion that the majority of the 80,000 Jews left in Poland would want to leave the country and that Poland must consequently be regarded as one of the chief possible sources of mass migration.

Czechoslovakia—The Jewish population of Bohemia and Moravia had dropped from a prewar figure of about 80,000 to 16,000, and the Jewish population of Slovakia, from 135,000 to 30,000. The remaining Jews of Carpatho-Ukraine (who had numbered about 100,000 before the war) were now Soviet citizens. All the anti-Jewish laws had been rescinded in

Bohemia and Moravia, and leaders of the Czech Jewish community believed that the Jews could again take their place in Czech national life. In Slovakia, however, anti-Semitism was still active. Zionism was consequently strong in Slovakia, and some 60% of its Jews wanted to emigrate.

Rumania —The Jewish population had dropped from its prewar figure of 850,000 to 335,000, yet Rumania still had the largest Jewish community in Europe outside the Soviet Union. 50% of Rumania's Jews were virtually destitute. Despite official condemnation of anti-Semitism, efforts to restore property and businesses had met with the same hostility as in Poland and Slovakia. Large numbers of Jews therefore desired to emigrate. Some 150,000 had applied for certificates to Palestine.

Hungary —The number of Hungarian Jews had fallen from a prewar figure of 200,000 to 100,000, and 90% of these survivors lived in Budapest, many in a semidestitute condition. Little had been done in the way of restitution, and anti-Semitism was increasing in Hungary. Only older people and those who were Socialists and Communists (some 30,000 to 40,000, or less than 25% of the Jewish population) wished to remain in Hungary, and, the committee reported, "as in Poland, the chief desire seems to be to get out." Between 50,000 and 60,000 Hungarian Jews had expressed their desire to go to Palestine.

Bulgaria —The number of Jews who had died in Bulgaria as a result of Nazi persecution was comparatively small, and the postwar Jewish population (45,000) was only a little below the prewar figure of 50,000. There was no anti-Semitism, but conditions were very bad, and the majority of non-Communist Jews wished to leave the country. 12,000 had applied to go to Palestine.

Yugoslavia —There were only 11,000 Jews left in Yugoslavia out of a prewar figure of 75,000. 2,750 of them wanted to emigrate to Palestine. Yugoslavia's Jews enjoyed full equality of status and shared in the economic and political rights of other Yugoslav citizens, and anti-Semitism was not evident.

Greece —The number of Jews in Greece had dropped from the prewar figure of 75,000 to 40,000. Only 2,000 of the former community of 56,000 were left in Salonika, the largest Jewish center. Anti-Semitism was not evident, but restitution went on slowly, and economic conditions were bad. About ½ the Jewish population was on relief. It was estimated that the number of potential emigrants numbered up to 50%, although that depended upon the progress of the country's economic recovery.

Italy —The prewar Jewish population of Italy was 46,000. Those who were Italian by birth did not desire to emigrate, but those who were migrants and displaced persons in Italy could not be assimilated under current economic conditions and regarded Italy only as a point of departure for Palestine.

France —There were 180,000 Jews in France after the war. 100,000 French citizens with full political and economic rights presented no special problem. The other 80,000 consisted of refugees and displaced persons, including a substantial number of orphaned children in the care of the French government and private American agencies. It was understood, however, that some 20,000 more recent refugees would not be allowed permanent residence in France and that their position would be further handicapped by the difficulty in securing papers to work or travel.

Belgium —The Jewish population had numbered 90,000 before the war and numbered 33,000 by the start of the first postwar year, 6,000 of these being German and Austrian refugees. The Belgian authorities were helpful, and there was no tendency towards large-scale emigration.

Netherlands —The Jewish population had fallen from 150,000 to a postwar figure of 30,000, including 6,000 German and Austrian refugees. The Netherlands government was helpful, and there was no tendency towards emigration, but the non-Dutch Jews had not acquired the right of permanent residence, and had only received the right of temporary asylum.

Switzerland —This country had provided asylum to about 35,000 Jews during the war. Most of these had come from France and Italy, and 24,500 had returned to their countries of origin, while 10,500 had remained. It was stated that 4,000 of this total might be able to remain permanently if funds were provided for their support. The rest could not be absorbed.

In all, the Jewish population of Europe (together with Britain and the USSR) had dropped from 9,946,200 in 1939 to 4,224,600 in 1946. 3,833,600 were nationals of the countries in which they were residing. 391,000 were refugees and displaced persons.

Arabs Oppose Committee's Recommendations

Arab opposition to the very existence of the Anglo-American Committee of Inquiry had been expressed from the outset. The Palestine Arabs' first decision had been to boycott its sessions. The Arab Higher Committee Jan. 6, 1946 had announced a flat rejection of the British proposal to permit interim Jewish immigration and had demanded that Palestine receive independence and that the grand mufti be returned to Palestine.

King Ibn Saud of Saudi Arabia Jan. 10 paid a state visit to King Farouk of Egypt, where he conducted discussions on Palestine with the king and with Premier Noukrashy Pasha. A joint statement was issued by the 2 monarchs Jan. 16. It read:

"We associate ourselves with all Moslem Arabs in their belief that Palestine is an Arab country and that it is the right of its people and the right of Moslem Arabs everywhere to preserve it as an Arab land. All the efforts by the Arab kings, heads of governments and peoples in support of the Palestinian Arabs were made to maintain the principles of justice.

"We confirm the constitution of the Arab League, which is that each Arab country has the right to decide its own future and enjoy independence. We desire our governments and peoples to go forward on the path of unity, to enter into agreements, create a rapprochement between them, and make their relations closer. The object of the Arab League was to create cooperation for the benefit of the Arab peoples. We desire that our league may always give an example of cooperation between a group of nations to maintain their security, liberty, and independence. Our intention is to cooperate with all other nations of the world on a basis of right, justice, and permanent peace. Our league will never think of being an aggressor against another nation."

To a delegation of Palestine Arabs, headed by Jamal el-Husseini, Ibn Saud said: "The question of the Arabs and Palestine is a question for Islam—all Arab countries, including my own." "My brother Farouk and I are with the league with all our strength." "What Farouk ratifies, I ratify, and what I ratify, Farouk ratifies."

In Jerusalem, the Arab Higher Committee ordered a one-day strike Feb. 2 in protest against the Anglo-American Committee's plan for interim Jewish immigration. While the strike was paralyzing the country, the Arab Higher Committee sent notes to Britain and the UN charging that Britain had violated its promise to the Arabs on the question of Jewish immigration.

By Feb. 1946, however, the Arabs had decided to accept the Anglo-American Committee and to present evidence to it. Meeting with the committee, then in session in London, Faris el-Khoury, the spokesman for 6 Arab League states (Yemen still had not formally joined) warned Feb. 1 that the Arabs would accept neither the partition of Palestine nor continued Jewish immigration. Testifying to the committee in Cairo Mar. 2, Abdul Rahman Azzam Pasha, secretary general of the Arab League, said that the league would oppose the creation of a Jewish state in Palestine with every means at its disposal, and he reiterated the demand for the creation of an independent Arab state in all of Palestine.

The U.S. State Department announced May 21 that the U.S. had asked for comments on the recommendations of the Anglo-American Committee from the governments of Egypt, Iraq, Lebanon, Syria, Trans-jordan, Saudi Arabia and Yemen as well as from representatives of Jewish and Arab parties, including the Jewish Agency and the Arab Higher Committee. (Unwilling to abandon American interests in the Arab States, Acting State Secy. Dean Acheson had promised representatives of 5 Arab states in Washington May 10 that the U.S. would keep a pledge made by Pres. Franklin D. Roosevelt to consult both Arabs and Jews before it agreed to any basic change in the Palestine administration.)

The Arabs had appeared extremely angered by the pro-Zionist sentiments expressed in the U.S. since the previous autumn. Outspokenly pro-Zionist assertions continued, however. Sen. Owen Brewster (R., Me.) said on a Washington broadcast May 11 that Britain had "bought" King Ibn Saud of Saudi Arabia with $20 million and had deliberately built him up as an Arab League leader. He urged a Jewish state as the best solution in Palestine. The Saudi Arabian legation in Washington protested May 14 to the State Department against Brewster's attack on the monarch.

The Arab Higher Committee, meeting in Jerusalem May 15, 1946, demanded the dissolution of the Jewish Agency as responsible for illegal immigration into Palestine. (This was the first meeting of the Arab Higher Committee in Jerusalem. The committee had been reconstructed in Nov. 1945 to represent all the Palestinian Arab parties in existence since 1939. Its prewar *de facto* leader, Jamal el-Husseini, interned in Southern Rhodesia in 1942, had returned to Palestine Feb. 7, 1946 and had taken over as committee chairman.) Under Husseini's aegis, the committee submitted 3 proposals to the U.S. and Britain: (a) the abrogation of the British mandate and cessation of all Jewish immigration; (b) the establishment of an Arab Palestine, and (c) the withdrawal of all foreign troops.

The Arab Higher Committee May 24, 1946 turned down an invitation by Gen. Sir Alan Cunningham, high commissioner for Palestine, to submit its views on the recommendations of the Anglo-American Committee of Inquiry. The Arab Higher Committee, repeating that the future of Palestine could be determined only by the Arabs, demanded an immediate halt to Jewish immigration and to land sales to Jews and called for the abrogation of the mandate, the withdrawal of British troops and the creation of a democratic Palestinian Arab state, which would become a member of the Arab League. In a note to the high commissioner, the Arab Higher Committee declared that Jewish immigration had converted Palestine "from a peaceful land to a raging volcano" and that the committee might be "unable to control the situation" if the government's policy did not change.

A split in the Palestinian Arab bloc was announced 5 days later. 5 of the 6 Palestinian Arab parties represented in the Higher Committee broke away from it and set up a rival organization, called the Arab Higher Front. The parties involved were (1) the National Defense Party, (2) the Reform Party, (3) the National Bloc, (4) the Arab Youth Congress and (5) the Istiqlal (Independence) Party. The reason for the break was said to be Jamal el-Husseini's refusal to approve the nominees of the Arab parties submitted to him as candidates for membership in the Higher Committee. Husseini, vice chairman of the Higher Committee, was the leader of the Palestinian Arab Party, which he claimed represented the majority of Arabs.

The announcement of the split came May 29, the day on which a conference of leaders and representatives of all the Arab states was convened, under the auspices of the Arab League and at the invitation of King Farouk of Egypt. The conference took place at Inshass, King Farouk's estate near Cairo, and those present included King Abdullah of Transjordan, the presidents of Syria and Lebanon, the regent of Iraq, the crown prince of Saudi Arabia, the representative of the imam of Yemen and Abdul Rahman Azzam Pasha, secretary general of the Arab League.

In a communique issued after the conference, it was stated that the issue of Palestine had been discussed "in all its aspects." Palestine was considered an Arab country, the communique said, and its future was of concern to all the Arab nations, which would oppose any further Jewish immigration as a violation of the British White Paper of 1939. The hope was expressed that "the 2 friendly democracies [the U.S. and Britain] would not do anything in connection with the Palestine problem which would compel the Arab world to retaliate." Touching on the newly created independent country of Tripolitania (later the northwestern province of Libya) and the British announcement of Britain's withdrawal from Egypt, the conference members said they hoped that these developments augured a new era of cordial relations between Egypt and Britain. The Arab states wanted to work for a lasting peace in the Middle East, they said.

The Council of the Arab League held a secret conference in Bludan, Syria, June 9-12, 1946. 32 delegates from the 7 member states were present, including a Palestinian Arab representative. The council June 13 issued a statement that contained a 10-point program calling for:

(1) The formation of a special "Palestine committee" to include representatives of all Arab states, to be entrusted with the task of conducting all affairs relating to Palestine.

(2) The formation of an Arab "supreme executive" for Palestine* consisting of Jamal el-Husseini, Ahmed Helmy Pasha, Dr. Hussein el-Khalidi and Emile el-Khoury.

(3) The demobilization of Zionist forces and the disarmament of Palestine (Jewish) terrorists.

(4) Enactment by the Arab nations of legislation that would take strong prohibitory measures against brokers and others selling land to Jews and against people aiding illegal Jewish immigration.

(5) The saving, by all means, of land in Palestine, and the utmost aid in this direction.

(6) Suggestions to Arab governments that they issue a special stamp, the proceeds of which would serve as a relief fund for the Palestinian Arabs.

(7) The creation of a "fund for Palestine" to which all Arab governments would contribute.

(8) The reorganization and extension of propaganda services.

(9) The reinforcement and extension of the boycott of Zionist goods and the organization of more stringent control.

The conferees urged the U.S. to withdraw from the Palestine issue and warned Britain that the Arab League would go before the UN if new talks failed. A secret resolution threatened to arm the Arabs unless Britain disarmed the Jews.

U.S., British & Jewish Reaction

The first official reaction to the Anglo-American Inquiry Committee's report came from Washington 10 days after the report had been issued. This was followed next day by the disclosure of the British government's position. The *yishuv*'s

---

* Not to be confused with the Arab Executive or, more properly, the Executive Committee of the Palestine Arab Council. The Arab Executive was created after the Arab riots of 1929 in an effort to unite the 2 main Palestinian Arab families and leaders of Arab nationalism, the Husseinis—led by the grand mufti—and the Nashashibis. Jamal el-Husseini, the mufti's cousin, was elected secretary of the Arab Executive, and it was dominated by the Husseinis. The Nashashibis organized a new party, the Nationalist, in Nov. 1923 to add weight to their cause. The 2 families' rivalry prevented the Palestinian Arabs from forming an Arab Agency that would operate on a par with the Jewish Agency for Palestine.

first reaction was expressed the same day by the Jewish
Agency.

Pres. Harry Truman Apr. 30, 1946 indorsed the
committee's short-term recommendations that 100,000
immigration permits be granted immediately and that the
Palestinian land-sale restrictions of 1940 be rescinded. He
pointed out that the committee had "recommended in fact the
abrogation of the White Paper of 1939."

The British government, however, was less sympathetic.
Prime Min. Clement R. Attlee May 1 gave a number of reasons
to the House of Commons why the government would refuse to
implement the recommendations of the committee it had
appointed jointly with U.S. Attlee declared that it "would not
be possible for the government of Palestine to admit so large a
body of immigrants" without American aid. He made the
admission of the immigrants dependent on the condition that
the "illegal armies in Palestine" (Haganah) be "disbanded and
their arms surrendered." Foreign Secy. Ernest Bevin June 12
made a similar statement at the annual Labor Party conference
in Bournemouth.

(The *yishuv* regarded these British statements as a call for
one-sided disarmament and as practically an invitation to
commit suicide—as British critics of the government in the
House of Commons debate May 1 also pointed out—since no
similar demand had been made about disbanding the armies of
the Arab League. These feelings were aggravated by
disclosures by Anglo-American Committee members that
Attlee's proposal making Haganah's disarmament a condition
for the admittance to Palestine of 100,000 European Jewish
displaced persons had been rejected by the committee as a
logical and moral impossibility.)

Bevin's speech at the Labor Party conference was stronger
than Attlee's in London. He told the party delegates that the
transfer of the 100,000 DPs to Palestine would cost the British
$800 million and that he would have "to put in another division
of troops there"—which he was not prepared to do—in order to
protect the new immigrants. Land in Palestine should be
publicly owned, and a Palestinian—not a Jewish or Arab—state
should be created, he said. Bevin attributed "the agitation in the
USA and particularly in New York for the 100,000 Jews to be
put into Palestine" to the fact that "they did not want to have

too many of them in New York." His statements received over-whelming applause.

Yishuv leaders were quick in pointing out that the transport and settlement of the immigrants were exclusively paid for by Zionist funds. Bevin retracted (indirectly) in an official government statement June 14 his original assertion on the cost to the British taxpayer.

Although the *yishuv*'s leaders had cooperated with the Anglo-American Committee of Inquiry by readily giving testimony at its sessions, they and other prominent *yishuv* spokesmen had placed little faith in the value of its forthcoming recommendations. *Ha'aretz* (*The Land*), a middle-class pro-gressive daily in Tel Aviv, observed Mar. 27 that committee questions had shown that the members were "grappling still with the same problems they had been trying to understand at the outset of the hearings." "It would seem," the paper said, "that they have not moved forward—and if they have, it is uncertain that they have not moved in the wrong direction." "This is borne out," it continued, "by the questions concerning the powers of the Jewish Agency and the results that would follow if recognition was withdrawn from it, or if it were actually forbidden."

Ha'aretz believed, it said, that the committee members' questions were not accidental. The questions, moreover, "left no room for doubt that the committee had heard strong arguments in favor of ending the [Jewish] Agency." *Haboker* (*Morning*), a right-wing Tel Aviv daily, concurred in this opinion.

Speaking in Nahalal, just west of Nazareth, Chaim Weizmann declared Apr. 9 that the Jews of Palestine "are now at the twilight hour and probably will be faced by new trials." "We will need great efforts to overcome the obstacles," he said. Skeptical of the committee's report, he added: "It is difficult to be a prophet in Palestine and say what the future holds and when our demands for a Jewish state will be realized.... Only by breaking out from the grips of inertia will we be able to emerge on the broad highway."

A preliminary Jewish Agency comment May 1 on the committee's report was that the document's greatest flaw was its failure to provide for the needs of the bulk of Jewish survivors in Europe, whose number far exceeded 100,000, and for Jews in non-European countries who wanted to enter

Palestine because their position had grown insecure where they dwelt.

While Arab reaction ranged from reserved judgment to open threats of direct action, and the Arabs in Cairo expressed shock at the possibility of large-scale Jewish immigration into Palestine, the Hebrew press was generally critical of the Anglo-American Committee's report and took the committee's conclusions as a dismissal of Jewish aspirations.

Other Developments

Pres. Truman declared June 14, 1946 that he had no intention of asking Congress to modify the U.S. immigration laws to admit a larger number of Jews into the U.S. He urged the British, moreover, to act on Palestine, and he created a special cabinet committee consisting of State Secy. James F. Byrnes, War Secy. Robert P. Patterson and Treasury Secy. John W. Snyder to advise him on the Palestine problem.

In New York June 13, speakers at an American Zionist rally had denounced British Foreign Secy. Bevin's Bournemouth remarks as "anti-Semitic, offensive vulgarity" and an affront to Truman. New York's Mayor William O'Dwyer said that Bevin "talks like Joe McWilliams [an anti-Semitic orator] and is just as wrong." Sens. Robert F. Wagner and James M. Mead of New York (both of them Democrats) cabled protests to Bevin June 15.

The British government felt impelled to issue a retraction June 14 and stated that Bevin's speech did not mean that the government had rejected the Anglo-American Committee's recommendations. Bevin's Bournemouth utterances, however, had reportedly instilled in the *yishuv* the fear that Britain would henceforth go "all out" against Haganah, the Jewish Agency and Zionism.

Grand Mufti Back in Mashreq

About this time the Middle East heard news that thrilled the Arab world—and embarrassed the British and French governments. In a press report form Beirut it was disclosed June 14, 1946 that the ex-grand mufti of Jerusalem, Haj Amin el-Husseini, whose sudden disappearance from France had caused an international controversy June 8, was in Syria at the home of ex-Premier Jamil Mardam, 15 miles from Damascus. Syria denied this report.

The French revealed June 8 that Husseini had left Orly Airport aboard a TWA Skymaster, had landed in Cairo and then had disappeared (carrying a counterfeit passport with the signature "Marcus Doualibi"). The mufti, although supposedly under surveillance at his villa near Versailles, where he had been living since his flight from Germany to Switzerland May 7, 1945 and deportation thence right after the war, had enjoyed the right to travel freely inside France.

Zionists in New York blamed the French and British governments as accomplices in this "escape," which Arab leaders throughout the Middle East hailed unanimously. The *N.Y. Post* announced that it was prepared to offer a $5,000 reward for Husseini's capture and indictment as a war criminal. The paper published documents obtained in Germany by the journalist Edgar Ansel Mowrer alleging that the mufti was "party to the murder of nearly 6 million European Jews."

Haj Amin el-Husseini had spent the war in Italy and Germany and had been sent after the war's end to France. He had fled imminent arrest in Jerusalem in 1937 for alleged involvement in terrorist activities. Other governments had also sought jurisdiction over him with a view to prosecution. The Yugoslav federal war-criminal commission had announced Aug. 22, 1945 that it would seek to try the mufti on the ground that he had organized during the German occupation an SS *(Schutzstaffel* ["protection staff"]—Hitler's elite guard) group of Bosnian Moslems who had handed Allied airmen over to the Germans. The British themselves were undecided about how to prosecute him. British Colonial Secy. George Hall had told the House of Commons Oct. 24, 1945 that he was unable to say "whether the mufti was to be treated as a traitor or a war criminal."

The French Foreign Ministry had stated officially Apr. 8, 1946 that the British government, without formally demanding the mufti's extradition, had requested several times that the French surrender the person of the mufti but that the French government could not do so without a properly formulated demand. The ministry added that the Anglo-French Extradition Convention of 1876 as applied to political refugees had not been invoked and that the mufti remained in France "under police protection for his personal safety"—but was not under arrest nor restricted in his movements. (It was announced in Paris Apr. 11 that the Lebanese government had informed France of its willingness to grant the mufti domicile in Lebanon.)

British Foreign Affairs Undersecy. Hector McNeil had told the House of Commons Apr. 15 that existing Anglo-French extradition agreements did not make the mufti's extradition possible, that such charges as those under which he might be tried were not extraditable offenses and that the mufti, technically speaking, was not a war criminal, as he was not an enemy national and had not served in any hostile armed forces.

No further official word of the mufti's whereabouts was forthcoming until June 20, when Egyptian Premier Ismail Sidky Pasha announced that the mufti had presented himself at the Abdin Palace in Cairo June 19 and that King Farouk, whose protection the mufti requested, had received "his eminence immediately." Egyptian Acting Foreign Min. Ahmed Lufti el Said Pasha asserted June 20 that the mufti would be considered a political refugee and that Egypt could not surrender him.

Prime Min. Clement R. Attlee informed the House of Commons in London June 20 that the British ambassador had received confirmation of the mufti's presence in Egypt from Sidky Pasha. The news of the mufti's flight from France had been relayed to Britain June 8 by British Amb.-to-France Duff Cooper. (French Foreign Min. Georges Bidault had delayed the report for 10 days because of French embarrassment over the mufti's success in leaving the impression that he was ill and still at his villa. It was announced in Paris June 9 that Rene Desvaux, Paris judiciary police chief assigned to the mufti's surveillance, had been dismissed.)

In Palestine, the mandatory government June 9 imposed strict censorship on all news of the mufti's movements. By then, however, the mufti's flight had become common knowledge in Palestine and throughout the Arab states.

STRUGGLE FOR IDENTITY

Summer of Strife & Terror

Terrorism was intensified in Palestine in the summer of 1946. The British reaction was an increase in repression, and these developments resulted in greater mutual bitterness.

In a serious new wave of terrorism, members of the Jewish underground illegal organizations, armed with bombs, grenades and automatic weapons, carried out a series of attacks on road and rail bridges in various parts of Palestine the night of June 16, 1946. They blew up the Allenby Bridge across the Jordan, the Wadi Gaza Bridge in southern Palestine, the Zid Bridge north of Haifa and a bridge near Metulla. A terrorist attack was also made that night on the Palestine Railway work shops at Haifa, where armed men blasted their way into the building with grenades and wrecked the main engine sheds and a power house. The attackers' escape route was blocked by British troops, and in the ensuing gun battle, 7 Jews were killed. The bodies of 2 more were found in the railway work shops.

In a countrywide hunt for the culprits, motorized British infantry, Palestine police and RAF units surrounded the Jewish settlement of Baar Ha'arava, near the Dead Sea, and despite resistance took away some 70 men and women for questioning. About 15 arrests were also made in and around Haifa.

Jewish gunmen June 18 broke into a British army canteen in Tel Aviv and kidnaped 5 British officers. 2 of the officers, who resisted, were struck on the head with iron piping. (2 more British officers were seriously wounded and hospitalized in Jerusalem that day when a gunman fired at them from a taxicab with a Thompson submachine gun. And the British military authorities announced June 18 that a Maj. Chadwick, a headquarters staff officer, had failed to arrive at a staff conference and was feared kidnaped. Chadwick escaped June 20 from the Bucharian quarter of Jerusalem after a captivity of 1½ days. An intensive search was pressed, but the British failed to locate the house where Irgun Zvai Leumi terrorists had held him hostage.)

British troops sealed off a section of Tel Aviv and
conducted a house-to-house search in quest of the 5 kidnaped
officers. The British command also imposed a 5 p.m. curfew
and ordered all Jewish-run hotels, cafes, restaurants, theaters
and other public places off limits to British troops. The Tel
Aviv Municipal Council and the Jewish Agency issued an
appeal to those responsible to release the officers and called the
kidnaping a detestable act.

British troops June 21 raided the Palestine Potash Works
at the Dead Sea, seizing a cache of arms. It was announced in
Jerusalem June 21 that there was evidence that the Irgun Zvai
Leumi had also planned to kidnap Lt. Gen. Sir Evelyn Barker,
military commander-in-chief of Palestine and Transjordan.

2 of the 5 officers kidnaped in Tel Aviv were released June
23. They said they had been chained for 5 days in a Tel Aviv
cellar by the Irgun Zvai Leumi. With their release, Haganah's
clandestine (Kol Yisrael ("Voice of Israel") radio transmitter
announced that 3 other officers would be kept as hostages for 2
Irgun members who had been sentenced to death in an arms
raid in March.

Mandatory authorities July 3 commuted to life imprisonment the death sentences of the 2 terrorists, Yosef Simkhon, 19,
and Michael Azbel, 24, who had been sentenced June 24 in
Jerusalem to be hanged for taking part in a raid on a British
military installation Mar. 6. The Irgun July 4 released in Tel
Aviv the remaining 3 British officers kidnaped June 18 as
hostages for the terrorists' lives. At the same time, the Irgun
issued a leaflet in which it said that "there is no alternative than
to fight." This broadside was taken as a virtual declaration of
war against the British.

The trial of 31 Irgun members—including a young
woman—charged with bearing arms and explosives had ended
June 27 with 30 receiving 15-year prison sentences and one
being sentenced to a life term. The defendants had refused during the proceedings to acknowledge the court's jurisdiction and
had resorted to reciting the 68th Psalm: "Let God arise, let His
enemies be scattered: let them also that hate Him flee before
Him. . . ." (This psalm was sung in King David's time and after-
ward whenever the Ark of the Covenant was being borne
forward in procession.)

British Crack Down on Yishuv

The British government appeared resolved to shelve all action on the Anglo-American Committee's recommendations. These proposals soon came to share the fate of the Royal Commission's report of 1937, whose proposals also had been ignored. Despite strong requests, Foreign Secy. Bevin refused to see committee members Richard Crossman (a Labor MP) and Sir Frederick Leggett (the British representative at the International Labor Office), who were urging that the committee's recommendations be put into immediate effect.

The British Laborites' view had at length come to coincide with the policy of the White Paper of 1939 that the *yishuv* should have a guaranteed minority status in an independent Palestinian Arab state linked to Britain by a pact of friendship—as were Transjordan and Iraq. A friendly Arab Palestine would be a bulwark against Russian penetration in the area, it was argued.

With this goal in mind, the British put into effect a plan of action submitted to the previous national coalition government in Britain by Sir Harold MacMichael, who had retired as high commissioner in Palestine in 1944. The plan called for the forcible disarmament of Haganah, the breakup of the Jewish trade union organization Histadrut and of the Jewish Agency and the arrest of many in the Jewish leadership in Palestine.

Supported by tanks and armored cars, British troops and Palestine police moved swiftly and without warning at dawn June 28, 1946, took over the Jewish centers of Tel Aviv, Haifa, Jerusalem and other towns and occupied the headquarters of the Jewish Agency in Jerusalem. Sir John Shaw, chief secretary of the Palestine government, announced that these operations constituted an effort to end the "state of anarchy" existing in Palestine and to enable law-abiding citizens to pursue their normal activities without fear of kidnaping, murder or bombing.

The Jewish Agency's premises in Jerusalem were heavily barricaded and fortified by the British, who also confiscated many Agency documents. British forces and police throughout Palestine arrested leading members of the Jewish Agency—including Moshe Shertok (head of the Agency's political bureau) in Tel Aviv; Dr. Bernard (later Dov) Joseph (the

Agency's legal adviser) in Nathanya; and in Jerusalem, Rabbi Yehuda Fishman (the Agency's acting chairman while David Ben-Gurion was in London) and David Remez, chairman of the Vaad Leumi and general secretary of the Histadrut (the Palestinian Jewish General Confederation of Labor).

3,000 officials of the Hebrew Labor Party, the trade unions, cooperatives and communal settlements and a number of Haganah members also were detained throughout the country. Top Haganah commanders escaped arrest by going underground. Most of Haganah's arms stores had been removed to new hiding places—because Haganah had known of the impending British action: the underground Kol Yisrael radio had broadcast the whole plan 2 weeks before it was put into operation.

27 settlements were surrounded and searched during the first days of the British operation by a task force amounting to 3 divisions. When the tanks or armored cars arrived to break down the gates of a settlement they encountered a new kind of resistance. According to one official communique, this took the form of "men and women lying on the ground with legs and arms interlocked and refusing to move." The resisters were dragged into barbed-wire cages for interrogation, but refused to give their names and answered all questions with the words: "I am one of the Jews of Palestine."

The government of Palestine June 30 announced the close of the first phase of the security operations and lifted curfew restrictions. In all, some 2,000 persons had been detained, Jewish casualties totalled 3 dead and 13 wounded and hospitalized, while one British soldier had been killed accidentally. A cache of arms and ammunition had been seized at Meshek Yagur, a Jewish settlement in Northern Palestine. This amounted to 14 machine guns, 5 mortars, a number of Thompson submachine guns, 314 rifles, bombs, 3,000 mortar shells, 200,000 rounds of ammunition and more than 500 pounds of explosives.

The British action provoked an outpouring of protest in Britain itself. Public criticism was aroused by reports of the passive resisters, and particularly by the arrest of Rabbi Fishman. The rabbi, 69, had been seized on a Saturday, had been denied the privilege of walking to jail (he was thus forced to desecrate Jewish law by riding on the Sabbath) and had been, according to a press statement, "walloped" by a soldier. The Colonial Office July 3 denied press and Jewish Agency allegations that Jews detained in its June 28 operations had undergone "3d-degree" torture and beatings. They also denied the alleged mistreatment of Fishman in the Jewish Agency building. The rabbi, they said, had refused to rise from his chair and had to be carried to a military vehicle, but he had not been maltreated or injured.

Prime Min. Clement Attlee, called on in Parliament to reply to criticism of official policies, said July 1:

> The House has been informed from time to time of acts of sabotage and terrorism in Palestine. In the face of these incidents the military and civil authorities have shown the greatest forbearance, and their action has hitherto been local or directed only against those immediately responsible for each particular incident. It has, however, become increasingly clear in recent months that these incidents form part of a concerted plan prepared and executed by highly developed military organizations with widespread ramifications throughout the country. The Anglo-American Committee called special attention to the development of illegal armed forces as a sinister feature in Palestine. The largest of these is the Haganah, about 70,000 strong, with a mobile striking force, the *Palmah**, some 5,000 strong.... In addition there are Jewish terrorist organizations—the Irgun Zvai Leumi, which has between 5,000 and 6,000 adherents trained in street fighting and sabotage, and the Stern Group, which specializes in assassination....
>
> The Jewish Agency have been repeatedly warned, both by the high commissioner and by his majesty's government, of the gravity of these developments and of the dangers to which they would lead.
>
> Accordingly, his majesty's government authorized the high commissioner to take all necessary steps to restore order and break up the illegal organizations, including the arrest of individuals believed to be responsible for the present campaign of violence. I am sorry to say that these included some of the leading members of the Jewish Agency.

Attlee added that the British government would publish the documents seized in the raid on the Agency's premises; he had already spoken about "evidence of a close connection between the Agency and the Haganah." He also said that the British government had informed the U.S. government of measures taken in Palestine, although Britain had not consulted the U.S. prior to taking action since it took the responsibility for its own

---

* The Palmah—*Plugot Mahatz* ("shock companies")—were the commando units of Haganah, subject to complete Haganah control but having an independent command. The Palmah commando units had been initiated and trained clandestinely in the 1930s by Orde Wingate, a British officer and deeply religious Christian whose particular belief led him to sympathize with Zionism. (Later, as a major general, Wingate commanded the famed Wingate's Raiders in Burma, where he was killed in a plane crash Mar. 24, 1944.)

actions. "These events," he concluded, "will not distract us from our examination of the Anglo-American Committee's recommendations."

Calling for an immediate debate on the action, Sidney S. Silverman (a Labor MP) moved that the House adjourn "to call attention to a matter of urgent public importance, namely, the arrest and detention of the executive members of the Jewish Agency ... and the occupation by armed force of its premises." He was backed by enough House members for a Parliamentary debate to take place.

In the debate that followed, several Labor members of Parliament expressed their opposition to Labor policy on Palestine. Silverman denounced the British government's measures as "plain, naked war upon the Jewish national home" and an effort to decommission the Jewish Agency. He said that the Agency had an equal right in Palestine with the British. It had been created by international law, and both the Agency and Britain were in Palestine under the mandate, Silverman declared. He called violence in Palestine the result of "desperation" and declared that the British Labor Party, like the Jewish Agency, was "committed up to the hilt" to the creation of the "Jewish national home." If the government would publicly announce that it accepted the recommendations of the Anglo-American Committee, he said, there would be immediate peace in Palestine.

A leading Laborite, Richard Crossman, who had been a member of the Anglo-American Committee, termed the government's policy "dangerous" and warned that it might lead to disaster. He said that the Jewish community in Palestine believed that "the only language the British government in Palestine understand is the language of force" and that the Jews had reached this conclusion during the Arab revolt of the 1930s, which after 3 years of violence had ended in complete appeasement. He said that the resistance movement in Palestine included the whole Jewish population. Sadly enough, however, this resistance was directed not against the Nazis but against Britain, the country that every Jew looked on as the Jews' best friend, Crossman declared. He urged the government to call on U.S. assistance in carrying out the Anglo-American Committee's report and recommendations.

Support for the government's policy was forthcoming, however, from the Independent member of Parliament D. L. Lipson of Cheltenham, who called the government's measures a "disciplinary action against Zionist lawbreakers," and from a Conservative member, Col. Oliver Stanley, who held that, if the government had genuine evidence of a plot by the Jewish Agency, the Agency, then, was declaring war on Britain. Concluding the debate, Attlee said: "Nothing can be more false than to say we have declared war on the Jews and Zionists."

Sidney Silverman withdrew a censure motion he had proposed to make.

Jewish Agency Accused of Abetting Terrorism

Attlee had assured the House of Commons that he would release evidence found in Jewish Agency files of the *Yishuv* leadership's complicity in terrorist activities against Britain. This information, published July 24, 1946, appeared in the form of a White Paper issued by the Colonial Office. Its conclusions were that:

● Haganah and its striking arm, the Palmah, under the political control of prominent members of the Jewish Agency, had engaged in "carefully planned movements of sabotage and violence under the guise of the Jewish Resistance Movement."

● The Irgun Zvai Leumi and Stern Group had been cooperating with the Haganah high command on some of these operations since the previous fall.

● Kol Yisrael, the underground Haganah radio, which claimed to be the "Voice of the Resistance Movement" and worked under the general direction of the Agency, had been supporting these organizations.

The Colonial Office said that its findings had been derived from 3 main sources: (1) Information contained in 7 telegrams (reproduced in the White Paper) that passed between London and Jerusalem between Sept. 23 and Nov. 3, 1945 and an 8th telegram May 12, 1946. (2) Various broadcasts by Kol Yisrael from Oct. 3, 1945 to June 23, 1946 that referred to specific acts of violence and sabotage. (3) Information found in the publications of the Stern Group, IZL and the "Jewish Resistance Movement" (Haganah), respectively: *Hamaas* (*The Deed*),

Herut (*Freedom*) and *Eshnav* (*Peephole*—Haganah's underground weekly).

The evidence related to: (a) Attacks on railways, police launches and the Haifa refinery, Oct. 31-Nov. 1, 1945. (b) Attacks on the Haifa radar station, Palestine mobile force camps and airfields, Feb. 20-25, 1946. (c) Attacks on road and rail bridges and railway workshops and the kidnaping of British officers, June 16-18, 1946.

Haganah, Irgun and the Stern Group were allegedly implicated in these actions. The Colonial Office deduced: The King David Hotel bombing "was carefully planned in advance as part of a deliberate policy. It was intended as a warning to h[is] m[ajesty's] government of the consequences that follow if they did not comply with the wishes of the *yishuv*.... The Jewish Agency Executive was not prepared to wait for a declaration of government policy but decided to cause 'one serious incident' to influence that policy."

The White Paper included texts of the telegrams. The first, sent to Jewish Agency heads in London by (Moshe) Sneh (the so-called "security member" of the Jewish Agency Executive) Sept. 23, 1945, read: "It is suggested that we do not wait for the official announcement but call upon all Jewry to warn the authorities and to raise the morale of the *yishuv*.... It has also been suggested that we cause one serious incident. We would then publish a declaration to the effect that it is only a warning and an indication of much more serious incidents that would threaten the safety of all British interests in the country, should the government decide against us.... The Stern Group have expressed their willingness to join us completely on the basis of our programme of activity. This time the intention seems serious. If there is such a union we may assume that we can prevent independent action even by the IZL [Irgun Zvai Leumi]."

The Agency Executive's approval of the action, according to the White Paper, was demonstrated in a telegram to London from Dr. Bernard Joseph (legal adviser to the Agency and one of those arrested in recent operations) Oct. 19, 1945. The telegram read: "Eliezar Kaplan [head of the Agency's financial department], basing himself on word from Hayyim* *via*

---

* Code names

Nwbw,* says that we should undertake nothing before you give us instructions to do [so]. He is opposed to any real action on our part until we hear from you. Other members, however, are of the opinion that it is necessary to back your political effort with activities which do not bear the character of a general conflict. It is essential that we should know at once whether such actions are likely to be useful or detrimental to your struggle. Should you be opposed to any action whatever, wire that we should wait for the arrival of Wlsly.* Should you agree to isolated actions, wire that you agree to sending deputation to the Dominions. If Hayyim meant us only avoid a general conflict, not isolated cases, send greetings to 'Chill'* [pronounced 'heel'] for the birth of his daughter."

According to the White Paper, Moshe Shertok (Sharett) had sent a reply from London to Dr. Joseph with the code expressions: "delegate Dominions" and "greetings to Chill," implying that it was desirable, while avoiding conflict, to indulge in isolated terrorist actions.

Later telegrams indicated that the Agency had obtained the cooperation of "dissident organizations." A telegram sent Nov. 5, 1945 from Jerusalem to London read: "We have come to a working arrangement with the dissident organizations according to which we shall assign certain tasks to them under our command. . . . The activities [of Oct. 31-Nov. 1] have made a great impression. The authorities are bewildered and have proclaimed a curfew on the roads at night. They are waiting for instructions from London. We are apprehensive of a general attack against the Haganah. We have taken the necessary security measures and are prepared for sacrifices. Confirm by telegram to Ada* inquiries about the health of her children."

In conclusion the Colonial Office stated: "The evidence contained in the foregoing is not, and is not intended to be, a complete statement of all the evidence in the possession of his majesty's government. Nor are the specific instances referred to by any means a complete list of all the incidents of violence and sabotage which have taken place in recent months. The fact is that in the first 6 months of 1946 there were nearly 50 separate incidents involving violence, and in many cases loss of life."

---

* Code names

The Colonial Office also cited numbers with regard to the Jewish paramilitary organizations in Palestine, labelling these estimates "too conservative" in reality. It described Haganah as: "an illegal and well-armed military organization organized under a central command," consisting of (a) a "state force" of settlers and townsfolk with an estimated strength of 40,000, (b) a "field army" based on the Jewish Settlement Police and trained in mobile operations with an estimated strength of 16,000, and (c) a "full-time" force (Palmah), permanently mobilized and possessing transport, with an estimated peacetime establishment of 2,000 and a "war establishment" of 6,000. The White Paper also said: "Something in the nature of conscription is in force [for Haganah], a year's service being obligatory for senior schoolchildren, male and female, between the ages of 17 and 18." The Irgun, operating under secret command, had a strength of 3,000-5,000, and the Stern Group a strength of 200-300 "dangerous fanatics"; these 2 groups had been fully cooperating for some time, and both were "equally committed to a policy of unrestrained extremism."

Reactions to the British Measures

Meeting in Jerusalem July 25, 1946, indignant executives of Zionist organizations and of the Vaad Leumi accused the Colonial Office of fabricating "a jumble of alleged telegrams" and insisted: "Not a single one of the alleged telegrams emanated from the Jewish Agency in Jerusalem. The Jewish Agency, which cannot accept the authenticity of these alleged telegrams, challenges the British government to prove that the Agency was responsible for their composition, authorization or dispatch."

Pres. Truman July 2 received Dr. Stephen S. Wise, the American Zionist leader, and U.S. Zionist members of the Jewish Agency for Palestine. The President, expressing his regret at the developments in Palestine and his hope that the Jewish leaders would soon be released, declared that the events must not be allowed to delay the execution of the policy of transporting the 100,000 Jewish immigrants to Palestine as recommended by the Anglo-American Committee. The American government, he said, was ready to assume technical and financial responsibility for the transportation of these immigrants.

5,000 British Jews marched through London July 7 in a mass demonstration ending in Trafalgar Square. Among their leaders was Thomas Gould, the only Jew to get the Victoria Cross in World War II. The marchers included hundreds of British Jewish ex-servicemen, several hundred orphaned children from the Nazi concentration camps and English-born Jewish agricultural workers training to work in Palestine. In Trafalgar Square they were addressed by prominent labor MPs critical of their party's policy, including Sidney Silverman, Barbara Syton Gould and Barnett Janner, as well as by Prof. Selig Brodetsky, head of the British Zionist Organization. In a resolution presented at 10 Downing Street, they called on the government to release the arrested Jewish Agency leaders, to implement the report of the Anglo-American Committee and to permit the immigration of 100,000 displaced Jews into Palestine as the report had recommended because "the establishment of a Jewish state in which Jews and Arabs shall live as free men under a democratic order is the only possible solution of the problems of the Jewish people and Palestine."

Dr. Chaim Weizmann, arriving in Jerusalem en route to London, issued a press statement July 9 condemning British policy and appealing to the British government for "speedy action such as will help us to counteract the counsels of despair now spreading among our people." Weizmann said in his press statement:

● "We are met today in the hour of grave crisis. The *yishuv,* for which we have toiled for 3 generations with so much love and devotion, is now in a state of siege, and our best sons and daughters imprisoned. In Europe, the remnants of our people, to whom Palestine is the last and only hope, are languishing behind barbed wire waiting for the slumbering conscience of the world to awaken and set them free." After a 6-year absence, he had found in Palestine that Haganah had for 8 months kept the strictest discipline and had cooperated with the government in controlling occasional extremist acts of terror.

● "My voice carried weight then. I was able to tell the *yishuv* leaders of Churchill's intentions to deal constructively with the Palestine problem following Germany's defeat. Then a great change swept over the political face of Britain, bringing to power a government more deeply committed to support the policy of Zionism than any other previous British government. That government has been in office for a year, and still the remnant of our people languishes behind barbed wire and there is no visible progress in the working out or application of a just and lasting solution to the Palestine problem. There is nothing but shifts, shufflings and procrastinations."

● There had been a marked slackening of tension in the *yishuv,* beginning with the publication of the Anglo-American Committee's report and lasting until Attlee made his statement "attaching an impossible condition to the implementation of the report"—*i.e.,* that Haganah disband. "Nothwithstanding Mr. Attlee's assertions to the contrary, I am deeply convinced that if the British government proceed immediately to implement the positive recommendations of the report, peace and quiet would reign in this country. But as one who has all his life regarded cooperation with Britain as the indispensable cornerstone of Zionist policy, I cannot help saying, however reluctantly, that the primary cause of the dreadful happenings here today lies not with the Jews but with those who have allowed the situation to drift into the present calamitous plight."

● "This should not be interpreted as meaning that I condone political violence. I abhor and repudiate it. I have used, and will continue to use, all my strength to eradicate it. I am the last to justify breaking the law, but even in administration of the law account is taken of extenuating circumstances." The Jews had helped Britain in both world wars; yet "now the mufti lives in a palace in Cairo while Shertok, the man who raised an army of 25,000 men to help Britain, is behind barbed wire."

● The mood of the *yishuv* had changed after Attlee's statement of May 1 to one of "bitter disappointment verging on despair." "The spirit that guides us—the weakest among the nations—is the same that guided Britain in the darkest hour of her history. And just as Britain triumphed against her adversaries, so we too shall triumph. Peace, justice and freedom are indivisible. A world half free and half slave will not endure. As long as the Jewish people are unredeemed, the world will remain shackled and crushed under the weight of its own injustice."

Arab Powers Oppose Creation of Jewish State

The 7 member states of the Arab League, meanwhile, had been circulating their arguments against a Jewish homeland in Palestine. The league disclosed in Cairo July 8, 1946 that the Arab states had sent notes to Washington and London in mid-June. It was asserted in the notes that American support of Zionism had had the effect of encouraging terrorism in Palestine and of imperiling peace in the Middle East.

UN Acting Secy. Gen. Arkady Sobolev revealed in New York July 24 that Egypt, Iraq, Syria, Transjordan, Saudi Arabia, Lebanon and Yemen—all Arab League members—had sent notes to the British government demanding that a new regime be installed in Palestine before the next UN General Assembly meeting. The notes, also received by the UN, were accompanied by a letter in which Egyptian Foreign Min. Ahmed Lufti el Said Pasha threatened to bring the issue before the General assembly if these demands were not met.

The Palestinian Arab Higher Committee July 10 attacked Pres. Truman's statement of July 2 that the U.S. was willing to assume technical and financial responsibility for the transport of 100,000 Jewish immigrants to Palestine. The committee declared that "Palestine is not a parcel of merchandise which can be bought in Wall Street for dollars or bartered for Jewish votes." It protested against the "flagrant, empty and irresponsible statements issued now and then by the President of the United States." It said: "The Arab Higher Committee wishes to assure Pres. Truman that it is not within his power or jurisdiction to determine the future destiny of this Arab country. If he is really in sympathy with the Jews and their plight in Christian Europe he should open the doors of the American continent, which can absorb not only 100,000 Jews but millions of them."

The Arab Higher Committee July 10 presented to the Palestine government a formal demand that the Jewish Agency be dissolved. It accused the Agency of encouraging illegal Jewish immigration and of subversive political activities. As the British released Rabbi Yehuda L. Fishman, the Agency's executive director, July 12 on the basis of his poor health, the Arab Higher Committee demanded subversion trials for the Agency's leaders.

The British Foreign Office, meanwhile, had announced
that it would arrange a meeting between the Labor government
and a U.S. mission on questions concerned with the recommen-
dations of the Anglo-American Committee's report. The
sessions, arranged by Cabinet Secy. Sir Norman Brook and
U.S. Amb.-to-Britain W. Averell Harriman, were conducted in
London July 12-26. The conferees were Henry Grady,
Goldthwaite Dorr and Henry Gaston, representing the U.S.
Cabinet Committee on Palestine that had been appointed by
Truman, and 3 British government representatives led by
Herbert Morrison. The 3 Americans at this meeting reported to
Washington that the British government had approved a plan
for the partition of Palestine on a federal basis, to be published
in due course. Truman recalled his representatives before the
meetings were scheduled to end.

British Release Some Yishuv Leaders

Mandatory authorities released Rabbi Yehuda Fishman,
acting chairman of the Jewish Agency, and several lesser
figures in the Agency from detention before mid-July 1946.
They did so after completing a thorough investigation of
Agency activities. The move was seen also as a conciliatory
gesture toward the *yishuv.* There had been no major instances
of terrorism in Palestine since June 18.

Arms searches throughout Palestine, meanwhile, had continued since the June 28 British raid on the Jewish Agency. An
official announcement July 5 from Jerusalem spoke of further
large quantities of arms found at Meshek Yagur, a settlement
near Haifa. Colonial Secy. George Hall told the British House
of Commons that this settlement was "literally honeycombed"
with arms caches, "some in bogus culverts and dummy sewers,
others beneath floors and above ceilings or in secret cupboards,
behind false panels, and some in children's dormitories." In all,
the British found 92 trench mortars, 5,267 mortar bombs, 5,017
grenades, 10 machine guns, 321 rifles, 78 pistols, 1,404 maga-
zines, 420,000 rounds of ammunition and quantities of
demolition explosives hidden in this settlement.

Lt. Gen. Sir Alan Cunningham, the high commissioner, announced the end of military operations July 11. The search of settlements ceased, and British troops were withdrawn from them. The curfew was lifted in Jerusalem, and the Jewish Agency building was evacuated.

The British authorities were still holding nearly 3,000 Jews arrested in the countrywide clamp-down June 29. None could be identified as a prominent terrorist or Haganah leader. The authorities began to release the prisoners in batches after Jews and government critics in Great Britain itself assailed the arrests with growing frequency as high-handed.

About 1,600 detainees at the Rafa camp went on a hunger strike July 16 in protest against the slow pace of their release. At Latrun, Moshe Shertok and Dr. Bernard Joseph, among others, went on a 24-hour hunger strike in sympathy with the Rafa prisoners. Most of the Jewish community followed suit Apr. 17 after the Vaad Leumi called a work stoppage and fast for 24 hours throughout Palestine. Jewish workers downed tools, and the *yishuv* observed a fast day.

Colonial Undersecy. Arthur Creech Jones announced in the House of Commons July 17 that, of the 2,675 Jews arrested in the operations, 677 had been released and 1,998 still remained under detention. (The Palestinian government July 29 released 138 more detainees from the Rafa and Latrun internment camps, including 50 women and 63 former members of the Jewish Brigade who had fought with the Allies in Europe.)

The London *Times* July 23 published a list of Jewish terrorist actions since the beginning of 1946. The incidents:

Jan. 1 —A series of attacks on government and army establishments in Jerusalem, Jaffa and Tel Aviv. Arms and explosives discovered by the police.

Jan. 13 —A train derailed and robbed at Hadera.

Jan. 19 —A police officer and an army captain killed in Jerusalem. Terrorists tried to blow up the broadcasting studios.

Jan. 20 —Givat Olga coastguard station, south of Haifa, blown up.

Jan. 21 —An attempted attack on RAF station at Mount Carmel.

Jan. 28 —Raids on RAF camp at Aqir; 200 machine guns stolen.

Feb. 3 —RAF camp at Tel Aviv raided by armed terrorists.

Feb. 5 —Abortive attack on Safad police headquarters.

Feb. 6 —British officer killed in terrorist raid on African soldiers' camp at Agrobank, near Jaffa.

Feb. 17 —Superintendent of police at Haifa attacked.

Feb. 20 —RAF radar station at Mount Carmel blown up (Haganah acknowledged responsibility).

Feb. 22 —Attacks with explosives on 3 Palestine police camps.

Feb. 26 —Extensive damage to aircraft and installations at RAF stations at Qastina, Petah Tiqva and Lydda.

Mar. 6 —Sarafand military camp attacked by terrorists.

Apr. 2 —Railways and bridges attacked by terrorists.

Apr. 23 —Simultaneous attacks on Ramat Gan police fortress and Tel Aviv railway station.

Apr. 25 —5 British soldiers and a British policeman killed in raid on Tel Aviv police station. 7 British soldiers killed in raid on car park between Jaffa and Tel Aviv.

June 10 —3 trains derailed and blown up between Jaffa and Jerusalem.

June 17 —Railway workshops near Haifa blown up and set afire. (Haganah claimed it had destroyed 11 bridges in the previous night's attacks.)

June 18 —5 British officers kidnaped in Tel Aviv. (2 later escaped; the remaining 3 were released July 4.)

King David Hotel Bombed

Terrorist explosives July 22, 1946 damaged the King David Hotel in Jerusalem. This 7-floor building, the seat of the British military headquarters in Palestine, contained the offices of the mandatory government secretariat. It was full of people, and casualties were numerous. Several government officials, including senior officers of the government of Palestine and office staff—Britons, Jews and Arabs, as well as British soldiers—were killed, injured or trapped under the debris.

British troops and Palestinian civilians searched for survivors for 48 hours. According to the official announcement Aug. 4, the victims totalled 91 dead and 45 injured. Among the dead were: the postmaster-general, 2 assistant secretaries, the economic adviser to the Palestine government and the commissioner for commerce and industry.

An immediate curfew was imposed in Jerusalem. Streets were barricaded, armored cars patrolled each quarter and the area around the hotel was cordoned off. In intensive searches in Jerusalem's Montefiore quarter, behind the hotel, the authorities picked up 446 Jews for interrogation and detained 30. A detailed report on the bombings, published July 22, said that 14 or 15 men, dressed as Bedouins, had alighted at the kitchen entrance of the hotel at 12:15 p.m. Holding the kitchen staff at gunpoint, they unloaded milk churns, one of which contained a time bomb. Sentries opened fire but the men succeeded in escaping, although one was wounded.

British forces July 23 again searched the Old City and discovered near the Jaffa Gate an abandoned car loaded with bombs, grenades, revolvers and Thompson submachine guns. In a nearby school they found a man shot dead and another, Aharon Abramovitch, suffering from gunshot wounds. Abramovitch had been a suspect in an attempt in early Aug. 1944 on the life of Sir Harold MacMichael, the former high commissioner, and had been released on parole in Sept. 1945. The British July 26 arrested 376 men and women suspected of complicity with terrorists.

The Irgun Zvai Leumi's underground radio, Kol Lochem Yisrael ("The Voice of Fighting Zion"), admitted responsibility for the bombing. In a broadcast July 23, it said that "the tragedy was not caused by Jewish soldiers, who carried out their duty courageously and with self-sacrifice, but by the British themselves, who disregarded a warning and refused to evacuate the building." The broadcast claimed that a warning of the coming explosion had been given 20 minutes beforehand by phone to the hotel switchboard, to newspaper offices and to the French consulate and that underground (Irgun) leaflets with similar statements had been sent to news agency offices in Jerusalem and secretly distributed in Tel Aviv and other towns. Later, however, it was reported that the French consulate had been alerted only several minutes before the explosion and that the local newspaper had been called 2 minutes after the explosion and told that "the Jewish resistance movement" was "going to blow up government offices."

Dr. Hussein el-Khalidi, secretary of the Arab Higher Committee, July 25 repeated its demand for the Jewish Agency's dissolution. Khalidi said that Arab organizations had been disbanded and individuals deported after a series of outrages in 1937. He asserted that the government was "shirking its responsibility" and that "if the Holy Land is to remain holy, it must be handed over to its lawful Arab owners, who will know how to maintain public security."

All Arab shops in Jerusalem were closed July 23 in a strike in protest against the bombing. The *yishuv* proclaimed a period of mourning, and the Vaad Leumi (Jewish National Council) issued a statement calling on the *yishuv* to "rise up against these horrible outrages." It condemned the "dastardly crime perpetrated by a gang of desperadoes" and expressed deepest condolences for the relatives of the victims. Dr. Chaim Weizmann, then in London for talks with British Prime Min. Attlee and Arthur Creech Jones, the new colonial secretary, strongly condemned this act of terrorism. The Palestine Jewish press equally condemned the Irgun.

Large-scale operations were begun in Tel Aviv July 30 to find the culprits in the King David Hotel bombing. The whole city was placed under curfew from 5 a.m. July 30 to 2 p.m. Aug. 2 while some 20,000 British troops and police made a house-to-house search. No craft were permitted to put out to sea, and anyone breaking the curfew (lifted intermittently for only a few hours to enable people to buy food) could be shot on sight. Essential services were maintained by the troops.

Gen. Sir Alan Cunningham, the high commissioner, said that these measures were the direct result of the King David Hotel attack. He asserted that the government had clear evidence that the terrorists concerned were in Tel Aviv. He promised that military action would be directed only against those responsible for violence. A search for arms was also launched.

The British unearthed a store of arms and equipment in an air raid shelter under the Great Synagogue in Tel Aviv. The items found included Sten-gun parts, revolvers, ammunition, British uniforms, stores of British army rations, forged Palestine government bearer bonds and forging equipment; weapons, explosives and ammunition were also found in 2 houses. A large arms dump with thousands of rounds of ammunition, mortar shells and hand-grenades, several hundred rifles and pistols were discovered behind false walls in a basement of a Jewish boys' school.

Arms caches were also discovered at the Ataroth settlement outside Jerusalem and in Jerusalem itself. A 3-day search of the Doroth and Ruhama settlements east of Gaza uncovered land mines, incendiary bombs, mortars, machine guns, Bren- and Sten-gun pistols and 15,000 rounds of ammunition, military maps, training pamphlets and other equipment. In Sdoth-Yom, a seaside settlement, a search by 3,000 troops to uproot illegal immigrants produced hidden diving suits and 300 passports of various nations.

A call to the *yishuv* to offer passive resistance to arms searches was made by the underground Haganah radio. In a series of phone calls Haganah warned that public offices in Jerusalem, including the registration office at the Palace Hotel, the British Overseas Airways Corp. (BOAC) office at the King David Hotel, the Palestine Broadcasting Service, the Law Courts, the Government printing press and the General Post Office buildings, would be blown up. They were evacuated but no explosives were found. All public buildings were surrounded by strong barbed-wire barricades. Armored cars and Bren-gun carriers maintained continuous patrols in the city.

The Colonial Office announced Aug. 2 that a search of discarded papers had dislodged a note in the handwriting of Moshe Sneh, a member of the Jewish Agency Executive, and 2 Haganah orders issued after the King David Hotel bombing. In the first of these orders Haganah called the explosions at the King David "the work of criminals." The same order instructed the population not to oppose the military searches by force. "In the event of the army's finding arms," the order continued, an armed attack was to be made to retrieve the arms "after the army left the settlement." It also told the farm settlements to remove their barricades and to avoid physical confrontation "in order to demonstrate rejection of the act in Jerusalem and not to incite the army." In the 2d order Haganah called on members to stand fast. It read: "In reply to our political struggle the British government has begun a military attack on the Jews of Palestine and on their achievements. Above all the attack is intended to break the Haganah and to seize its men in order to make the Jewish community incapable of resisting the policy which will destroy Zionism. The struggle for the Haganah now embodies the battle of the Jews for their freedom, their honor and Zionism."

A total of 120,000 Jews aged between 15 and 50 were interrogated—a process to which the *yishuv* (according to British reports) submitted with good humor and resignation. 767 men and 20 women suspects were detained for further questioning.

British Parliamentary Debate

The British Labor government at the end of July 1946 held a formal, full-dress Parliamentary debate on Palestine. Highlights of the debate were remarks of ex-Prime Min. Winston Churchill and the disclosure of the government's cantonization plan for Palestine.

This plan had been discussed at meetings of British representatives with representatives of Pres. Truman's Cabinet Committee on Palestine. It was presented July 31 by Herbert Morrison, lord privy seal, in a statement at the opening of the 2-day House of Commons debate on Palestine. The plan, according to a statement made during the debate by Col. Oliver Stanley, Conservative ex-colonial secretary, was based on a scheme prepared by the Colonial Office before the Labor Party had come to power, and it had already been rejected by the Anglo-American Committee of Inquiry. It was never officially published but was given in outline to the House of Commons.

From the *yishuv*'s point of view, its key features were a ban on Jewish settlement in 83% of Palestine and provisions to make the availability of the remaining 17% dependent on the ruling of the British high commissioner. The plan had not been accepted at the Anglo-American discussions since Truman had recalled the 3 U.S. members before the meetings were scheduled to end.

Subsequent information revealed the details of the "Morrison Plan." Basically, it provided for the cantonization, or federalization, of Palestine into 4 areas: a semiautonomous Arab province, a semiautonomous Jewish province and 2 districts—the district of Jerusalem and the Negev district administered by the British government. The Jewish province was to include eastern Galilee, the Emek and the coastal plain from Haifa to Tel Aviv; the district of Jerusalem was to embrace Jerusalem, Bethlehem and their immediate environs; the Negev district was to consist of an uninhabited triangle of desert in the south of Palestine. The Arab province was to consist of the remainder of Palestine. Jaffa would be an Arab enclave not contiguous with but administratively attached to the Arab province. The Jewish area would amount to 1,700 square miles, *i.e.,* 17% of Palestine; the Arab area to 4,050 square miles, *i.e.,* 40%; the British area to 4,360 square miles, *i.e.* 43%. It was estimated that the population of the Jewish area would number about 775,000 persons (including 300,000 non-Jews), that of the Arab area 740,000 (including 13,000 Jews), that of the British area 72,000 persons and that of the Jerusalem area 194,000 (including 100,000 Jews). The Jaffa enclave would have 66,000 Arabs.

Morrison gave this explanation of the self-government proposals:

The provincial boundaries would be purely administrative boundaries, defining the area within which a local legislature would be empowered to legislate on certain subjects and a local executive to administer its laws. They would have no significance as regards defense, customs or communications, but, in order to give finality, the boundaries, once fixed, would not be susceptible of change except by agreement between the 2 provinces....

The provincial governments would have power of legislation and administration within their areas with regard to a wide range of subjects of primarily provincial concern. They would also have power to limit the number and determine the qualifications of persons who may take up permanent residence in their territories after the introduction of the plan... The provincial governments would have the necessary power to raise money for the purpose of carrying out their functions.

There would be reserved to the central government exclusive authority as to defense, foreign relations, customs and excise. In addition, there would be reserved initially to the central government exclusive authority as to the administration of law and order, including the police and courts, and a limited number of subjects of all-Palestine importance. The central government would have all powers not expressly granted to the provinces by the instrument of government. An elected legislative chamber would be established in each province. An Executive, consisting of a chief minister and a council of ministers, would be appointed in each province by the high commissioner from among the members of the legislative chamber, after consultation with its leaders. Bills passed by the legislative chambers would require the assent of the high commissioner. This, however, would not be withheld unless the bill is inconsistent with the instrument of government whose provisions would afford safeguards for the peace of Palestine and for the rights of minorities.

It would also be necessary to reserve to the high commissioner ʿan emergency power to intervene if a provincial government fails to perform, or exceeds, its proper functions. The executive and legislative functions of the central government would initially be exercised by the high commissioner, assisted by a nominated executive council. Certain of the departments of the central government would be headed, as soon as the high commissioner deems practical, by Palestinians. The high commissioner would establish a development planning board and a tariff board composed of representatives of the central government and of each province. In the Jerusalem district, a council would be established with powers similar to those of a municipal council. The majority of its members would be elected, but certain members would be nominated by the high commissioner. The Negev district would be administered, for the time being, by the central government.

Morrison said that the central government would have final control over immigration but that this control would be exercised on the basis of the recommendations of the provincial governments and that "so long as the economic absorptive capacity of the province was not exceeded, the central government would authorize the immigration desired by the provincial government."

Morrison said: "As part of this plan it would become possible to accept the recommendations of the Anglo-American Committee for the immediate admission of 100,000 Jewish immigrants and for continuing immigration thereafter. The [6] experts [had] prepared a plan for the movement of 100,000 Jews from Europe to the Jewish area of Palestine, and this plan could be set in motion as soon as it was decided to put into effect the scheme as a whole." It was proposed to select the immigrants primarily from Germany, Austria and Italy, with prior consideration given those having wintered in collection centers there. From countries of eastern and southeastern Europe, only orphan children would be eligible for immigration. The U.S. government would be asked to undertake sole responsibility for the sea transport of these refugees and to provide their food for the first 2 months after their arrival in Palestine. The money needed for the transfer and settlement was to "be found from reparations, contributions by world Jewry and [from] loans."

The plan also called for a program to improve the economic and social conditions of the Palestinian Arabs. The U.S. government was to "be asked to make a substantial grant to be used principally for financing Arab development projects not suitable for self-liquidating loans and for assisting in meeting extraordinary expenditure during the transition period," Morrison said, "while Great Britain should be asked to take ultimate responsibility for meeting Palestine's annual budgetary deficit up to the time when increased revenues made this unnecessary."

Morrison listed what he considered the advantages of the plan to all involved: It would give the Jews a large measure of control over immigration in their own province. The land transfers regulations, and odious to Jews, would be repealed. The Arab province would be free to refuse permission to Jews to buy land, but the area of the Jewish province would be larger than the White Paper "free" zone. The Arabs would be freed from any fear of Jewish domination. They would achieve immediately a large measure of autonomy, but the way would remain open for development towards either partition or federal unity.

Morrison also added comments on the general situation in Palestine. He reminded the House of the recent King David Hotel bombing, "a tragedy that must have moved the most war-hardened amongst us." The greatest obstacle in the police and military search for the culprits had been the refusal of the *yishuv* to cooperate with the authorities, he asserted, and the government had therefore concluded that "radical action was needed against the organizers of illegal armed forces and the organizations they control."

Morrison then referred to a letter sent to British staff and field officers by Lt. Gen. Sir Evelyn Barker after the bombing. The letter prohibited British soldiers from associating with Jews and warned that any association in the way of duty should be as brief as possible and kept to the business at hand. Such a policy, Barker wrote, would have a chastening effect on "the race ... by striking at their pockets and showing our contempt for them." The government felt that these instructions were justified, Morrison said, although it could not associate itself with the terms used in Barker's letter.

Morrison accused the Jewish Agency of complicity in terrorism. "The leaders of the Jewish community in Palestine have, we feel bound to say, failed to preserve their movement from the contagion of these false ideals," he said. He cited the Anglo-American Committee report on how "the Jewish Agency had ceased to provide that cooperation with the mandatory government which is the duty expressly laid upon them by the mandate." He reminded the House of Commons of the Colonial Office White Paper's charges of Jewish Agency complicity in terrorism.

Morrison asserted that his plan was an outcome of the deliberations of the Morrison-Grady meetings and that it represented a follow-through on the recommendations made by the Anglo-American Committee of Inquiry. The "expert delegations" (as he termed the British and U.S. representatives) had proposed, he said, that Britain and the U.S. should seek to create conditions favorable to the resettlement of a substantial number of Jews in Europe itself and to eradicate anti-Semitism, and this was being done. Britain would also urge that the UN, at its forthcoming General Assembly meeting, appeal to countries to accept displaced persons, including Jews, from Europe, and Britain would make a similar appeal to its dominions, Morrison said.

Morrison was followed to the floor by: Col. Oliver Stanley, ex-colonial secretary, who advocated the outright partition of Palestine in preference to "the cautious and intermediate step of federation"; Laborite Richard Crossman, who rejected the Morrison plan as "out of the question," suggested that it was motivated by the exigency that "we had to get our troops out of Egypt and wanted to put them somewhere else" and urged British authorities to free and cooperate with Palestinian Jewish leaders then in jail; the independent member Kenneth Lindsay, who urged that a bipartisan commission of government representatives together with Conservative leader Anthony Eden go to the Middle East before the crisis worsened; and Laborite George Wigg, who recommended that an envoy of cabinet status be sent to advise Gen. Sir Alan Gordon Cunningham and Lt. Gen. Sir Evelyn Barker on policy, which, by definition, was a political and not a military problem.

The first speaker Aug. 1 was Trade Board Pres. Sir Stafford Cripps, who said that the Labor government's plan was an attempt to help "the High Court of Parliament ... exercise with impartiality a wise and equitable judgment" in the dilemma. "By partition ... we could not achieve a quick decision" in the problem, for both sides equally opposed this solution, Cripps said. In the existing circumstances, however, the government believed that a quick decision was absolutely essential, Cripps declared.

Cripps also said: The terms of a new trusteeship agreement, which would supersede the mandate, would be worked out by the UN. Meanwhile, the British government would begin immediate discussions with representatives of the Jewish communities of various countries and Arabs from the Arab states as well as from Palestine. Both sides would be given a wide power of selection, and the Jewish Agency would not be bypassed. The U.S. did not wish to participate in the discussions although it would be represented by observers. The ex-grand mufti of Jerusalem would not be invited, although if the Arabs wished him to attend, a final decision could be made later.

At about this time it was learned from wire service reports out of Washington that (Pres. Truman had disapproved the Morrison-Grady plan.)

Churchill Speaks Out

Ex-Prime Min. Winston Churchill, taking the floor Aug. 1 as both his own and his (Conservative) party's spokesman, told the House the history of his position on the matter of a Jewish national home in Palestine ever since he personally had drafted the Declaration of 1922 as colonial secretary. Churchill said:

● The Declaration of 1922 did not make Palestine a Jewish national home but only recorded that a Jewish national home in Palestine was to be set up. It had been understood that Jewish immigration was to be allowed in accordance with the economic absorptive capacity of the country and that the mandatory power was to be the final judge of what this capacity was. Under the mandate, not only had the Jewish population increased from about 80,000 to nearly 600,000, but the Arab population, living in the areas colonized and enriched by the Jews, had doubled to 500,000. This showed that both groups had gained a marked advantage from the Zionist policy pursued and developed by Britain. Churchill disagreed with Sir Stafford Cripps that the past 25 years had been the most unkind or unhappy Palestine had known; in fact, "it would hardly be possible to state the opposite of the truth more compendiously." The British mandatory period in Palestine was the brightest Palestine had known and was full of hope.

● The White Paper of 1939 was "a negation of Zionist policy—an integral condition of the mandate." The White Paper had been violently received both by Jews in Palestine and by world Jewry. During the war Churchill had wanted the Jewish community in Palestine to be armed, in order to free British units and to help in the defense of the Holy Land. The horrible persecutions of Jews by the Nazis had left no doubt about which side Jews were on. Nevertheless, Churchill would not wish to be thought inconsiderate of the Arabs; they had had very fair treatment by the British. The British asked little enough for the Jews—"a national home in the historic Holy Land, in which they had the power and the virtue of conferring many blessings for the enjoyment of both Jew and Arab." Churchill agreed that the claims of the Zionists had gone beyond anything agreed on by the mandatory power, and he felt that this was causing alarm and unrest among the Arabs.

● "At the general election the Labor Party, which was believed to champion the Zionist cause, gained a large majority. During that election the most strenuous pro-Zionist speeches and declarations were made. Many of their most important leaders were known to be supporters of the Zionist cause, and their success was naturally regarded by the Jewish community in Palestine as a prelude to the fulfillment of the pledges which had been made to them. However, when the months slipped by and no decided policy or declaration was made by the present government, deep and bitter resentment spread throughout the Palestinian Jewish community, and violent protests were made by the Zionist supporters in the United States. The disappointment and disillusionment of the Jews at the procrastination and indecision of the British Labor government is no excuse for the dark and deadly crimes of the fanatical extremists. Those miscreants and murderers should be rooted out and punished with the full severity of the law. But the expectation which had been aroused by the Labor Party and the revulsion of feeling are facts."

● If, after the war had been won in 1945, he had received the chance of continuing to guide the course of events, Churchill would have carried forward the Zionist cause as he conceived it to be. It was unimaginable, however, that there would be enough room in Palestine for the numbers of Jews wanting to leave postwar Europe. The notion that the Jews' problems could be solved or even helped by a great transfer of the European Jews to Palestine was "too silly to consider." Besides, they might find it best to stay in Europe.

● "We had no idea, when the war came to an end, of the millions that had been slaughtered. That dawned on us gradually after the struggle was over." If that many had perished, however, the room for their survivors had certainly increased, and there had to be much heritable property that these could claim. The alternative was a postwar Europe empty of Jews. "Are we not to hope that some tolerance will be established in racial matters in Europe and that some law will prevail" whereby at least a portion of that heritage would not be denied to those Jews coming forward to claim it? The "crude idea" of letting all of Europe's Jews pass over into Palestine bore no relation to the problem.

● The British mandate had been "a thankless task." Britain had developed no interests in Palestine; it had never sought or made anything out of the country but had only "discharged a painful, costly, laborious and inconvenient duty for more than 25 years with a very great measure of success." Jews all over the world should not forget that quickly. If uncontrollable elements existed in the Zionist movement or the Jewish Agency and if they struck at their "best and only effective friend," the Zionist cause would inevitably suffer. Jewish warfare against the British in Palestine would, if protracted, automatically release Britain from all obligations and would destroy Britain's inclination to make future efforts. He felt that many people in Britain were approaching that attitude already.

● Churchill "earnestly" hoped that the Labor government would respect the authority of Dr. Chaim Weizmann, the "ablest and wisest leader of Zionism," his whole life having been devoted to the cause and his son having been killed "in the battle for our common freedom." The government should maintain contact with Weizmann and show the *yishuv* in what great esteem the British held him. "In that case we should have the best opportunity" of progressing toward a solution.

● Almost any solution in which the U.S. would join Britain could be made to work. All those processes of inquiry, negotiation and discussion had only caused prolonged and dangerous delays. If success were not attained (success being Anglo-American cooperation on equal terms in carrying out a Zionist policy within the limits defined), then Britain would have to face a deplorable failure in its conduct of affairs in Palestine.

● The single, reasonable, rightful and compulsive lever of Britain's Palestine policy was its sincere readiness to lay its mandate at the feet of the UN and to evacuate a country with which it had no connection or tradition. Once having made it clear that Britain had no interests in remaining in Palestine and that it refused to carry this harsh, invidious burden single-handed, then all kinds of good solutions for Jew and Arab alike, based on the cooperation and resources of the English-speaking world, would immediately come into the field of possibility.

● Because of its precipitous abandonment of its treaty rights in Egypt, the British Labor government had been forced to look for a strong base for an arsenal and a "jumping-off ground" in Palestine in order to protect the Suez Canal. Britain was apparently ready to leave 400 million Indians to fall into a bloody civil war—a civil war compared to which anything that could happen in Palestine would be "microscopic"—yet it was not ready to leave Palestine. The makers of British policy insisted that the one place where Britain was at all costs and at all conveniences to hold on and fight it out to the death was Palestine. Britain was to be at war with the Jews of Palestine— and if necessary with the Arabs of Palestine—because, the world would say, having been driven out of Eygpt, it needed to secure a satisfactory strategic base from which to pursue its imperial aims.

● As positive action, the British government should say that if the U.S. would not share the burden of the Zionist cause as defined or agreed, Britain would serve notice that it would return its mandate to the UN and evacuate Palestine within a specified period. At the same time it should inform Egypt that it stood by its treaty rights and that it would maintain the position in the Canal zone.

Other Members & Peers' Positions

Among other speakers during the debate in the House was the Laborite Sidney Silverman, himself a Jew, who Aug. 1 called on those who sympathized with Lt. Gen. Sir Evelyn Barker's nonassociation policy "to have the same kind of under-standing in regard to the feelings of people in Palestine and elsewhere who have lost so many of their relatives in Europe and who are overstrained" both by their past ordeal and by their dwindling prospects. Silverman agreed that Europeans should create conditions tolerable enough to encourage Jews who wished to do so to remain and help rebuild the war-torn continent. He argued, however, that Jews ought not to be compelled to stay if they wanted to leave.

Silverman said that he had found these 3 "fatal defects" in the Morrison plan: (1) The proposal that 100,000 Jews should be allowed into Palestine within 12 months of the (Morrison) plan's coming into operation meant, in reality, within 12 months of the day when the Arabs agreed to admit them. (2) If the issue of immigration certificates were left to the central government and the governor acted on the advice of the projected executive council, which would have Arab members, there would be friction and delay. (3) The national home could not be created within too limited an area; there was no need to take Arab land, since the Negev in the south was available; though the Negev was desert, the Jews said they would be able to cultivate it, and they were willing "to take the victims of Nazism, whom nobody else wants, out in the desert that nobody else wants and make it the flower of civilization, as they have made Palestine in the last 25 years."

Non-Zionist Daniel L. Lipson, speaking Aug. 1 as an independent member, came out against terrorism. He said: There was no justification in Judaism for murder and outrage. The terrorists had done an injury to the Jews such as Hitler had not been able to do. Hitler had destroyed their bodies, but the terrorists had inflicted an indelible stain on the name of Jews. If they persisted, they would destroy the Jewish soul. He felt that there would be no future in Palestine if gangster rule prevailed. He favored the Morrison plan, which (a) could work if there was the will to work it and (b) did not close the door to the possibility of realizing what most people must appreciate as the best solution for Palestine—the creation of a Palestinian state in which Jews and Arabs could cooperate. To suggest that Jews should leave Europe was a policy of defeatism and despair and would mean the triumph of Hitlerism. The U.S. was taking a morally indefensible position in asking the Arabs to take 100,000 Jews into Palestine while themselves refusing to take more Jews into the U.S. He hoped that the present plan for

Palestine would be accompanied by a real effort to find a home for displaced Jews "so that Jews everywhere may enjoy at long last peace, security and an equal opportunity for the full life which Jews enjoy wherever the Union Jack flies."

Clement Davies, the Liberal leader, recalled July 31 that while members of the current government had condemned the 1939 White Paper in June 1945 and had defined the Balfour Declaration as envisaging a Jewish national home with control over its own affairs, *i.e.,* a Jewish state, nothing had been done to implement this view. He said that the language used by Ernest Bevin at the Labor Party Conference in Bournemouth was "unworthy of him," that the current proposals could be, at best, only short-term policy and that the question should be brought before the UN as a matter of urgency.

Spokesmen for Britain's 3 major parties in the House thus indicated that their parties considered the mandate unworkable and wished to end it within the shortest possible period, although only on certain conditions. This attitude was also reflected in the House of Lords, where the government's proposals were announced July 31 by Lord Addison, the dominions secretary.

The ensuing debate in the House of Lords brought out the views of individuals who had been important in shaping British policy in Palestine and in carrying it out. Lord Samuel, the first British high commissioner in Palestine, blamed Britain's current troubles on the White Paper of 1939. Samuel July 31 drew parallels between the current British rule in Palestine and the rule of the Romans and between the Irgun Zvai Leumi and the Zealots of the Roman era; he said: "There was much heroism, much willingness for self-sacrifice in a cheerful spirit, to challenge the might of the Roman empire. The Zealots were slaughtered to the last man, woman and child, and for the Jewish people it was complete destruction. They were wiped out from the land and dispersed over the world from that day to this, full of heroism but no achivement. Let the Jews beware of treading again along this course. If there are more outrages such as the recent one it will not be only bridges or workshops or administrative headquarters that will be destroyed, it will be the national home itself, because its moral and spiritual founda-tions will be blown to pieces, and without them it cannot stand." Samuel added that he supported the British proposals, which he termed "a wise course."

Lord Rothschild, as a symbol of traditional Jewry, expressed his coreligionists' abhorrence of war and violence but pointed out July 31 that almost all young Jews in Palestine had parents and relatives among the 6 million murdered by the Nazis. This explained the desperation that had led to the events of the past few months in Palestine, he said. Added to the suffering was the fact that many Jews felt that the British had betrayed previous promises. They remembered the heroic deeds of Jewish resistance members during the war, Rothschild held, and, therefore, when the scales seemed once more to be weighted against them, the last tenuous threads had snapped and they said: "There is no hope: therefore, let us die fighting, as we did against Hitler."

Lord Robert C. Morrison, a member of the Anglo-American Committee of Inquiry, registered his personal regret at Pres. Truman's failure to support the joint efforts of the Morrison-Grady group. Morrison asserted that true progress was not served by "one nation telling another nation what to do but by sharing the task of carrying out the new policy formulated by the committee, half of whose members were appointed by the President himself."

Truman Holds off from Plan

The White House July 31 issued a statement reporting that Pres. Truman had "been considering certain recommendations to the alternates of the Cabinet Committee [on Palestine— *i.e.,* the 3 American spokesmen at the July discussions in London] with regard to Palestine and [had] decided, in view of the complexity of the matter, to request Amb. [Henry F.] Grady and his associates to return to Washington to discuss the matter with . . . [Truman] in detail." "The President hopes," the statement continued, "that further discussions will result in decisions which will alleviate the situation of the persecuted Jews and at the same time, contribute to the ultimate solution of the longer-term problem of Palestine." Truman, however, was still adamant in calling for the immediate admission into Palestine of the 100,000 displaced European Jews in refugee centers.

Truman's move caught the British government by surprise. Members of the government reportedly had not expected this turn of events when the President had called Amb. Grady and his colleagues back to Washington from the London talks July 26. Prime Min. Clement Attlee flew to London from Paris Aug. 1 for cabinet discussions.

Acting U.S. State Secy. Dean Acheson later in August said in a statement that the State Department "has been very active indeed on the matter of Palestine" and was "in constant communication with the British Foreign Office on the subject." Acheson declined to elaborate beyond saying that "it is a delicate and explosive situation which has to be handled with wisdom, restraint and care."

There was official confirmation in London that Truman's comments on the federalization plan for Palestine had been received. Charles Ross, the President's press secretary, described the communication as "certain suggestions to be thrown into the discussion on the Palestine plan which the President thought would be helpful." Ross added that Truman had not proposed any kind of "formal plan."

Yishuv & Palestinian Arabs Reject Plan

Both the Jews and the Arabs were practically unanimous in rejecting the Morrison Plan. Jewish Agency Pres. Chaim Weizmann assailed the plan in London July 28, 1946, and the Agency Executive in Paris Aug. 5 condemned it as "illusory." Vice Chairman Jamal el-Husseini of the Arab Higher Committee rejected the plan in Jerusalem Aug. 8.

Jewish objections were directed especially against the restrictions of the Jewish national home to a narrow zone of settlement, against what they protested was the illusory character of provincial self-government and, in particular, against the provisions relating to immigration. By the subtraction of western Galilee, the Negev, the Jewish part of Jerusalem and the Dead Sea concession from the Jewish province, the *yishuv's* capacity to absorb large-scale Jewish immigration was severely restricted, Jewish spokesmen noted. The plan was generally viewed as a design for perpetuating British rule by conceding to Jews and Arabs a negligible measure of local self-government in parts of the country and essentially leaving Britain a free hand over the whole of Palestine.

At its meeting in Paris, the Jewish Agency Executive announced Aug. 5 that it regarded "the British proposals, as based on the meetings of the [Anglo-U.S.] Committee of 6 and announced by Mr. Morrison in the House of Commons, as unacceptable as a basis for discussion." An Agency spokesman described the British plan as offering "no independence"; he asserted that "self-government in the proposed separate provinces would be illusory."

The Morrison Plan, as outlined July 31 in the House of Commons, contained 2 critically important provisions. One would call both Jews and Arabs to a conference in London, where the plan would be discussed and, if found acceptable, embodied in a future trusteeship agreement for Palestine. The other was that the implementation of the plan depended on U.S. cooperation—and, by implication, that the admission of the 100,000 Jews was dependent on Jewish acceptance of the plan.

The Jewish Agency, addressing itself to this aspect of the plan, argued that "the Anglo-American Committee had recommended (a) that 100,000 permits be authorized *immediately* for the admission of European Jews into Palestine; (b) that these certificates be issued as far as possible in 1946; and (c) that actual immigration be pushed forward as rapidly as conditions would permit (Recommendation No. 2)." The Morrison Plan, instead of implementing these recommendations, in fact abandoned them, the Agency maintained. The plan made the authorization of the 100,000 permits contingent on the acceptance by Jews and Arabs of a new and mutually unsatisfactory constitutional order in Palestine. This was tantamount to putting off the admission of the 100,000 "to the Greek calends," the Agency held. While the area into which future Jewish immigrants could move would be limited to 17% of western Palestine, the high commissioner would retain overriding jurisdiction to determine Jewish immigration in accordance with what, at his discretion, he judged to be the economic absorptive capacity of the area at any time. The Agency warned that past experience had shown that the principle could be so interpreted as to permit the most arbitrary limitation of Jewish immigration.

The Jewish Agency also assailed the provisions for financing resettlement and development plans. The Agency pointed out that Jewish requirements for the immigration and absorption of the 100,000 refugees were estimated to amount to £70 million ($336 million), and the Arab needs for improvement purposes to £15-£20 million ($72-$96 million), plus another £10 million ($48 million) "for loans." There were plans for the U.S. to lend—through the International Bank or other lending institutions—$250 million to the Arab states for the economic development of the Middle East, including Palestine but with no special emphasis on Palestine. In addition, it was expected that Pres. Truman would ask Congress for a $50 million grant to be spent exclusively for Arab projects in the Arab province. (Truman, however, had abandoned the Morrison Plan completely.)

The Arab feelings about the British proposal were expressed Aug. 8 by Jamal el-Husseini, deputy chairman of the Arab Higher Committee, on his return from Alexandria, where he had engaged in talks between Higher Committee and Arab League officials. Husseini called on the British high commissioner, Gen. Sir Alan Cunningham, who extended to him the British government's invitation to the Palestinian Arabs to attend a conference in London on the Palestine question. Refusing to accept the invitation on behalf of the Arab Higher Committee, Husseini replied that no discussions were acceptable that were based on the proposed federal plan. He also raised the problem of illegal Jewish immigration and demanded the release of detained Arab political prisoners.

The British government had first announced in London July 25 that Jewish and Arab representatives from Palestine and those from the Arab League countries would be invited to London for a round-table conference on the Palestine question. The British hoped that such a gathering could achieve at least the aim of persuading both sides to consider the Morrison-Grady plan evolved at Anglo-American talks for settling the issue. It also was hoped that such a conference would wind up before the 2d UN General Assembly session due to begin Sept. 23 in New York.

Ahmed Bey el-Shukeiri, head of the Arab League Office*
in Jerusalem, said Aug. 8 that the whole Arab world totally
opposed the British plan to create 4 provinces and a federal
government in Palestine. He said that "all diplomatic and
political means are to be mobilized to defeat these proposals."
Should these efforts fail, he said, there would be "endless ways
and means for further action." He said he thought the Arabs
would agree to participate in talks if the British could assure
them that the Jews would not take part and that the federal
plan would not be the agenda for these talks. Husseini said the
ex-grand mufti would be the legitimate leader of any
Palestinian delegation, even if he were absent in Alexandria.
Challenging Russia's pro-Zionist attitude, Husseini accused
Zionism of being "a racial, capitalist government" and said
that "if Russia would defend our cause, it would be appreci-
ated."

Sir Alan Cunningham met with Husseini again Aug. 10
and told him that although the British government planned to
use the federal plan as a basis in the negotiations at the London
conference, their delegates would be free to present counterproposals. The British government was not committed to
putting a federal plan into effect, notwithstanding the result of
the conference, Cunningham declared. Husseini Aug. 11 proceeded to Alexandria for a meeting of the foreign ministers of
the Arab League Aug. 12-13. There they announced Aug. 14
that they had reached unanimous agreement on coordinating
policy and on the selection of the Arab candidates for seats in
the UN. They also decided that each Arab country would be
bound in its UN decisions by the decisions of the Council of the
Arab League taken at its Bludan meeting, and by a refusal to
consider partition as an acceptable solution for the problems of
the peoples in Palestine.

---

* The Arab Office was established in 1945 by Mussa el-Alami, a nonparty member of the Arab League, on league instructions and with league funds. His
mission was to set up propaganda offices in Jerusalem, Washington and
London from which to promote the Arab cause. Arab Office policies were
generally sympathetic to the policies of the grand mufti.

2nd

Crisis Over 'Aliyah Beth' Immigration

A nocturnal war of wits between the *yishuv* and the British authorities had begun before midsummer of 1946 on Palestine's beaches, where illegal immigrants generally managed to slip past the British police nets to merge with the population in the cities and settlements. But British vigilance at sea, where Britain reserved the right to board suspect ships approaching Palestine waters, could not be defeated by the *yishuv.* In early Aug. 1946 what came to be known as *Aliyah Beth* (the 2d immigration) precipitated a serious new crisis between the *yishuv* and the mandatory authorities.

The British authorities towards the end of July had been alerted to the approach of a fleet of small craft carrying large numbers of Jewish immigrants. 2 former corvettes, the *Haganah* and the *Josiah Wedgewood,* as well as a sailing vessel, the *Jewish Soldier* (in a sinking condition), appeared at Haifa carrying a total of some 3,300 people. More ships were reported nearing Palestine Aug. 5. These attempted to elude the British navy patrols and to land their passengers in secret with the assistance of Haganah.

2 small sailing vessels, the *Henrietta Szold* and the *Yagour,* each carrying more than 600 passengers, were spotted by RAF planes Aug. 12 and towed into Haifa. 2 more sailing ships, the *Fenice,* with 650 immigrants, and the *San Pisero* (renamed *The 23* in commemoration of 23 Jews from Haifa who vanished in Syria during the war on a mission against Vichy France), with more than 800 immigrants aboard, met the same end. Meanwhile, about 200 immigrants were caught while landing on a beach north of Tel Aviv from an unidentified small sailing vessel.

Reporters who visited the *Haganah* and the *Josiah Wedgewood* called them "floating slums." Passengers were cramped in 3-tiered wooden bunks and in rough shelters from the bridge down to the holds in the most squalid conditions. The *Haganah* was said to be carrying 2,678 people, most of whom, including large numbers of young people and pregnant women, had come from Rumania, Hungary or Poland, had been in concentration camps and had been roaming over Western Europe since the end of the war. They had waited in Italy for 8 months before sailing and had been at sea for nearly 3 weeks.

Some 1,000 of the aged, the sick and the pregnant women were permitted to disembark Aug. 3. The others were kept on board, and they received food supplies from the Palestinian government until they were removed to the Athlit Clearance Camp.

The British government announced in London Aug. 8 that it had protested to Moscow and Bucharest against the connivance of Russian members of the Allied Control Commission for Rumania in the organized shipment of refugees from Rumanian ports to Palestine. British protests to the French, Czechoslovak, Greek and Italian governments demanded their cooperation in halting this traffic.

A dramatic report in the London *Times* Aug. 9 spoke of a "European-wide conspiracy to bring Jewish immigrants to Palestine." The *Times'* diplomatic correspondent reported that immigrant ships came from Antwerp, northern and southern Italy, inlets on the Dalmation coast, Greece and the Black Sea. Chartering these ships and fitting them with bunks ("which will pack human beings as tight as sardines"), providing them with false papers and well-paid crews was an operation costing millions of dollars and commanding the devotion and skill of a general staff of the various organizations known to be engaged in the operations, the reporter declared. Selecting the immigrants in Poland, Hungary and Austria in the right proportions of young people and pregnant women (who usually formed about 20% of the total), transporting them across frontiers, paying their train fares and assembling them in the Mediterranean ports to which they were taken by trucks and summoned on board the waiting ships by roll-call—all this marked an organization with European ramifications and practical experience in underground work.

The Anglo-American Committee of Inquiry had already cited, in its report, evidence of such a "grapevine" organization stretching across Europe, but the organized exodus had been strongly denied by Jewish spokesmen. The *Times* report contained the assertion that, while the motive driving these thousands of Jews westward from eastern Europe was fear, and the magnet drawing them south was the belief that somehow they would get to Palestine and that British humanitarianism would finally allow them to enter Palestine, those who organized the movement seemed to be dominated by no such humanitarian motives—a charge that outraged Jewish opinion in London.

These monthly totals of illegal immigrants who had arrived in Palestinian waters since Dec. 1945 were disclosed in London Aug. 12: Dec. 1945—252; Jan. 1946—911; February—15; March—973; April—90; May—1,662; June—1,743; July—3,800.

The Jewish Agency Executive, meeting in Paris Aug. 13, repudiated the British charges that immigration was being deliberately organized. Its statement read: "Under the impact of anti-Semitic terror in eastern Europe the existence of which the British government explicitly acknowledge, the Jews are leaving the countries which can no longer provide them with any assurance of a life of decency, peace, and security. The British government's assertion that this movement of escape has been artificially created is a distortion of the known and acknowledged facts. To close the doors of Palestine against refugees from terror is to deny the last remaining hope of freedom and the enjoyment of human rights to liberty."

Britain took added steps to halt the flood of illegal immigrants and to detain them outside Palestine pending a decision on their future. The new policy was outlined in a communique from the cabinet Aug. 12. Accusing the *yishuv* of operating "a closely knit network of agents" "to maintain the traffic in illegal immigration," the Labor government, in its communique, called the operation "a source of grave danger to law and order in Palestine" and the cause of "greatly increased tension between the Arab and Jewish communities." It concluded:

"His Majesty's government can no longer tolerate this attempt to force their hand in framing a new policy for Palestine. They have made urgent representations to the governments of the countries from which the immigrants are dispatched in order to stop the traffic at its source. In addition, instructions have been given to the Palestine authorities that the reception into Palestine of illegal immigrants must cease. Accordingly, immigrants arriving illegally will henceforward be conveyed to Cyprus or elsewhere and housed in camps there until a decision can be taken as to their future. Meanwhile, it is fully understood that many of the illegal immigrants concerned have come through conditions of great hardship in circumstances not under their control, and all reasonable measures will be taken for their health and well-being."

Prague radio announced that the Polish-Czechoslovak frontier had been closed to check the mass exodus of Jews from Poland, where Jews were crossing the border at the rate of 3,000 daily.

British correspondents in Vienna reported Aug. 14 that as a result of the British efforts to halt illegal immigration, the number of Jewish newcomers to Vienna that day was only 200, whereas nearly 15,000 had arrived between Aug. 1 and 13. About 15,000 Jews had entered Vienna during July and 7,000 had come in June. Many had been living in eastern Poland before the war and had been taken to the interior of Soviet Russia when these provinces were absorbed by the Soviet Union in 1940. The Polish-Soviet agreement on the repatriation of former Polish citizens had given these Jews the chance to return to Poland. A pogrom in Kielce July 4 and other serious instances of anti-Semitism encountered there, however, had driven many of them away with the hope of reaching Palestine via the Mediterranean ports.

The Italian government announced Aug. 13 that as a result of the British note, measures were being taken immediately to check illegal traffic of immigrants from Italy to Palestine. Later, Italy notified the U.S. government that it would accept 10,000 Jewish refugees from Austria on a temporary basis. The U.S. suggested that Italy provide temporary shelter for 25,000.

The government's communique on its new deportation policy drew an immediate response from the Jewish Agency, which said in a statement: "If the British government were sincerely anxious to preserve the peace of Palestine, it could never have authorized such an action or issued so inflammatory a statement.... The Royal Navy, the British Army and the Royal Air Force are today mobilized against a few thousand helpless mortals who are trying to reach the only country in the world where they have friends, where their families are waiting to receive them and where they would have the opportunity of building up their lives anew.... The Palestine immigration regulations, under which it is sought to exclude these new arrivals, have no foundation in law. The breach of the law lies with those who enforce the regulations, and not with those who seek to enter the country in their despite. ... At a time when, more than ever, restraint and conciliation are called for in Palestine, the British government has done its best to arouse feelings of bitterness and hatred. If it persists along this course, the chances of arriving at an agreed and peaceful settlement of the Palestine issue will disappear altogether. They have already been greatly reduced by the British government's latest action against these hapless refugees and by the deliberately misleading terms of the statement by which the government attempted to save its face."

The 3,000 immigrants who were then being detained at the Athlit Clearance Camp on the Mediterranean coast just south of Haifa represented the full quota of legal entries for 2 months. Thus, only a few special permits for normal entry were to be issued during that period, according to the precedent established by Britain. Some 1,500 immigrants were being detained on 2 ships in Haifa harbor, and a new ship had been reported approaching the port, while 6 others were known to be on the way. The ships flew a variety of flags, including those of Mexico, Panama and Costa Rica. Many of them, when confiscated, were found to be scarcely seaworthy. All were very seriously overcrowded.

The 1,500 immigrants aboard the *Henrietta Szold* and the *Yagour* Aug. 13 were transferred to the British steamers *Empire Rival* and *Empire Heywood.* The whole port of Haifa was closed by the British army's First Infantry Division after a curfew had been proclaimed in the city for fear of a possible riot by Haifa's Jews. The *Yagour* was towed to dock, but when a naval party tried to board the *Henrietta Szold* from small launches, the immigrants, both men and women, hit the sailors with sticks, clubs, bottles and cans and inflicted slight injuries on several of them. A larger naval detail, its members wearing steel helments, went aboard from a seagoing tug and met no resistance.

As the ships with the transferred immigrants were about to sail Aug. 13, Haganah's underground Kol Yisrael radio urged the Jewish residents of Haifa to make a "mass break" out of their homes and pour onto the streets in violation of the curfew. In the violent demonstration that ensued, 3 Jews were killed and 19 injured as 200 or so attempted to breach the barricades at Hadar Carmel, a suburb of Haifa.

The Jewish community in Jerusalem stopped all work Aug. 13 from 5 p.m. to midnight in protest against sending immigrants to Cyprus. The Elected Assembly—which administered the *yishuv*'s own domestic matters through the Vaad Leumi, its presidium—called a plenary session in Jerusalem, where it was resolved to start a campaign of political noncooperation Aug. 19. At public meetings in Tel Aviv, Haifa and Jerusalem members of the *yishuv* voiced bitter disappointment at the British actions. After the funeral Aug. 14 of the 3 victims of the previous day's clash, Jews in Haifa posted protest placards on outdoor walls. A police charge, with batons, took place in Haifa to prevent a large crowd from storming the port area, while in Tel Aviv 20,000 people marched through the city in anti-British demonstrations.

The *Empire Rival* and *Empire Heywood* arrived in Cyprus Aug. 14. 658 men, 451 women and 177 children landed at Famagusta Aug. 14 and 15. To the Jewish immigrants, the British arrangements in Cyprus looked much like a renewed concentration camp existence, complete with barbed wire and guards.

The British boarding party coming aboard *The 23* in Haifa's harbor Aug. 18 to transfer its passengers was initially driven off the vessel but the immigrants were later tear-gassed and forced to leave the ship. After the transfer, an explosion occurred in the hold of the *Empire Heywood;* an immigrant had tried to blow a hole in the ship's bottom. While the *Empire Heywood,* with 600 passengers aboard, remained in Haifa, the *Empire Rival* sailed for Cyprus. When the *Empire Rival* returned from Cyprus after discharging 542 men, 237 women and 5 children, several explosions occurred aboard the ship, one opening a hole the area of whose aperture was 24 square feet. Authorities intensified warship patrols in the harbor thereafter.

The *Empire Heywood* Aug. 26 transferred 370 more Jewish men, 219 Jewish women and 11 Jewish children from Haifa to Famagusta. British authorities Sept. 2 sighted *The 4 Freedoms,* a vessel of about 400 tons carrying 1,200 immigrants from Poland, Hungary, Germany, Rumania and Austria, nearing Tel Aviv. Among the passengers were 160 pregnant women and 200 mostly orphan children. The British brought the ship into Haifa harbor. The ship was taking seawater in 4 places, and the passengers had been without fresh water for the last few days of their voyage, with several ill from drinking seawater. Some 70 were taken ashore and hospitalized. The rest, some on stretchers, were transferred to the *Empire Heywood* and taken to Famagusta, with the British army providing food, water, blankets, clothing and medical aid.

While the *yishuv* was up in arms against the forcible shipping of illegal immigrants to camps in Cyprus, the British military authorities began the trial in Haifa of 18 young men and 4 young women alleged to be members of the Stern Group. They were accused of participation in the blowing up of railway shops at Haifa and of firing on British troops the night of June 16. The defendants obstructed the proceedings by loud singing in court. A spokesman declared that they regarded themselves as soldiers and "prisoners of war" and did not recognize the jurisdiction of the court. The 18 men were sentenced Aug. 16 to death by hanging and the 4 girls to life imprisonment.

Protest meetings and posters in the streets of Tel Aviv, signed by the Stern Group, bore the slogan "Blood for Blood" and threatened retaliation. It was announced Aug. 29 that Lt. Gen. Sir Evelyn Barker had commuted the death sentences to life imprisonment. (Earlier, the Palestinian government had announced that 4 other suspected Jewish terrorists had been deported to Eritrea.)

Yishuv & Palestinian Arabs Unrepresented

Great Britain's Labor government had proposed a blueprint—the Morrison plan—for resolving the greatest crisis of the country's 24-year-old mandate in Palestine. In Palestine, however, neither Jew nor Arab would accept it—or even go to London when invited to discuss it. Only Palestine's neighboring Arab lands accepted Britain's invitation and sent representatives to London early in September. There they discussed the Palestine question for 3 weeks before the conference was adjourned until winter.

Shortly after the arrest of the Jewish Agency leaders, a majority of the members of the Jewish Agency Executive from Jerusalem, London and New York had met in July 1946 in Paris, where the peace conference of Allied Foreign Ministers was to take place. They discussed the situation, and representatives of the several Zionist parties in the U.S. joined them in their deliberations. The Executive had declared the Morrison cantonization plan to be unacceptable as a basis of discussion. On the other hand, the members said they were "prepared to discuss a proposal for the establishment of a viable Jewish state in an adequate area of Palestine."

Those at the meeting proposed these demands: (a) the immediate grant of 100,000 immigration permits and the immediate beginning of the transportation of the 100,000 to Palestine; (b) the grant of immediate full autonomy (in appointing its administration and in the economic field) to the area of Palestine to be designated as the territory of the future Jewish state; (c) the grant to the administration of each area of the right to control its immigration.

Copies of these resolutions were sent to the British and American governments. Pres. Truman indorsed them and informed the British government that he did so. Britain, however, stuck to the Morrison Plan and to its condition that a conference be convened to discuss it.

The British Foreign Office announced Aug. 26 that the planned British conference, with the participation of Arab and Jewish representatives, would begin Sept. 9 and that invitations had been issued to the governments of the Arab states, to the Jewish Agency, to the Arab Higher Committee for Palestine and to Azzam Pasha, secretary general of the Arab League, who would come to London in an individual capacity.

Jamal Husseini, the vice chairman of the Arab Higher Committee, who Aug. 8 had rejected an informal invitation on the committee's behalf, replied Aug. 26 that "there is no real hope to be expected from the outcome of these talks." Accepting the invitation nevertheless, he requested that the other 4 members of the committee, including the ex-grand mufti of Jerusalem, its chairman, also be invited. The member states of the Arab League (which had decided Aug. 12 to accept the invitation after the clampdown on Jewish immigration) Aug. 22 sent a note to London asking Britain to recognize the mufti as the leader of the Palestinian Arabs and saying that recognition of his leadership was "essential."

Gen. Sir Alan Cunningham, the high commissioner, saw Dr. Hussein el-Khalidi, the committee's secretary, and informed him Aug. 29 that the British government, although it would welcome the other 4 members of the committee and other Arab delegates, could not invite the mufti. The other 4 members told Cunningham Sept. 1 that they refused to attend the conference. They said that the Palestinian Arabs had "unanimously chosen" the mufti and that they believed that this "hostility to their leader" was "the result of Zionist influence."

The Zionists were debating whether to participate in the London conference. Dr. Chaim Weizmann, in his capacity as president of the Jewish Agency, discussed the situation with 5 members of the Jewish Agency Executive then in London. George Hall, the British colonial secretary, met Aug. 14 with Weizmann, Dr. Nahum Goldmann, Rabbi Stephen S. Wise and other members of the Jewish Agency Executive at the Colonial Office. According to a report by Weizmann later, the meeting was conducted in a "most friendly spirit," but nothing much came of it. Hall then left for Paris to brief Ernest Bevin there, and both met with 2 American Jewish leaders—Rabbi Wise and Dr. Goldmann—and Berl Locker. (Locker was a Jewish Agency representative in Britain and a member of the Agency Executive.) The aim of Hall and Bevin was to discuss an official letter from the Jewish Agency, signed by Weizmann and outlining the conditions under which the Agency would consent to attend the conference in order to discuss the cantonization plan outlined by Morrison. A Jewish Agency spokesman in Jerusalem said that the plans for Jewish noncooperation with the British campaign would be postponed.

Pres. Truman, who had rejected the Morrison Plan, issued a statement Aug. 16 in which he supported the idea of the conference. The U.S. document said:

"Although the President has been exchanging views with Mr. Attlee on the subject, this government has not presented any plan of its own for a solution of the problem of Palestine. It is the sincere hope of the President, however, that, as a result of the proposed conversations between the British government and Jewish and Arab representatives, a fair solution of the problem of Palestine can be found and immediate steps can be taken to alleviate the situation of displaced Jews in Europe. It is clear that no settlement of the Palestine problem can be achieved which will be fully satisfactory to all the parties concerned, and that, if this problem is to be solved in a manner which will bring peace and prosperity to Palestine, it must be approached in a spirit of conciliation. It is also evident that a solution of the Palestine question will not in itself solve the broader problem of the hundreds of thousands of displaced persons in Europe. The President has been giving this problem his special attention, and hopes that arrangements can be entered into which will make it possible for various countries, including the U.S.A., to admit many of these persons as permanent residents. The President, on his part, is contemplating seeking the approval of Congress for special legislation authorizing the entry into the U.S.A. of a fixed number of these persons, including Jews."

Truman had already told the British that he could neither accept nor reject the cantonization plan without "the support of the American people" (a reference to the Congressional elections scheduled for that fall). But he had advised Britain, as the mandatory power, to "take such action as seemed wise in the circumstances."

The Jewish Agency's first reply to the British invitation had been that (a) the Agency could not negotiate on the federal plan unless Zionist control over Jewish immigration became a part of it and (b) the Agency would need full freedom to name its own delegates to the conference (including, presumably, those of its members still detained at Latrun). It also wanted—in consultation with the British—to invite delegates from other Jewish organizations.

Dr. Nahum Goldmann, who was in touch with the British, flew to Paris in a vain effort to try to persuade David Ben-Gurion, the Agency's chairman, to come to London. Ben-Gurion sent Berl Locker to Jerusalem to report to the Palestinian members of the Agency's Executive and to attend a meeting of the Zionist Inner General Council. He was allowed to visit the Agency leaders in detention at Latrun. This was the first time they were permitted by the British to meet with their colleagues, and they were equally firm about boycotting the London conference.

The Zionist Inner General Council then met in Jerusalem Sept. 1-2 to review the political issues and the negotiations. By a vote of 16 to 6 the council adopted a resolution to the effect that it had heard the report of the Agency Executive on the negotiations with the British concerning the Agency's participation in the London conference and noted the Agency's intention to bring the result of the negotiations before the council when the talks were completed. The 6 dissident votes expressed the opinion of those who felt that the Agency's attitude was too conciliatory.

Goldmann submitted fresh proposals to Foreign Secy. Ernest Bevin Aug. 30 in a final effort to obtain conditions making the invitation more palatable to the Jewish Agency. These proposals contained some modifications of the Agency's original plan, which had envisaged partition in 2 to 3 years. Under the original plan, the Jews had hoped to receive an area that included the coastal plain, the plain of Esdraelon and all of Galilee, plus a revisionary right to a part of the Negev. The Jewish Agency had not yet revealed whether its representatives would attend the conference, and the British, therefore, began Sept. 4 to issue invitations to non-Agency Jewish organizations and prominent Jews in Britain and Palestine.

Of the 4 invited Arab leaders outside the Arab Higher Committee, 2—Suleiman Bey Tuqan (Mayor of Nablus) and Anton Attalah, a Christian Arab lawyer—declined the invitation. With the refusal of the Palestinian Arabs to send delegates to the London conference unless the ex-grand mufti were at their head, Weizmann told British Colonial Secy. George Hall that the Jewish Agency also was not prepared to send delegates to the conference. In a letter released Sept. 6, Weizmann declared that the Agency would participate only on certain conditions. The main ones were that: (a) The discussions would be on the basis of "the establishment of a viable Jewish state in an adequate area of Palestine." (b) The Agency would be accorded "full freedom" to nominate its own delegates, and these might include people currently under detention. (c) The Agency would be the channel for invitations to all non-Agency Jewish delegates.

Weizmann said that the Agency wanted to do "everything possible in cooperation with the British government "to reach a satisfactory solution of the Palestine problem which would ensure lasting peace in that country." He added, however, that the federalization plan would be repudiated by the entire Jewish people, since it would deprive the Jews of their rights under the mandate in 85% of western Palestine. Moreover, the plan did not provide for genuine self-government and did not secure freedom of Jewish immigration and settlement.

George Hall responded that his government, "in convening a conference of both Arabs and Jews on a subject vital to both peoples, cannot possibly allow one party alone to lay down the agenda of the proceedings."

The British sent invitations to the acting chief rabbi of Great Britain and to these Jewish organizations in Britain: the Board of Deputies of British Jews, the Anglo-Jewish Association and the Agaduth Yisrael World Organization. In Palestine, invitations went to Chief Rabbi Isaac Halevi Herzog, Chief Rabbi Ben-Zion Meir Hay Uziel, Itzhak Ben Zvi of Vaad Leumi, Joseph Sprinzak of the Jewish Agency Executive, Golda Meyerson (later Meir) of Histadrut, Mordecai Bentov (Hashomer Hatzair), Israel Rockach (mayor of Tel Aviv) and Rabbi Isaac Meyer Levin (Agaduth Yisrael). No definite replies had been received by the time the conference opened Sept. 9.

Kings Ibn Saud of Arabia and Abdullah of Transjordan again tried to persuade the Palestinian Arabs to attend but could not.

Conference Begins

The London conference opened Sept. 9 at Lancaster House, with delegates from all of the 7 states of the Arab League attending but without representation by the Palestinian Arabs or the Jewish Agency. It adjourned Oct. 2. Abdul Rahman Azzam Pasha, secretary general of the Arab League, was present in a consultative capacity.

The London conference thus took place without the participation of the only 2 genuinely interested parties—the Jews and Arabs of Palestine. The British delegation consisted of Ernest Bevin (foreign secretary), George Hall (colonial secretary), Sir Norman Brook (additional secretary to the Cabinet), Arthur Creech Jones (undersecretary for the colonies) and Sir George Gater (permanent undersecretary, Colonial Office).

The conference proceedings began formally Sept. 9 with an address by Prime Min. Clement Attlee, who presented British policy on Palestine. He said:

It has always been the intention of his majesty's government to call the governments of the Arab countries into consultation before arriving at any final conclusion as to the future of Palestine.... It is my earnest hope that, as the result of this conference, the way may be cleared towards some acceptable solution of this intractable problem. I much regret that the Arabs of Palestine have decided not to send representatives, but, knowing how near this question of Palestine is to the hearts of the neighboring Arab countries, I feel fully satisfied that, even if there are no Palestinian delegates, the Arab point of view is adequately and effectively represented by the present gathering.

I need hardly tell you how much his majesty's government deplore the state of unrest and disturbance into which Palestine has been plunged. It is a state which cannot be permitted to continue, and it is incumbent on us all to make every effort to promote such a settlement of the underlying issues as will establish peace and prosperity in the land. It is for this purpose that the conference has been convened. I do not believe that it is, as is sometimes stated, a problem for which no solution is possible....

His majesty's government have themselves put forward a plan which seems to them to be well worthy of consideration. Discussion of this plan will be the first item on the conference agenda....

There are 3 matters which I would earnestly ask you to bear in mind. First, I would suggest that too much time should not be devoted to the discussion of past history. We live in an ever-changing world and must face facts as they exist today. No plan, however firmly rooted in the past, which fails to give due weight to the existing situation is likely to provide a solution of our difficulties. Secondly, I would urge the importance of recognizing that no settlement is possible in Palestine unless each community is prepared to take account of the other's interests and to make the concessions necessary for peace.... Finally, we must all remember that the Palestine problem cannot be treated in isolation but must be regarded against the wider background of world policy. Palestine is a tiny country, but everything that happens in it has reactions in a far wider sphere. To plan for Palestine while ignoring these reactions would be to shut one's eyes to realities; the structure might seem worthy, but the foundations would be on sand....

Anything that affects the Arab peoples is a matter of interest to the British people, and in the same way the destiny of Britain is, I believe, a matter of importance to the Arabs. We are associated in a natural partnership. Sometimes it has seemed that the harmony of this partnership is threatened by the impact upon it of events in Palestine. It is my earnest hope that we shall succeed in removing that danger by frankly explaining our difficulties to one another and searching together for a solution to which you and we can honorably agree....

The fact that we are thus met together shows the extent to which his majesty's government recognize that Palestine is a subject of legitimate interests and concern to all the Arab peoples.

Arab League's Stance Against Zionism

Faris el-Khoury, chairman of the Syrian Chamber of Deputies and leader of the Syrian delegation, stated the Arab position Sept. 10. He contrasted the political successes of the Arabs in Arab countries other than Palestine with the current situation in Palestine. Khoury said:

Palestine alone has been required to be an instrument in the realization of the dreams and ambitions of political Zionism.... The confusion between the world Jewish problem and Palestine has had the most unfortunate results. The Jewish problem, as such, is of world concern and requires worldwide solution. Palestine has nothing to do with this problem, nor can any solution be found in Palestine....

What we are concerned with is that the Arabs of Palestine shall not lose their inherent rights: that Palestine, with its sisters the Arab states, shall have its rights recognized; and that no part of Palestine shall be cut off to make a home or state for a body of immigrants belonging to different nationalities, though they may be of the same religion. On that basis and within those limits we have come to exchange opinions and engage in discussions in a spirit of friendship and cooperation with Great Britain, hoping that we may together find the right way and that peace may remain in the Arab world and in the world at large.

Colonial Secy. George Hall outlined the Morrison Plan proposal to grant provincial autonomy under a federal arrangement. It was promptly rejected by all the 7 Arab delegations, who submitted counterproposals. A committee of the heads of the Arab delegations was then appointed to study the Arab proposals in detail. Emir Feisal of Saudi Arabia and Emir Saif el-Islam Ahmed of Yemen did not take part, however. Arab League Secy. Gen. Abdul Rahman Azzam Pasha and Sir Norman Brook (as the British representative) served as the committee's chief coordinators. This *ad hoc* committee submitted its report to the conference Oct. 2, and the conference was then adjourned until Dec. 16 to give the British government further time for consideration of the Arab proposals.

The Arab states had proposed Sept. 10 that Britain relinquish the mandate and designate an independent Palestinian state by 1948. The *ad hoc* committee developed this proposal with the following interim recommendations:

● The high commissioner for Palestine should establish a provisional government of 7 Arab and 3 Jewish ministers, all of Palestinian nationality. The administration's legislative and executive powers should be transferred to them, although the high commissioner would keep a veto power until the transition was effected.

● The provisional government should make up a voting roll based on universal adult male suffrage and hold elections for a constituent assembly of 60 members—no more than 20 of them Jews—reflecting proportionate representation.

● The provisional government should prepare and submit to the constituent assembly a draft constitution whose terms would be reconsidered and revised in accordance with the assembly's debates.

● Following the adoption of the constitution, the provisional government should hold parliamentary elections. The first head of the newly independent state of Palestine would then be appointed by the procedure laid down in the constitution. He would assume full powers under it. A treaty of alliance would be concluded between Britain and Palestine.

● While the constitution was being drafted, both the provisional government and the constituent assembly would be bound by certain directives issued by the high commissioner to ensure the incorporation in the constitution of 12 irreducible principles.

These 12 principles were:

(a) Palestine is to be a unitary state (*i.e.,* not a federal state).

(b) Applicants for naturalization must have been legal residents of Palestine for a continuous period of 10 years.

(c) Full rights of citizenship should be accorded to those born in Palestine, those who had gained Palestinian citizenship by naturalization before May 1939, those acquiring it thereafter under the existing regulations (if permanently resident for 10 years) and those who obtain it in future under the new laws.

(d) The sanctity of all holy places must be preserved and freedom of religious practices guaranteed.

(e) The guarantees concerning the holy places must be included in any declaration of independence by the projected Palestinian state to the UN General Assembly.

(f) The right of religious bodies and others to maintain private schools and universities is to be guaranteed, subject to the compulsory teaching of Arabic in the schools.

(g) Jews are to be permitted to use Hebrew as a 2d official language in districts where they constitute an absolute majority.

(h) All important sections of the population must be adequately represented—but in no case should the number of Jews in the legislature exceed ⅓ of the total number of members. There must be a proportionate reflection of this distribution in the administration and executive arm.

(i) As many Palestinians as practicable shall receive a part in the administration during the transition period, and "every effort should be made to complete these stages with the least possible delay, notwithstanding the noncooperation of any section of Palestinian citizens."

(j) All Jewish immigration into Palestine is to be immediately and completely banned; existing restrictions on land transfer are to remain in force unless and until changed by legislation, for which the majority consent of the Arab members of the legislature would be needed.

(k) The guarantees of Jewish rights should not be changed without the majority consent of the Jewish members of the legislature.

(l) A supreme court shall be set up to determine whether any legislation is inconsistent with the constitution; every Palestinian shall be entitled to recourse to this tribunal.

Conference Adjourns

On the adjournment of the conference Oct. 2, Arab League Secy. Gen. Abdul Rahman Azzam Pasha said that the Arab delegations were dispersing "in a more cheerful mood" than the one in which they had come. He said he hoped that the Jews in Palestine would "realize that the Arabs had gone a long way to meet them" and that the *yishuv*'s representatives would be at the conference when it reconvened.

It appeared that the Arab states wanted an alternative scheme for Palestine's future, based on their own terms and definitions. But they did not speak for the Arabs of Palestine. The organ of the latter, the Arab Higher Committee, remained obstinate in its boycott of the conference. This boycott indicated that the Palestinian Arabs would not accept its decisions. According to an Associated Press report Sept. 30 from Jerusalem, the Higher Committee had set up in Alexandria, Egypt a Palestinian Arab "shadow government" with Haj Amin el-Husseini, the exiled grand mufti of Jerusalem, as "president of the republic" and with Higher Committee Vice Chairman Jamal Bey el-Husseini, his cousin, as premier and foreign minister.

The Zionist leaders were at least as adamant in their opposition to the conference. The British Foreign Office had approached a number of Jewish public figures with anti-Zionist views and had invited their participation in the conference. To the Jewish Agency, this meant that Britain was trying to create a puppet Jewish Agency, a kind of British satellite. Moreover, Foreign Secy. Bevin during September seemed to be working under the impression that Agency leaders who had not been arrested and who had come to London for "informal talks," where they were offered the release of their colleagues if they gave up promoting illegal immigration, would be willing to agree to his offer. The Jewish Agency's determination not to do so appeared to be fortified by the news that a Palestinian Arab "shadow government" had been set up in Alexandria.

Truman Statement

In a statement cabled by Pres. Truman to Prime Min. Attlee on *Yom Kippur,* the Jewish Day of Atonement (Oct. 4, 1946), Truman urged once again that "substantial immigration" of Jewish displaced persons in Europe begin "at once." He pledged U.S. help in transporting them to Palestine. The President, recapitulating the events leading up to the London Conference said:

(1) In view of the fact that winter will come before the conference is resumed, I believe and urge that substantial immigration to Palestine cannot await the solution of the Palestine problem and should begin at once. Preparations for this movement have already been made by the government and it is ready to lend its immediate assistance.

(2) I state again, as I have on previous occasions, that the immigration laws of other countries, including the United States, should be liberal with a view to the admission of displaced persons. I am prepared to make such a recommendation to Congress and to continue as energetically as possible collaboration with other countries on the whole problem of displaced persons.

(3) Furthermore, should a workable solution for Palestine be devised, I would be willing to recommend to Congress a plan for economic assistance for the development of the country.

In the light of the terrible ordeal which the Jewish people of Europe endured in the recent war and the crisis now existing, I cannot believe that a program of immediate action along the lines suggested above could not be worked out with the cooperation of all the people concerned. The Administration will continue to do everything it can to this end.

Truman's statement was reaffirmed Oct. 24 in this letter by State Secy. James Byrnes to Rabbi Stephen Wise, an American member of the Jewish Agency Executive.

I have received your letter in which you were good enough to mention the helpfulness of the President's recent statement on the subject of Palestine and the DPs in Europe.

In the letter you also referred to certain rumors which allege a difference of opinion between the President and the State Department regarding these matters and ask for clarification.

I am happy to assure you that the rumors to which you refer have no basis in fact.

The statement by the President on Oct. 4 regarding Palestine and Jewish immigration into Palestine is, of course, an expression of policy of this government.

With this policy I am in hearty accord. The importance which this government attaches to the matter and the deep personal concern of the President over the condition of DPs in Europe—a concern which I share—is shown by the fact that on this occasion and several previous occasions, the President has himself expressed the views of the government.

The State Department and the Foreign Service are endeavoring loyally and wholeheartedly to do their part in the implementation of the policies regarding Palestine and the associated problems, and they will continue to do so.

In a circular letter to U.S. diplomats in the Middle East, the U.S. government noted that their activities should henceforth be guided by the President's Oct. 4 statement.

The British tried to delay the release of the Truman statement until Foreign Secy. Bevin could be consulted, but Truman would not wait. The U.S. release of the statement drew a sharp admonition from Britain. An official spokesman said: "The British government has been working hard to bring the Jews and Arabs together. It is not correct that the discussions have been broken off. Consultations with the Jews are actually in progress at this moment. It is, in the British government's view, most unfortunate that a statement of this kind should have been made. It may well jeopardize a settlement of this difficult problem."

The British publicly accused Truman of acting on internal political considerations, with an eye on the coming elections in New York and its important Jewish vote. A spokesman for Prime Min. Attlee Oct. 4 called Truman's intervention "unfortunate." He asserted that negotiations with the Arab delegations had been suspended only temporarily and that negotiations had been proceeding smoothly with Dr. Chaim Weizmann. Attlee, however, did not pursue his disagreement with Truman and let the matter drop; he refused to publish his correspondence with the President, in which he had remonstrated with Truman on the matter. It was disclosed in London Oct. 11, however, that Truman had answered Attlee by reiterating his firm stand in favor of admitting 100,000 European Jewish refugees. At the same time, he rejected the suggestion that the publication of his position had jeopardized the London conference's prospects of success.

The Jewish Agency issued a statement in which it maintained that neither Truman's demand for immigration nor his support for a Jewish state in an adequate area of Palestine were new, nor could either be regarded as a "sudden intervention." The Agency added that the absence of Jews from the London conference was not the reason for its failure to achieve a quick solution to the Palestine problem.

The Arab Higher Committee in Jerusalem issued a declaration in which it warned that "increasing U.S. interests in all Arab and Moslem countries will be jeopardized by the President's ill-considered statements on Jewish immigration into Palestine." It said that the President needed "the Jewish vote" and therefore disregarded "the Arabs of Palestine," who, with "their brethren in neighboring countries, are resolved to oppose Pres. Truman's hostile policy by all means at their disposal."

In New York State, Gov. Thomas E. Dewey (R.) and ex-Gov. Herbert H. Lehman (D.), the latter running for the Senate, urged in campaign speeches Oct. 6 that immediate large-scale Jewish immigration into Palestine begin at once.

The Iraqi government Oct. 6, in notes handed to the British embassy and to the U.S. legation in Baghdad, expressed Crown Prince Abdul-Ilah's displeasure at the President's position. The Saudi Arabian legation in London issued the text of a message to Truman in which King Ibn Saud expressed "great surprise" at the President's statement of Oct. 4 and called for the "stopping of Zionist aggression."

Stalemate over Immigration

Despite the Jewish Agency's nonparticipation in the first stage of the London conference, the talks between Jewish Agency leaders and the British during Sept. 1946 had led Britain to believe that it was on the verge of a settlement with the *yishuv*. British Foreign Secy. Bevin had often asserted that the Jewish Agency was very largely dominated by its New York members, but evidence indicated increasingly that the real power and leadership were in the hands of the Zionist Inner General Council in Jerusalem. The leaders of this inner council made it plain that they were not prepared to make concessions to Britain without an increase in the monthly immigration quota; but the Foreign Office had already told the Arab states that Jewish immigration would not be increased—at any rate, not before the London conference reconvened. At the same time, the British war on illegal immigrants rankled deeply with the *yishuv* and made compromise harder to achieve.

The Vaad Leumi (Jewish Agency's National Council Executive), together with the municipal and rural councils, had resolved Sept. 9 the date of the London conference's opening, on an immediate allocation of $400,000 to aid illegal immigration "without regard to the [1939] White Paper." In another resolution, the Vaad Leumi had called for noncooperation with the Palestinian mandatory administration's advisory bodies. The Jewish municipalities, local councils and community councils met in all the towns and villages of Jewish Palestine and agreed to allocate part of their annual budgets to help illegal immigrants slip into the country. At these meetings, the Jewish Agency spokesman said, the *yishuv* was taking "political action whereby these bodies will identify themselves with all kinds of immigration—legal or illegal."

Britain, nevertheless, indicated that it aimed at achieving some kind of agreement to reduce tension in the *yishuv* as a preliminary measure to getting Zionist participation in the 2d stage of the London conference. The mandatory authority, however, refused to discuss any increase in the immigration quota despite the Agency's insistence that this was at the root of *yishuv* disaffection. The British demanded the Agency's cooperation in curbing terrorism. The Agency insisted on the release of its 3 leading members, detained at Latrun without formal charge or trial, and on an end to severe repressive measures by the British security forces; it also asked for a halt in arms searches in outlying settlements, where no terrorism existed.

The Jewish Agency was incensed by the military searches, particularly those that had taken place at the settlements of Dorot and Ruhama, on the border of the Negev, where the British uncovered arms and munitions caches Aug. 30. Not a single room had been left intact in the latter settlement after a 6-day search, and this settlement had twice been destroyed by Arab rioters before the British troops arrived. "Scrapers and bulldozers had been used in the search," according to an Agency account. "The newly built meteorological station was a heap of rubble. Clothing was ripped and scattered all over the place. In the secretary's office, typewriters, duplicating machines and other equipment were smashed, while scraps of iron had been dropped down the drill shafts used for well-boring. The grain silo was dismantled, a tractor set on fire. The entire store of winter clothing, valued at about £5,000 [$24,000], as well as watches, cameras and other valuables were removed; sewing machines were smashed to bits. Trees, including saplings, were uprooted. In Dorot, too, a great deal of wanton damage was caused. As no act of sabotage or terrorism had occurred in that part of Palestine, the object of the search could only be defensive weapons."

"The Jewish community as well as the agricultural settlements have never denied that there are arms for defense purposes," said Mrs. Golda Meyerson, acting head of the Jewish Agency's Political Department, at a press conference held Sept. 1. "To take away these arms actually means an invitation to destroy Ruhama for the 3d time. We cannot give up these arms, because our experience in the past gives us no certainty that anyone else will, in time of trouble, be able to guarantee us any defense."

Terrorist acts by Jewish extremists grew in number in the bitter atmosphere engendered by the British policy and by the deportation of immigrants appearing at Haifa harbor in often unseaworthy blockade-running vessels.

Terrorists Sept. 8 attacked transport and communications installations, among them a railroad bridge at Bat Galin and a railroad signal box in Haifa, where an Arab boy was killed. They also set off explosions along 3 pipelines into the Consolidated oil refinery, but the resultant fire was put out quickly.

2 gunmen shot and killed a Palestinian police officer outside a Haifa hotel in broad daylight Sept. 9. The victim, an Englishman, had spotted and arrested Itzhak Jazarnitsky, 2d-in-command of the Stern Group, in Jerusalem Aug. 2.

Later Sept. 9, terrorists shot to death a British army sergeant north of Tel Aviv, blew up a railroad bridge and signal box in Tel Aviv, cut the railroad line between Tel Aviv and Jaffa in a number of locales but failed in an attempt to destroy railroad crossing barriers on Tel Aviv's main road. Terrorists also planted explosives at an administrative headquarters of the mandatory government in Tel Aviv. A British security officer and an Arab policeman were killed in the blast,

and the officer's wife and a Jewish deputy superintendent of
police were wounded, as were 4 others.

The Irgun Zvai Leumi Sept. 10 claimed credit for the railroad sabotage and called it a protest against the London
conference.

Haganah Breaks with Terrorists

A triple bank robbery Sept. 13 confirmed the *yishuv*'s
regular underground military arm, Haganah, in its growing
resolve to dissociate itself from the 2 extremist units, the Irgun
and the Stern Group. Early that day terrorists held up the
Ottoman Bank in Tel Aviv, escaping with £5,000 ($24,000),
while confederates were robbing its branch and the Arab Bank
in Jaffa. In ensuing gunfights 2 Arab policemen, 2 Arab
passersby and one Jew were killed. The British imposed curfews
in both cities and arrested 36 Jews.

Haganah's underground radio Sept. 14 denounced the Sept.
13 killings as "senseless outrages." The Irgun's underground
radio confirmed Sept. 15 that Haganah had broken with it and
the Stern Group over this latest violence. According to the
Irgun broadcast, "a new era" in Palestinian history had begun
"for the Jewish resistance"; the Irgun promised to carry out its
violent attacks henceforth without letup. (Terrorists struck the
same day, attacking a coastal police post near Tel Aviv. The
authorities there drove them off.)

The Jewish Agency's Executive Sept. 15 officially termed
the extremist attacks a "form of gangsterism" and attributed
them to "elements not accepting the discipline of the organized
Jewish community." The Executive especially expressed regret
at the loss of Arab life and deplored the increase in Arab-Jewish
hostility thus occasioned—"particularly since, even in the days
of strained relations, the Jews made every effort to prevent
suffering and injury to people with whom we have no quarrel."

Haganah's break with the extremists became official
Zionist policy Oct. 29, when the Zionist Inner General Council
categorically denounced the extremists' policy and the "bloodshed caused by groups of terrorists defying national discipline."
It urged the *yishuv* to stop assisting or supporting them. The
council went on record in declaring that "the Zionist movement
has always rejected and continues to reject terrorist bloodshed

as an instrument of political struggle." "The banner of Zionism must be kept pure and unbesmirched," the council said. "The Zionist Inner Council denounces without reservation the ... groups of terrorists who ... thereby place themselves outside the ranks of the organized community. The[ir] deeds defile the struggle of the Jewish people and distort its character; they strengthen the hands of the opponents of Zionism and the enemies of the Jewish people. The council calls upon the *yishuv* to isolate these groups and to deny them all encouragement, support and assistance."

The Palestinian Arab Party of Jamal Bey el-Husseini, meanwhile, announced in Jerusalem Sept. 16 that it was organizing an army to defend Arabs against Zionist terrorism.

That terrorism, however, resumed Sept. 20, when part of Haifa's eastern railroad station was blown up. No one was injured, and police sealed off the station at once. It was soon learned that 4 armed Jews had rolled a large cylinder of explosives into the station. The drum was labeled "Danger, Mines" in 3 languages. 3 days later, terrorists similarly destroyed an engine and 2 cars of a fuel train near Hadera in the Plain of Sharon. Later Sept. 23 a squad of uniformed men killed an Arab sentry guarding the Lydda-Jaffa railroad bridge. In the month's final outburst, terrorists gunned down and killed a British army sergeant on a motorcycle from a passing car on the Lydda-Petah Tiqva road, shortly after terrorists had wounded a girl in a jeep on the same road.

The immigration struggle continued. A detail from the British naval minesweeper *Rowena* met with stiff resistance from Jewish passengers on the bark *Palmach* when the British seamen tried to board the vessel sometime before dawn Sept. 22. One British sailor shot a Jewish passenger to death, and the detail resorted to tear gas to quell the resistance. 32 of the passengers jumped overboard during transfer operations in Haifa harbor Sept. 23 but were fished out by launches. The British steamship *Ocean Vigour* Sept. 24 took 585 illegal immigrants from the *Palmach* to Cyprus, where they were interned at Caraolos.

Hatred between Briton and Jew had become another aspect of the increasingly troubled situation in urban Palestine, where, in Oct. 1946, terrorism took a toll of 12 lives, all of them British. Extremists began mining roads and highways Oct. 8

over which British military traffic had to pass. Yisrael Scheib and Nathan Mor's Stern Group Oct. 21 began distributing handbills bearing threats to kill certain British soldiers and policemen.

Animosity reached such a pitch as to set off a storm of Jewish protest over so small an incident as the refusal of a British battalion commander to allow reporters to watch a roundup of suspects after 3 bomb explosions in the center of Jerusalem. Lt. Col. Richard H. L. Webb of the First Battalion, Argyll & Sutherland Highland Regiment, was heard by the reporters Oct. 24 to call the Jews a "dispicable race." Webb was relieved of his command Oct. 29 in a move taken by the *yishuv* as a British gesture at mollifying the Jews.

MacMillan Succeeds Barker as Military Commander

The British government had already made a personnel change at the highest command level. The government Oct. 22, 1946 recalled Lt. Gen. Sir Evelyn Barker from his post as military commander in Palestine and named Maj. Gen. G. H. A. MacMillan to succeed him. Barker under fire for an allegedly anti-Semitic remark after the bombing of the King David Hotel, received the top post of the British Eastern Command in England.

British vigilance toward illegal immigration attempts continued unabated. The British minesweeper *Moon* Oct. 21 intercepted the blockage-running vessel *Alma* off northern Palestine and towed it into Haifa. From there the steamers *Ocean Vigour* and *Empire Heywood* took its 819 passengers to internment in Cyprus.

Because of British policy on immigration, Haganah took up a posture opposing the mandatory authorities as well as the extremists. In an underground radio broadcast Oct. 25, a Kol Yisrael spokesman denied that Haganah would oppose the terrorists militarily. He said Haganah preferred to oppose terrorism with "education and civic measures" and would not collaborate with the mandatory government against the terrorists so "long as the British government continues to prohibit immigration and pursues a policy of searches and arrests."

British Release Zionist & Arab Leaders

British Colonial Secy. Arthur Creech Jones told the House of Commons Nov. 5, 1946 that the 8 Jewish Agency leaders detained in Palestine and several Palestinian Arabs detained in the Seychelles Islands would be freed. The Labor government's move, Creech Jones said, was an act of reciprocation for the Zionist Inner General Council's disavowal Oct. 29 of terror as a method of protest. He added that the British government had decided to accept the council's statement "as an earnest of the intention of the Jewish Agency and of representative Jewish institutions in Palestine to dissociate themselves entirely from the campaign of violence and to do their utmost to root out this evil."

In announcing the release of the Palestinian Arab leaders, Creech Jones said that "in the light of ... representations" made to the British government by the Arab delegates to the London conference "and as a gesture of goodwill at this time, when important decisions on the future of Palestine are in the balance,... [the government had] decided to release these detainees and to permit their return to Palestine." The British had already released 2 other Arabs for reasons of health from internment in the Seychelles and, through the mandatory government, would grant an amnesty to "certain other Arabs," he added.

Creech Jones said that although Jewish terrorists detained in Eritrea would not be released, 2,550 of the Jews suspected of complicity in Haganah activities and 779 of the Jews detained after the King David Hotel bombing had been freed.

Among the 8 Jewish Agency leaders released from the Latrun jail were Moshe Shertok, director of the Agency's Political Department, and Dr. Bernard Joseph, legal adviser to the Agency. 129 others were then freed from Rafa camp. Those leaders abroad when the arrests occurred June 29 were pronounced free to return home. Curfews in Jerusalem and other towns were lifted. It also was announced in Jerusalem that 20 Palestinian Arab leaders had received amnesty. Among them were Mohammed Munif Husseini, nephew of the exiled grand mufti of Jerusalem, and 2 cousins.

Terrorists Declare Open War on Britain

2 bombs exploded early Oct. 31, 1946 outside the British embassy in Rome. 2 Italian pedestrians were hurt, one seriously, and the embassy was badly damaged. In a letter to Italian Premier Alcide De Gasperi, released Nov. 4 to the press, the "Supreme Command of Irgun Zvai Leumi" claimed responsibility and said that this was "the opening of the Jewish military front outside Palestine." According to this Irgun leadership message, "Britain has declared a war of extermination on our people all over the world.... The armed forces of the eternal people will reply with war everywhere until our stolen fatherland is freed."

19 soldiers were injured when a truck was blown up near Tel Aviv Nov. 2. A troop furlough train was derailed by a mine near Lydda Nov. 7. An explosion at a railroad station near Petah Tiqva killed one Arab policeman Nov. 10. A mine on a railroad track at Beit Safafa near Jerusalem exploded Nov. 13, killing 2 British and 4 Arab railroad policemen. 2 trucks exploded in the center of Jerusalem the same day. 3 policemen and an RAF sergeant were killed by a land mine in Tel Aviv Nov. 17. A Jewish detective was shot to death Nov. 19 on the main street of Tel Aviv.

Railroad employes staged a work stoppage Nov. 19 in protest against dangerous conditions resulting from the mining of railroad tracks. (The Irgun Nov. 22 suspended its attacks on railroads because the transportation was needed for the citrus harvest.) The Palestine Inland Revenue Department's offices in Jerusalem were blown up Nov. 20, and the blast killed a Jewish policeman. Palestinian police fought Stern Group terrorists in the streets of Jerusalem Nov. 30 after terrorist attempts to destroy police barracks and other public buildings with mines and grenades; 8 people were injured, 52 arrested and a curfew imposed.

4 soldiers were killed Dec. 2 when their jeep was blown up on the Jaffa road outside Jerusalem. Armed terrorists failed in an attempt to rob a bank messenger in Tel Aviv Dec. 3. Explosives in a truck driven by a terrorist in British uniform who had false identification papers exploded in the Sarafand military camp Dec. 5 near Jaffa; 2 British soldiers were killed.

A truck went over a land mine on the Haifa-Tel Aviv road Dec. 6, and 5 soldiers were injured.

British Maj. Paddy Brett was kidnaped from Nathanya Dec. 29 in reprisal for the flogging of a Jew convicted of complicity in the robbery attempt on the Ottoman Bank in Jaffa Sept. 13; Maj. Brett received 20 lashes from an Irgun punishment squad and was released. 2 British sergeants in Tel Aviv Dec. 29 also were kidnaped, received 18 lashes each and were then let go.

The Irgun's radio Jan. 1, 1947 announced a step-up in "night attacks on British army transport" in reprisal for the condemnation to death of Dov Bela Gruner, 33, that day for his role in the Irgun attack on a police outpost at Ramat Gan Apr. 23, 1946.* Terrorists Jan. 2 attacked British police and military headquarters at Citrus House in Tel Aviv; terrorists also blew up a Bren gun carrier near Haifa Jan. 2, killing 4 British soldiers.

British forces had carried out intensive searches in Nathanya, Lydda and Rishon-le-Zion for terrorists Dec. 30, 1946 and had arrested one of Maj. Brett's attackers. British troops surrounded the Hadera and Kfar Attah settlements near Haifa Jan. 5, 1947, detaining 33 persons and seizing 3 mines and a quantity of arms. A surprise raid at Rishon-le-Zion by British troops Jan. 8 netted 18 terrorists.

Yishuv Condemns Terrorists

At a joint session in Jerusalem Dec. 4, 1946, the Jewish Agency and the Vaad Leumi had reiterated their stand against terrorism. The 2 organs declared that the terrorists, "in defiance of the Zionist Inner General Council's appeal of Oct. 29," were "continuing to use murder and terror as a political weapon." They called for the immediate end of these activities and drew "the entire *yishuv*'s urgent attention to the grave dangers and disasters that threaten it if the terror[ist] outrages of these isolated groups do not immediately cease."

---

* Gruner had fought as a British army lance corporal in Africa and Italy during World War II.

This plea, however, failed to satisfy Sir Harry Gurney, the acting high commissioner for Palestine. Gurney summoned Rabbi Yehuda Fishman, acting head of the Jewish Agency, and Yitzhak Ben Zvi of the Vaad Leumi to the government house in Jerusalem Jan. 3, 1947 and demanded that the *yishuv* cooperate in ending terrorism. Gurney threatened to invoke "drastic measures" (such as martial law) if the incidents did not cease.

British soldiers were ordered to wear arms at all times and were forbidden to frequent restaurants or cafes at any time. Haganah's secret radio Jan. 5 again condemned the terrorists and called for an end to the violence, but that same day 11 British soldiers were injured in a grenade attack on a train in Egypt carrying troops into Palestine.

High Commissioner Sir Alan Cunningham arrived in London Jan. 3 for consultations on action against terrorism. He conferred with Arthur Creech Jones, Clement Attlee and Ernest Bevin. Field Marshal Bernard Montgomery, chief of the Imperial General Staff, was present at the first meeting. David Ben-Gurion, in his capacity as chairman of the Jewish Agency, arrived in London at the beginning of 1947 and met with Creech Jones Jan. 2 and 8. During these talks he told the colonial secretary of the decision of the Zionist Congress— which had met in Basel in Dec. 1946—not to take part in the forthcoming 2d stage of the London conference. In Jerusalem later, Ben-Gurion discussed the terrorists' activities with Lt. Gen. Cunningham, who returned Jan. 17 from London (riding down a road later found to have been mined).

In raids on Rishon-le-Zion and Rehovoth Jan. 8, British mandatory police arrested 32 persons suspected of being members of the Irgun's "Black Squad," but Sir Harry Gurney revoked a flogging sentence imposed on Aharon Cohen, a captured Irgun member, after the Irgun threatened retaliation.

After a 10-day lull in violence, a man drove a truck filled with explosives into the central police complex in Haifa Jan. 12; explosions there killed 2 British policemen and 2 Arab constables and injured 140 others. The terrorist escaped. The Stern Group claimed responsibility for the attack. British soldiers and police Jan. 13 screened 872 persons in Haifa and detained 19 for further questioning as Arabs and Jews condemned the bombing.

The British military high command Jan. 13 issued orders to the 3d Division to transfer its headquarters from the Suez Canal Zone to Palestine. A military court in Jerusalem Jan. 14 sentenced Yehuda Katz, 17, to life imprisonment for his part in the attempted robbery of a bank in Jaffa Sept. 13, 1946 in quest of funds for the extremist underground movement.

Yishuv Outlaws Anti-Jewish Terrorists

The Jewish Agency's leaders Jan. 20, 1947 again condemned terrorism and outlawed terrorists who directed violence against Jews. The Vaad Leumi, at its session in Jerusalem Jan. 20, unanimously adopted a resolution calling on the *yishuv* to resist the terrorists by force.

Vaad Leumi Chairman David Remez warned that physical power would be used when necessary against Irgun and Stern Group operatives. He said: "We shall use force to protect ourselves from intimidation practiced for the purpose of obtaining financial assistance; from coercion of teachers and pupils; from threats issued against Jewish policemen, and from force used against drivers to get their vehicles. We do not desire internecine warfare; it is not our wish that Jews should fight Jews. It is wrong that such an internal struggle should be placed upon us simultaneously with outside factors. We hope that the sincere call which goes out from our hearts to the whole *yishuv* for unity and discipline shall be heard, heeded and adhered to."

Mrs. Golda Meyerson (Meir), head of the Jewish Agency's Political Department, declared in an appeal to the terrorist organizations: "We call on you once more to stop terrorism now, or we will stop you by force. We do not want civil war, but it has reached a state where the Jewish population in Palestine must decide that this situation cannot continue. We cannot continue to live in a state in which small groups decide what is to be the policy of the nation—groups guilty of extortion, intimidation of children, robbery at pistol point and murder of innocent persons."

The mandatory authorities indicated, however, that they still did not consider the Agency's stand to be sufficiently forceful and clearcut. Chief Secy. Sir Harry Gurney of the Palestinian government announced Jan. 22 in Jerusalem that the British mandatory administration would tax the *yishuv* $2.4 million to pay for damages from sabotage by terrorists.

The mandatory government's pressure on the *yishuv* moderates brought an angry response from many American Jews. Dr. Abba Hillel Silver, president of the Zionist Organization of America, said at his group's national mobilization conference in Chicago Jan. 26 that Britain was to blame for the terrorism in Palestine. British policy, he said, consisted of "broken promises, ruthless tyranny and brutal actions of injustice" toward the *yishuv*.

The U.S. government deprived the Political Action Committee for Palestine, Inc. of its tax exemption, a committee spokesman disclosed in New York Jan. 8. The reason given was that the organization had "sought to influence legislation" by campaigning against a U.S. loan to Britain. The spokesman denied that the committee had given financial aid to the Jewish underground and expressed regret at its inability to do so. (After visiting Palestine, Committee Chairman Joseph C. Baldwin recommended in a 12,000-word message to Pres. Truman Jan. 18 that Palestine become an independent, all-Jewish state.)

The British, acting against another American pro-Zionist lobby Jan. 17, deported Johan J. Smertenko, vice president of the American League for a Free Palestine. They shipped him from Croydon Airfield outside London to Paris aboard the same plane on which he had arrived Jan. 16 in defiance of a British request to stay out of the country. He had denounced British "terror" in Palestine.

Extremist terrorism continued. Armed men Jan. 26 kidnaped Maj. H. A. I. Collins, 48, a banker and retired military officer, from his apartment in Jerusalem and beat him senseless in reprisal for a military court's confirmation of the death sentence imposed Jan. 1 on Dov Gruner of the Irgun. Terrorists Jan. 27 kidnaped Ralph Windham, chief judge of the Tel Aviv District Court, in his robe and wig while he was hearing a case. As in most of the terrorist outbursts in Jan. 1947, Gruner's death sentence again was the avowed motive. After Sir Alan Cunningham announced a stay of execution for Gruner until Feb. 4, the terrorists released Judge Windham wigless but unharmed Jan. 28. Maj. Collins was found unconscious Jan. 29 on the grounds of a Jerusalem hospital.

Cunningham Jan. 31 ordered the immediate evacuation from Palestine of the wives and children of all British personnel in the land and the departure for home of certain nonessential male civilians. More than 1,600 persons left Palestine under these circumstances in the next 96 hours.

Debate in Commons

A debate on the situation in Palestine took place in the British House of Commons Jan. 31, 1947. It was opened by a Conservative member, Col. Oliver Stanley, speaking for the opposition. He complained that the government had not had a policy in Palestine for the past 18 months and that hardly a week had passed since the King David Hotel bombing without the loss of British life. He attributed Maj. Collins' and Judge Windham's release to terrorists' initiatives rather than to an official show of force; he asserted that the government had retreated before their threats.

Stanley said: "You cannot have a situation where the administration of justice and the punishment of offenders are being dictated by the criminals. Sooner than that this country should have to endure further humiliation of this character, I would prefer that we should clear out of Palestine and tell the people of the world that we are unable to carry out our mandate. Yet I believe that that would be a disaster and that such a retreat would only be the signal for a bloody civil war. But whatever the final policy, any chance of its success will depend upon a firm hand and resolute authority in Palestine. Only so will our policy have any chance of rallying to its side what moderate men there may be in either communit[y]..."

Stanley argued that the Jewish Agency and Haganah, despite their disavowal of the 2 terrorist groups' policies, bore "a great responsibility" for Irgun and Stern Group excesses. "If there had been active cooperation, the terrorism of Irgun could not have continued," he said. Any further "deterioration will lead to further loss of British lives and in the end to turning the biblical land into a bloody hell for British, Jews and Arabs alike," he warned.

3 Labor members also criticized the government. Laborite Richard Crossman called the Irgun a right-wing fascist organization that had been resisted from the start by Jewish labor. He argued that the British policy of "half repression and half conciliation" had bolstered the Irgun and weakened the moderates. Crossman added: "We should appreciate the position of the moderate Jew in Palestine. He is between the devil and the deep sea. He knows about the destruction of his country, but how is he to cooperate with the British authorities when terrorism is as great a power in Palestine as the British government today? Ruthless measures of repression without a policy will produce war in Palestine, for which Irgun has been working for 7 years, and will destroy the last position of moderate and intelligent Jews who stand by this country. I believe it is a futile illusion that one can find an agreed solution between Jew and Arab. The mandate is unworkable."

Barnett Janner agreed that the government had to do everything possible to combat terrorism and keep order, but he expressed doubt that this goal could be achieved merely by military action. If immigration into Palestine were available to more displaced Jews from Europe, terrorism would fail as a policy and cease almost at once, Janner asserted.

Laborite Sidney Silverman condemned terrorism as "morally wrong, wicked and without justification," but he said that the *yishuv*'s young men and women had opted for terrorism because of "the utter failure of the government to show them any hope." The government must decide for itself on a "constructive policy . . . and apply it fearlessly," he said.

Conservative member Sir Reginald E. Manningham-Buller (like Crossman, a member of the Anglo-American Committee of Inquiry) took the government to task for its lack of a resolute stand since the Anglo-American Committee had issued its report Apr. 30, 1946. Meanwhile, he said, the government had let matters "drift into a series of discarded plans and indecisive conferences." He charged the government with "vacillating" in its pursuit of justice and said that moderate Jews would welcome the introduction of stern measures against the terrorists.

Winston Churchill, leader of the Opposition, summed up Conservative opinion. He said: "We have very great difficulty in conducting squalid warfare with terrorists, and that is why I submit that every effort should be made to avoid getting into such warfare. If warfare has broken out, every effort should be made to bring it to an end. It is quite certain that what is going on now in Palestine is doing a great deal of harm to our reputation all over the world. This struggle could have been avoided if promises had not been made by members opposite at the election on a wide scale. Promises were made far beyond those to which a responsible government would commit itself, and the performance has been a vacuum, a gaping void, a senseless abyss. We have not advanced one single step either in making good our pledges to those to whom we have given them, or in reaching some broader solution, or in disembarrassing ourselves of burdens and obligations—burdens we cannot bear and obligations we have shown ourselves unable or unwilling to discharge. If you should be drawn into a quarrel, you must bear yourself so that your opponent may beware of you. Pugnacity and willpower cannot be dispensed with. It is a dreadful thing to be drawn into a quarrel and cowed out of doing your duty.... What are you to say about altering the course of justice because criminals threaten to add to their crimes? .... You cannot wonder that you will be defeated and humiliated if you allow threats of maltreatment to turn you from the administration of the law as it would otherwise have been carried out."

Churchill charged that Britain had at least 100,000 men in Palestine who could be more usefully employed at home in bolstering industry. Each year, he said, the government was spending in Palestine £30 million to £40 million ($144 million to $192 million) "which could be employed much better on this island." He asked and answered 3 questions:

... How long are you going to stay there [in Palestine], and stay there for what? Is it in order that, on a threat of killing hostages, we show ourselves unable to execute a sentence duly pronounced by the competent tribunal? Let us stay in the [Suez] Canal zone and have no further interest in the strategic position of Palestine. I never thought we had a strategic interest there. We have broken our pledges to the Jews. We have not fulfilled promises made at the election, and having found ourselves unable to carry out our policy we have no right to stay there for motives of policy. It is said we must stay because if we go there will be civil war. I think it very likely, but is that a reason why we should stay? We do not propose to stay in India. The responsibility for stopping civil war in Palestine ought to be borne by the United Nations and not by this overburdened country.

There is a conference, and unless it produces a solution which it is in our power to enforce effectively we should definitely give notice that, unless the U.S.A. comes in with us on a 50-50 basis in all the bloodshed, odium, trouble, and worry, we will lay our mandate at the feet of the United Nations. We really cannot go about in all directions, taking on burdens which drain the remaining strength of Britain, and which are beyond any duty we have undertaken in the international field. I trust the government will make perfectly certain that the willpower of the British state is not conquered by brigands and bandits and that at the earliest possible moment, unless we have the aid of the U.S.A., we will give due notice that we will divest ourselves of a responsibility we are failing to discharge and which in the process is covering us with blood and shame....

The debate ended inconclusively with this final statement by Arthur Creech Jones: "The conference is sitting in London, and other consultations are going on. Therefore it would be unfortunate if in the midst of these discussions I were to refer to the problem of long-term policy and discuss it at any length. We share with all members the feeling of humiliation and are conscious that the prestige of Britain is assailed when terrorist outrages of this kind are perpetrated in territory for whose administration we carry responsibility. I would remind the House that the facts are not quite as stated by members when they allege that people have not been brought to punishment for the crimes which they have committed. During 1946, 22 Jews were sentenced to death, but the sentences were commuted to long terms of imprisonment up to a maximum of 20 years. There have been 83 Jewish terrorists who have been convicted by military courts for carrying or discharging firearms; all have been sentenced to long terms of imprisonment. 26 have actually been killed and 28 wounded during action with the police and military."

The Labor government had "given its unreserved support to the high commissioner and the military authorities in applying all possible measures for rooting out terrorism as well as securing law and order," Creech Jones added, but "unless you get the cooperation and good will of the people you cannot completely eradicate terrorism in any community."

First among the measures thereafter taken by the mandatory government was an ultimatum to the Vaad Leumi Feb. 3. It gave the *yishuv* 7 days in which to volunteer its security forces to assist the government in hunting down the terrorists. The government was making this request "on the express direction of the high commissioner," the note read. It was signed by Sir Harry Gurney, as the Palestine government's chief secretary, on behalf of Lt. Gen. Sir Alan Cunningham. It was addressed to Mrs. Golda Meyerson (Meir). She promptly declared that the Jewish Agency was not willing to turn the 600,000 Jews in Palestine into informers.

The Jewish Agency Executive, meeting Feb. 4, expressed anger at the government's references to Jewish resolutions "purporting to condemn bloodshed and terrorism" as implying a "charge of insincerity." Chairman David Remez, addressing the Vaad Leumi Feb. 5, said: "The keys to cooperation are with the Palestine government. The government also holds the keys to the immigration of Jewish survivors from Europe, to recolonization of the promised land and to sovereignty of the Jewish nation. We were shocked at receiving an ultimatum from the Palestine government at a time when discussions were taking place in London between our representatives and the British government for a solution of the problems of Palestine which may well renew the friendly and faithful ties between Jews and the British people. We will, however, never accept the demand to hand over the terrorists to the authorities. Although fully aware of the grave consequences of our refusal to offer more cooperation with the Palestine government against the terrorists than that already made, we regret we are unable to accept the ultimatum."

The British district commissioner, James Huey Pollock, Feb. 4 disclosed a plan for the military occupation of 3 sections of Jerusalem and ordered nearly 1,000 Jews to evacuate the Rehaviah, Schneler and German quarters by noon Feb. 6. While the Vaad Leumi rejected the British ultimatum, the Irgun Zvai Leumi passed out notes asserting that it would "fight to the last breath" against the British authority. Preparing for military action, the British Feb. 5 ordered resident families out of sections of Tel Aviv and Haifa that they planned to fortify as security areas.

Illegal Immigration Continues

The main reason given by extremists for their acts of terrorism was the British restrictions on Jewish immigration.

This tide of immigration, declared illegal by Britain, kept rolling steadily towards Palestine's shores through the last months of 1946.

The *San Dimitrio,* a Panamanian-registry steamship of 700 tons, was intercepted by a naval patrol off Cyprus and brought into Haifa Nov. 1, 1946 with 1,279 immigrants aboard. The ship had sailed from the French port of Le Ciotat 2 weeks earlier; the passengers later overpowered the Panamanian crew and seized control of the vessel. In Haifa, they put up a fierce fight against British naval boarding parties, who used tear gas to overcome them. The immigrants were transferred to the *Empire Heywood* and *Ocean Vigour* and taken to Cyprus.

The ship *Lochita,* renamed the *Jewish Assembly,* flying the Zionist flag, put into Haifa from France Nov. 25 with more than 3,300 immigrants, the largest number yet in one ship to reach Palestine's shores. Strong resistance was put up against British forces, who used tear gas and fire hoses to board the ship. 20 British soldiers and 22 Jews were injured. The immigrants were transferred to Cyprus in the *Empire Heywood, Empire Rival* and *Ocean Vigour.*

A 3d ship, with 800 people aboard, ran aground Dec. 8 on the Greek island of Syrina. Supplies were dropped to it by aircraft; the British destroyer *Chevron* and a Greek destroyer rescued all aboard Dec. 10 and took them to Cyprus.

In an effort to cut off a source of illegal immigrant transport, the British government had drawn France's attention to conditions at Le Ciotat, used as an "escape" port for Jews trying to enter Palestine illegally. A French Foreign Ministry statement said Nov. 7, 1946 that talks were going on with the British over the matter and that the French government would make sure that immigrants passing through France had valid visas for their ultimate destination. The French spokesman said however, that France would not "herd displaced persons into concentration camps and jails like common criminals." France had "neither the desire nor sufficient police to put one policeman behind every unfortunate person passing through this country," he declared.

The British authorities announced Nov. 12 that 1,500 Jewish refugees held in Cyprus would be allowed into Palestine before Jan. 16, 1947 (when this quota was to be halved). The mandatory government disclosed Dec. 16, 1946 that more than 11,500 Jews then detained in camps in Cyprus and Palestine had received immigration certificates under the 1945 quota of 18,000. It then announced that the monthly quota would henceforth be divided equally between Cyprus and the British zone of western Germany.

A writ of *habeas corpus* was applied for Nov. 25, 1946 on behalf of the passengers aboard the *Jewish Assembly.* This action challenged Britain's right to detain incoming Jews on Cyprus as illegal immigrants. The application was considered by the Palestine High Court Nov. 27-29 and rejected by unanimous decision. The government of Palestine said Nov. 29 that it regretted the necessity to transfer the immigrants, and it admitted having caused heartache and inconvenience. But it asserted that no country could allow them to enter in such numbers after giving repeated warnings that they would not be permitted to set foot there. These immigration attempts, the government added, only defeated efforts by the government and Jewish moderates to improve conditions.

Despite the British action, attempts to smuggle in illegal immigrants were increased. Dr. Emanuel Neumann, vice president of the Zionist Organization of America, declared in London in Jan. 1947 that U.S. Zionists would spend "millions" to finance "illegal" immigration of Jews to Palestine. A Haganah spokesman claimed in Paris that 21,878 Jews had entered Palestine "illegally" during the past 15 months.

The 22d Zionist Congress

The 2d stage of the London conference had been put off until early in 1947 to enable the Jewish Agency to refer the question of its attendance to the 22d Zionist Congress, which met in Basel, Switzerland in mid-Dec. 1946.

Significant changes had taken place in the Zionist movement's composition. Since the eve of World War II, the Jewish population of the world had been cut from almost 17 million to about 11 million. Yet, probably because of the Nazi holocaust and the failure of the UN to provide for the rehabilitation of European Jewish survivors, world Zionist enrollment had more than doubled—topping 2 million in 1946. The number of countries with Zionist branches had risen to 63, with the U.S. replacing Poland as the chief Zionist center; almost half the members of the movement lived on the North American continent. The Zionist movement's political character had also changed. Disillusionment and uncertainty combined with disgust at British policies in Palestine had toughened Zionist stands.

The political debate, which occupied most of the 16-day session of the congress Dec. 9-24, left the Jewish Agency more than ever determined to stamp out terrorism. Dr. Chaim Weizmann denounced terrorism and warned that the growth of this "cancer in the body politic of Palestinian Jewry" must be checked, "for, if not, it will devour the [Zionist] movement and the *yishuv* and will destroy all that we have built up." The congress adopted this resolution: "While upholding the right of the *yishuv* to resist the policies of the present oppressive regime in Palestine, the congress condemns murder and the shedding of innocent blood as a means of political warfare. The terrorist campaign, to which certain dissident groups in Palestine have resorted in defiance of Jewish national authority, serves to distort the true character of the *yishuv* in the eyes of the world and to defeat rather than promote its legitimate struggle. The congress pledges the full support of the Zionist movement to the *yishuv* in its efforts against terrorism. It calls upon the members of the dissident organizations to desist from further bloodshed and to submit to the national discipline of the organized *yishuv* and the Zionist movement."

The congress also reaffirmed the full Zionist program claiming Palestine as a Jewish state. A motion to prevent the Jewish Agency Executive from discussing a plan for a Jewish state in a part of Palestine was turned back by a large majority. The congress aired Jewish resentment at the British government's failure to repudiate the 1939 White Paper and implement the short-term recommendations of the Anglo-American Committee of Inquiry. The Morrison Plan was rejected as "a travesty of Britain's obligations under the mandate, designed to divide Palestine into Arab, Jewish and British provinces, all of which would be under the unfettered control of the British administration."

The congress went on record with an assertion that "Jewish statehood is the only form in which the original purpose of the mandate for Palestine can be fulfilled in the event of the mandate's termination." It declared its opposition to any new trusteeship over Palestine "by which the establishment of the Jewish state would be prevented or postponed," and it appealed to the UN and to all its member states "to support the Jewish people in its claim for statehood in Palestine and a place in the family of nations."

In regard to the London conference, due shortly to be resumed, the congress refused to empower the Jewish Agency Executive to exercise its own discretion. Instead, a majority ruled that in the existing circumstances the Zionist movement could not take part in the conference but that the Inner General Council would reconsider the matter if the situation changed.

The Jewish Agency Executive thus did not formally participate in any stage of the London conference but held informal talks during the 2d stage of the conference in January-February 1947 with members of the British government. The Agency leaders indicated that they had become convinced that Britain was not ready to concede the Jewish claim to statehood or even to the control of immigration into a part of Palestine and that the Foreign Office had retreated from even the limited concessions contained in the Morrison Plan. Towards the end of these talks, the British government disclosed to the Agency the proposals submitted by the British delegation at the London conference Feb. 7, 1947. These proposals subsequently became known as the Bevin Plan.

LONDON CONFERENCE—PART II

Bevin Plan

Britain's conference on Palestine, boycotted by *yishuv* leaders, reconvened in London Jan. 27, 1947 and ended Feb. 14. The Palestinian Arabs, who had refused to attend the first part of the conference, sent representatives—but only after the Arab Higher Committee accepted the invitation extended Jan. 10 to Jamal el-Husseini, its deputy chairman. Nevertheless, the Higher Committee issued a statement Jan. 14 to the effect that the Palestinian Arabs were "resolutely opposed to partition in any form and at any price." This was plain notice of their continued rejection of the Morrison Plan.

Husseini brought with him to the conference the committee's secretary, Dr. Hussein Khalidi, and the committee member Emile el-Khoury, secretary of Husseini's Palestinian Arab Party. Arab League representatives attending included Foreign Min. Fadhil Jamali of Iraq, Lebanese Min.-to-Britain Camille Chamoun, Saudi Arabian Min.-to-Britain Sheikh Hafiz Wahba, Education Min. Adil Arslan of Syria, Syrian Min.-to-Britain. Najeeb el-Almanazi, Syrian Rep.-to-UN Security Council Faris el-Khoury, Transjordanian Min.-to-Egypt Fawzi Mulki, Transjordanian Min.-to-Britain Abdul Majid Haidar and Imam Abdullah of Yemen.

Executive Chairman David Ben-Gurion of the Jewish Agency had arrived in London Jan. 19 and had conferred with British Foreign Secy. Ernest Bevin and Colonial Secy. Arthur Creech Jones Jan. 29. It was reported in London that the British cabinet decided that same day to work for the partition of Palestine.

Faris el-Khoury, leader of the Syrian delegation to the conference, issued a statement Feb. 4 on behalf of all the Arab states and the Palestinian Arabs. He said that no discussions could be entered into that involved any plan for the partition of Palestine or that provided for the establishment there of a Jewish state. Despite this announcement, Britain offered its new proposals on Palestine to the Arab delegations and the

Jewish Agency Feb. 7 as a possible basis for negotiation. The new plan, submitted to the Arabs and the Agency by Foreign Secy. Bevin, came to bear his name—although it was in essence only a modified version of the already rejected Morrison Plan.

A British memo on the new plan, dated Feb. 7, 1947, said: "The British delegation cannot accept the contention of the Jewish Agency that the rate of Jewish immigration into Palestine as a whole should be determined by the Jews alone. Nor can they accept the demand of the Arab delegations that all Jewish immigration should cease forthwith. They do not contemplate either a settlement which would bring to an end the development of a Jewish national home or the admission of Jewish immigrants without reference to the effect of their entry on the rights and position of the country's population. The provisions made for future Jewish immigration must rest upon consideration for the well-being of Palestine as a whole. With this end in view, the trusteeship agreement would provide for Jewish immigration at a rate of 4,000 monthly for a period of 2 years. This would guarantee the entry of approximately 100,000 additional Jewish immigrants. During the remainder of the period of trusteeship, the continuance of immigration and the rate of entry would be determined, with due regard to the principle of economic absorptive capacity, by the high commissioner in consultation with his advisory council. In the event of disagreement, the final decision would rest with an arbitration tribunal appointed by the United Nations."

These proposals were designed, according to the memo, "to give the 2 peoples an opportunity of demonstrating their ability to work together for the good of Palestine as a whole and so provide a stable foundation for an independent state."

The Jewish Agency's leadership a week later pointed out what it considered to be flaws in the Bevin Plan and communicated these objections in a memo dated Feb. 13, that contained a critical analysis of the plan and the Jewish Agency's alternative proposals.

The Agency argued: "... There are 3 vital interests that the Executive of the Jewish Agency seeks to preserve in any settlement that may be devised for the solution of the Palestine problem. These are: (A) Freedom of Jewish immigration into Palestine up to the country's economic absorptive capacity. (B) Freedom to settle on the land, including state lands and waste lands not required for public purposes, and to develop the country's potentialities. (C) Freedom to develop the Jewish national home to the position of a self-governing independent Jewish state."

The Agency said "The proposals contained in the memorandum are incompatible with all 3 basic purposes of the mandate: immigration, land settlement and ultimate statehood," firstly, because the memo "provides for the immigration of 96,000 Jews at the rate of 4,000 a month over a period of 2 years. The Executive of the Jewish Agency begs to recall that 20 months have elapsed since the proposal to admit 100,000 Jews immediately was first submitted to his majesty's government. The Anglo-American Committee of Inquiry recommended their quickest possible transfer, and even the Morrison Plan, which the Jewish Agency regarded as unacceptable, provided for the entry of 100,000 within a year. The memorandum further provides that, after the first 2 years, it shall be open to the high commissioner in consultation with his advisory council, composed of Arab as well as Jewish representatives, to determine whether immigration should at all continue even into the Jewish areas and, if so, at what rate. This provision replaces the positive injunction of the mandate to 'facilitate Jewish immigration under suitable conditions,' which injunction, as laid down by the Council of the League of Nations, signified that immigration is to proceed up to the economic absorptive capacity of the country."

On the issue of Jewish land settlement the Agency held that "it is especially incongruous to discriminate against Jews in the right of access and settlement in the country designated by history and international law as the Jewish national home." It protested that the existing land legislation created a situation in which "in the bulk of the country the Arab local authorities would be free to prevent the transfer of land to Jews." It asserted that "when the Jewish population reaches some 700,000 to 800,000, it would come under the domination of the Arab majority, whereupon Jewish immigration would cease." "The Executive of the Jewish Agency can in no way agree that this measure is in accordance either with the purpose or the provisions of the mandate," the Agency declared.

"To condemn the Jewish national home to the position of a permanent minority," the Agency said, "would not merely be contrary to the clear intention of the mandate: the denial of statehood and independence to the Jewish people even in its homeland would constitute a grave historic injustice. On the other hand, if the Arabs of Palestine found themselves in a minority, their position would not similarly affect the Arab people as a whole, since it enjoys independence and sovereignty in a number of countries covering an area vastly greater than Palestine."

The Agency asserted that "for all these reasons, the Jewish Agency cannot accept the proposals contained in the memorandum as a basis for further discussions and will find itself constrained to oppose the conclusion of a trusteeship agreement envisaged in the memorandum."

The agency's alternative proposals were:

"(a) That, in accordance with the original intentions of the Balfour Declaration and the mandate, large-scale Jewish immigration and settlement should be effected, with the result that Palestine would become a Jewish state....

"(b) That if, for any reason, his majesty's government ... would prefer for the time being to continue the mandatory regime, the Jewish Agency would urge that ... Jewish immigration be regulated up to the full extent of the country's economic absorptive capacity, that close settlement of Jews on the land be encouraged, and that no part of the country be closed to Jewish land purchase and settlement....

"(c) That, in the event of a final settlement being required immediately, the Jewish Agency would be ready...to consider a compromise scheme for the setting up of a 'viable Jewish state in an adequate area of Palestine.' ... The state should have complete control over immigration and development and be represented in the United Nations. Such a state, too, would be based on complete equality for all citizens with the necessary safeguards for religious, cultural and linguistic needs."

These counterproposals were rejected by the British government.

Following talks with Bevin and Creech Jones, the Arab delegations rejected the new British plan. With neither side willing to budge, the Bevin Plan faded out of sight.

Britain Refers Problem to UN

British Foreign Secy. Bevin, in a statement in the House of Commons Feb. 18, 1947, surveyed the late discussions on Palestine and then confessed that Britain had run out of ideas on how to handle the problem. He said: "The conference with the Arabs and the consultations with the Zionist Organization about the future of Palestine, which have been proceeding in London, have come to an end because it has become clear that there is no prospect of reaching by this means any settlement even broadly acceptable to the 2 communities in Palestine."

Since neither side was willing to accept either the federal plan or the plan for a unitary Palestine, Bevin concluded, Britain, after intensive and extensive discussions with both sides, could find "no prospect of resolving this conflict by any settlement negotiated between the parties."

"If the conflict is to be resolved by arbitrary decision," Bevin continued, "that is not a decision which his majesty's government are empowered, as mandatory, to take. His majesty's government have of themselves no power under the terms of the mandate to award the country either to the Arabs or the Jews, or even to partition it between them. In these circumstances we have decided that we are unable either to accept the scheme put forward by the Arabs or by the Jews or to impose a solution of our own. We have, therefore, reached the conclusion that the only course open to us is to submit the problem to the United Nations. We intend to place before them an historical account of the way in which his majesty's government have discharged their trust in Palestine over the last 25 years. We shall explain that the mandate has proved to be unworkable in practice and that the obligations undertaken to the 2 communities in Palestine have proved to be irreconcilable. We shall describe the various proposals put forward for dealing with the situation—the Arab plan, Zionist aspirations, the proposals of the Anglo-American Committee, and the various proposals which we ourselves have put forward. We shall then ask the United Nations to consider our report and to recommend the settlement of the problem. We do not intend ourselves to recommend any particular solution."

Bevin explained to the House the dilemma that the Labor government found impossible to solve after the failure of the Morrison and Bevin plans. According to his account:

From the outset both Arabs and Jews declined to accept as a basis for discussion the provincial autonomy plan put forward by his majesty's government. The Arabs put forward an alternative proposal under which Palestine would achieve early independence as a unitary state with a permanent Arab majority. His majesty's government, seeing no prospect of negotiating a settlement on that basis, put forward new proposals of their own. These envisaged the establishment of local areas, Arab and Jewish, with a substantial degree of autonomy within a unitary state, with a central government in which both Arabs and Jews would share.... This plan, while consistent with the principles of the mandate, had an element which had hitherto been lacking in the administration of Palestine—namely, a practical promise of evolution towards independence by building up during a 5-year period of trusteeship political institutions rooted in the lives of the people. These proposals were rejected outright by both the Arab delegation and the representatives of the Jewish Agency, even as a basis for discussion.

It is important that the House should understand the reasons which prompted the 2 sides to reject this solution. For the Arabs the fundamental point is that Palestine should no longer be denied the independence which has now been attained by every other Arab state, and that in accordance with the accepted principles of democracy the elected majority should be free to determine the future destiny of the country. They regard the further expansion of the Jewish national home as jeopardizing the attainment of national independence by the Arabs of Palestine, which all the Arab states desire, and are therefore unwilling to contemplate further Jewish immigration. They are equally opposed to the creation of a Jewish state in any part of Palestine.

The Jewish Agency, on the other hand, have made it clear that their fundamental aim is the creation of an independent Jewish state in Palestine. With this in view they first proposed that his majesty's government should continue to administer the mandate on a basis which would enable them to continue to expand the Jewish national home until such time as they had attained by immigration a numerical majority in Palestine and could demand the creation of an independent Jewish state over the country as a whole. When it was made clear that his majesty's government were unable to maintain in Palestine a mandatory administration under the protection of which such a policy should be carried out, the Jewish Agency indicated that, while still maintaining the justice of their full claims, they would be prepared to consider as a compromise the creation of "a viable Jewish state in an adequate area of Palestine." While they were not themselves willing to propose a plan of partition, they were prepared to consider such a proposal if advanced by his majesty's government.

His majesty's government have thus been faced with an irreconcilable conflict of principles. There are in Palestine about 1,200,000 Arabs and 600,000 Jews. For the Jews, the essential point is the creation of a sovereign Jewish state. For the Arabs, the essential point is to resist the establishment of Jewish sovereignty in any part of Palestine....

In Bevin's 2d statement on Palestine, made during House of Commons debate Feb. 25, he said that the issues on which the UN was asked to decide were: "(1) Shall the claims of the Jews be admitted that Palestine is to be a Jewish state? (2) Shall the claims of the Arabs be admitted that it is to be an Arab state with safeguards for the Jews, under the decision for a national home? (3) Shall it be a Palestinian state, in which the interests of both communities are as carefully balanced and protected as possible?"

On the problem of Jewish immigration, Bevin claimed that since Dec. 1945 a total of 21,000 Jews had entered Palestine over and above the 75,000 provided for in the White Paper of 1939; this represented a rate exceeded only 5 times in the history of the mandate and one well above the average for the whole mandatory period. But, he added: "It might have been possible to increase that rate if the bitterness of feeling had not been accentuated by American pressure for an immediate increase to 100,000. I do not desire to create any ill-feeling with the U.S.A. I have done all I can to promote the best possible relations with them as with other countries, but I should have been happier if they had had regard to the fact that we were the mandatory power and were carrying the responsibility. If only they had waited to ask what we were doing we could have told them, but instead a person named Earl Harrison was sent out to collect certain information, and a document was issued which destroyed the basis of good feeling which the colonial secretary and I were endeavoring to produce in the Arab states and which set the whole thing back. However, it was recognized that American interest had to be taken into account and they were invited to join in forming an Anglo-American committee of inquiry. I have been severely criticized in America for not accepting the committee's report, but none of the report was accepted by the U.S.A. except the one point about the admission of 100,000 Jews. I was always prepared to stand for the report as a whole and its 10 points, though as events turned out that would not have settled the Palestine problem, and we had to continue our efforts to work out a policy."

Bevin recounted the history of his efforts between sessions of the London conference to induce the *yishuv*'s side to discuss with the Arabs the future of the Palestinian mandate in which the British were preparing to relinquish their predominant part.

He shed some light on the circumstances surrounding Pres. Truman's statement of Oct. 4, 1946, in which Truman again urged that the mandatory government at once admit 100,000 European Jewish refugees to Palestine. Bevin said:

I did reach a stage in meeting the Jews separately in which I advanced the idea of an interim arrangement leading ultimately to self-government. I indicated that I did not mind whether it was 5 or 10 or 3 years, or whatever it was. At that stage things looked more hopeful. There was a feeling when they left me in the Foreign Office that day that I had the right approach at last. But what happened? I went back to the Paris peace conference between the Allies and Italy, Hungary, Rumania and Bulgaria and next day the prime minister telephoned me at midnight and told me that the President of the U.S. was going to issue another statement on the 100,000.

I think the country and the world ought to know this. I went next morning to the Secretary of State, Mr. [James F.] Byrnes, and told him how far I had got the day before. I believed we were on the road if only they would leave us alone. I begged that the statement be not issued, but I was told that if it was not issued by Mr. Truman a competitive statement would be issued by Mr. [Thomas E.] Dewey [Republican candidate opposing Truman in the U.S. Presidential election]. In international affairs I cannot settle things if my problem is made the subject of local elections. . . .

However, the statement was issued and the representatives with whom I was dealing and I had to call . . . [our talks] off because the whole thing was spoilt. I had to open the conference with the Arabs alone, and they put the point to me that they wanted finality. They wanted to determine what the future of Palestine was to be. The Jews also want finality, provided it takes the form of a Jewish state. But they would be prepared to see British rule continued as a protecting power provided it was clearly aiming at a Jewish sovereign state.

The conference was suspended . . . [early in October]. The United Nations were meeting in New York. While there I discussed the matter with Mr. Byrnes, and he made a public statement saying that the basis upon which Great Britian was proposing to hold the conference in his view merited the attendance of the Jews as well as the Arabs. Even that from America produced no results.

Bevin turned his fire on the Zionists, declaring: "If it were only a question of alleviating Europe of 100,000 Jews, I believe a settlement could be found. Unfortunately, that is not the position. From the Zionist point of view the 100,000 is only a beginning, and the Jewish Agency talks in terms of millions. I believe the Arabs could be persuaded to agree to 100,000 Jewish immigrants on humanitarian grounds having regard to the European situation, if immigration after that were to be determined by the elected representatives of the people of Palestine."

Bevin concluded by saying: "The claim made by the Arabs is very difficult to answer. Why should an external agency largely financed from America determine how many people should come into Palestine and interfere with the economy of the Arabs who had been there for 2,000 years? The Arabs said they were not going to be pushed out by an external agency from a country which they regarded as their own and in which they had been living for as long as England had been a Christian country. The Arabs would accept the national home, although not the Balfour Declaration or the mandate, within a unitary state. That gives an Arab majority. I have argued with both Jews and Arabs. What is it we have got to solve? Are the Jews a state or are they a religion? I have got to face the question of Catholics, Moslems, and everybody else. This is a difficult thing to decide. I cannot believe that if there is a unitary state in Palestine every Arab will vote for an Arab candidate or every Jew for a Jewish candidate. No one is elected to this House either as a Jew or a Christian. One is elected as a representative. Therefore, one will have Communists, Socialists and Conservatives. It may be that there will be some liberalism, even in Palestine. There is no doubt that people will form views which will crystallize. Therefore the Arabs argue, 'Leave it to the intelligence of the people who live in the state.' The Jews say that if that is done they will be tolerated as a minority. I cannot alter the balance of people in a state; that is impossible, any more than one can alter it between Nehru and Jinnah in India. The numbers are there and one cannot alter that in any country."

The problem, Bevin argued Feb. 25, might have been solved by conferring dominion status on Palestine; but it was too late for that, he said, and there was no other road open but the establishment of a (UN) trusteeship leading to independence. He foresaw still more violent controversies on the proposals for partitioning the country. The best partition scheme that he had seen would leave 450,000 Jews under Arab rule and 360,000 Arabs under Jewish rule, he said.

In the ensuing debate, Laborite Richard Crossman suggested that Jew and Arab "fight this out themselves, even though it involves some bloodshed." Laborite Ben Levy called Bevin's speech "the best exposition of the Arab cause that I have heard." Gen. Sir G. D. Jeffreys, a Conservative member, demanded a "sustained offensive" against terrorism in Palestine "regardless of the inconvenience ... which might ... fall upon the Jewish population."

The feelings of some persons in the U.S. were also aroused by Bevin's sentiments. Rep. Sol Bloom (D., N.Y.) said Feb. 25 that the statement was "stupid, stupid, stupid.... Everything he said is just not true." Rep. Charles A. Eaton, (R., N.J.) called Bevin's remarks "fraught with passion and fear." Rep. Emanuel Cellar (D., N.Y.) denounced his words as "a damnable lie."

In an unprecedented action, the White House Feb. 26 issued a statement terming Bevin's charge that "America's interest in Palestine and settlement of Jews there is motivated by partisan and local politics ... most unfortunate and misleading." The White House asserted that Pres. Truman's statement of Oct. 4, 1946 had merely "affirmed the attitude toward Palestine ... which the U.S. government had publicly expressed since the summer of 1945" and which was "already fully known to all parties to the Palestine negotiations.... America's interest in Palestine ... is a deep and abiding interest shared by our people without regard to their political affiliation."

Sen. Owen Brewster (R., Me.), Robert A. Taft (R., O.), Alben W. Barkley (D., Ky.) and Albert W. Hawkes (R., N.J.) Feb. 26 also assailed Bevin, while other denunciations came from such Zionist leaders in the American Jewish community as Rabbis Abba Hillel Silver and Stephen S. Wise and Col. Morris J. Mendelsohn.

Bevin told the House of Commons, Feb. 27 that "while there may have been some misunderstanding over the matter debated in the House 2 days ago ..., our relations with the U.S. are of the most cordial character.... We ... shall not allow any wedge to be driven between our 2 countries and to disturb our friendship."

The British request to place the Palestine question on the agenda of the forthcoming regular session of the UN General Assembly was formally transmitted to Secy. Gen. Trygve Lie Apr. 2, 1947. Accompanying the request was a proposal that a special session be convened to enable the British government to prepare a report on its administration of the mandate and to make recommendations for the future status of the territory. It was announced from Lake Success Apr. 13 that a majority of

the 55 member states (including the U.S., Soviet Union, France
and China) had agreed to the British request for a special
session of the UN General Assembly, which was slated to open
Apr. 28.

Terrorism Takes Wide Toll

The first half of 1947 became in Palestine a time of
heightened disorder, often close to anarchy. Palestine's
inhabitants, Jews and Arabs alike, suffered most.

Adding to assaults on the tenuous fabric of social peace
and civil order, terrorists resumed their activities Feb. 20 after
a 3-week midwinter lull by blowing up the Iraq Petroleum Co.'s
pipeline in northern Palestine—an economic objective—besides
staging an inconclusive attack on an RAF base near Hadera.
After an 8-day interval, the terrorists quickened the pace to at
least one attack each week until Apr. 7; they resumed this
practice from mid-April until June.

The British authorities had prepared themselves for an
increase in violence. The mandatory government Feb. 3 had
given the Jewish Agency and the Vaad Leumi one week in
which to reply to official demands for their complete
cooperation against the terrorists. Taking no chances, British
authorities Feb. 8 converted all the main residential quarters of
Jerusalem and the government buildings into strongly fortified
"security areas" and placed them under military control. The
British evicted more than 1,000 Jewish residents but furnished
them no emergency accommodations; troops then cordoned off
the sector with barbed wire and set up machine-gun emplace-
ments at strategic points.

The Jewish Agency and Vaad Leumi Feb. 10 made public
their answer to the mandatory government's demands. Both
groups stressed that they could not go beyond their previous
assurances of proper orderly conduct and disavowals of the
terrorism for their own part until the British offered an acceptable solution to the political problem. As an earnest of its own
good faith, the Jewish Agency informed the government that it
had already resolved on a means of destroying the terrorists'
effectiveness "by preventing any aid from being rendered to
them and by assuring effective assistance to those resisting
coercion and intimidation."

The British had already resolved to mete out to all terrorists the most severe punishments sanctioned by law. The Jerusalem Military Court Feb. 10 sentenced to death 3 Jewish terrorists—Dov Ben Salman Rosenbaum, 24, Eliezer Ben Zion Kashani, 23, and Mordecai Ben Abraham Alkoshi, 21—and condemned a 4th, Chaim Gorovelsky, 17, to life imprisonment. The 4 had confessed to being members of the Irgun and had said that they had been charged with a "mission of revenge." When taken into custody by a British patrol Dec. 29, 1946 they were found to be carrying firearms—a capital offense—and whips. They were seized after 2 British sergeants had been flogged.

Lt. Gen. G. H. A. MacMillan, who succeeded Gen. Sir Evelyn Barker as military commander in Palestine Feb. 13, stayed the 3 men's executions Feb. 18 pending the outcome of an appeal to the British royal privy council from a 4th terrorist under capital sentence, the Irgunist Dov Bela Gruner. MacMillan took stern measures, however, after a series of terrorist raids Mar. 1 that resulted in 30 deaths. The military commander imposed martial law in Tel Aviv, Ramat Gan, Petah Tiqva, Bnei Brak and the Jewish sections of Jerusalem and ordered a rigorous curfew on 240,000 members of the *yishuv*. (The attacks Mar. 1 were thought to be coordinated. In Jerusalem alone, about 30 terrorists blew up an officers' club, killing 19 men and injuring 26.)

For more than 2 weeks Tel Aviv, Jewish Jerusalem and the other 3 municipalities had no postal, telegraph, phone and motor transport services. No goods were allowed to enter or to leave the martial-law area, and no one was admitted to it except by special permit. Workers living in the areas could not go to work outside, while those living outside were not allowed to enter. The same applied to school children and teachers. This unprecedented collective punishment caused repercussions throughout Palestine. Nevertheless, martial law did not deter the terrorists.

The sufferers included the mass of the Jewish community. Searches took place at all times and places; old and young, forced against a wall, had to stand with uplifted arms, and sometimes soldiers manhandled their victims. During the weeks of statutory martial law the *yishuv* made bitter complaints of thefts and other illegalities on the part of the soldiers, including

misbehavior against women; some of these charges were subsequently admitted by the military authorities. In a number of
cases people were shot at by soldiers in the street, sometimes
with fatal results. A 4-year-old girl was shot and killed and her
mother was wounded late Mar. 2 when they appeared on a
balcony in Jerusalem.

Before the curfew was lifted Mar. 17, several terrorist
incidents occurred. Terrorists Mar. 4 boobytrapped an army
vehicle injuring 4 persons near Rishon-le-Zion, and terrorists
blew up an RAF truck near Aqir. British troops detained 32
persons in Hadera Mar. 7 and found 2 flamethrowers in a
search for arms. Terrorists attacked the British military headquarters in Tel Aviv Mar. 8 and killed a British soldier, but 4
terrorists were killed. Terrorists Mar. 10 killed a British soldier
and wounded 6 others in a raid on an army camp. Explosions in
a British military camp in Jerusalem Mar. 12 killed one soldier
and wounded 8 others. Terrorists threw incendiary bombs at an
oil train on the Tel Aviv-Haifa line the night of Mar. 12; that
same night terrorists derailed a freight train on the Jerusalem-
Haifa line.

The Palestine government Mar. 13 announced the capture
of 78 terrorists with help from the Jewish community. Martial
law was lifted Mar. 17 in the areas on which it had been
imposed at the beginning of March. The Jewish Agency
Executive Mar. 18 repeated its appeal to the *yishuv* to combat
terrorism but declared that it would not cooperate with the
government under the current conditions of immigration. The
Agency Executive also declared that it would not stop
individuals from informing the authorities on terrorists,
however.

Terrorists resumed their attacks the night of Mar. 28-29,
killing a British army officer and a policeman from ambush
near Ramleh. In Tel Aviv, meanwhile, assailants fled after
beating to death in the street a Jewish policeman who had
worked as a detective in the mandatory government.

There were no reports of terrorism in the first part of Apr.
1947. The Haifa Jewish community was ordered to pay for
close to $4.8 million worth of damage done at the Shell Co. oil
refinery Mar. 31 in Haifa. David Ben-Gurion, in a strongly
worded warning to the terrorists, declared at a meeting of the
Vaad Leumi Apr. 1 that the Jewish people would have to take

up arms against those who "only understand the use of force." "We have got to liquidate them and protect ourselves from going down a path the end of which no one can foresee," Ben-Gurion said. He stressed, however, that until Britain revised its immigration policy, there could be no cooperation with the British in an antiterrorist campaign.

Dov Gruner Executed

British military authorities hanged Dov Bela Gruner, 33, and 3 other Irgun terrorists about 4 a.m. Wednesday, Apr. 16, 1947 inside Acre Prison on the Bay of Haifa. Those executed with Gruner were Dov Ben Salman Rosenbaum, 24, Eliezer Ben Zion Kashani, 23, and Mordecai Ben Abraham Alkoshi, 21, captured with whips and firearms the night of Dec. 29, 1946 during a sweeping British search of the Nathanya, Lydda and Rishon-le-Zion areas. The British clamped a curfew on Haifa, Tel Aviv, Petah Tiqva and Jerusalem for several hours after the executions.

For Gruner, the execution ended months of appeals by relatives, friends and influential *yishuv* officials on Gruner's behalf. The Palestine High Court Apr. 7 had rejected such an appeal made by Mayor Israel Rokach of Tel Aviv. Gruner's uncle Frank Gruner had taken a petition for a stay of execution to the judicial committee of the British Royal Privy Council in London, which dismissed the petition Mar. 26.

Within hours of the executions, the Irgun's underground radio announced that "10 British senior officers will be hanged in the streets of Palestine for our martyrs murdered by the British today." In London, police reported that a time bomb was discovered in the Colonial Office and removed before it could explode.

Terrorists Grapple with British

The terrorists intensified their attacks on the British military and mandatory authorities after Gruner's execution and the British continued to deal severely with terrorists.

The British military command Apr. 17, 1947 confirmed the death sentences of Moshe Ben Abraham Barazani, 21, and Meir Ben Eliezer Feinstein, 21. Barazani had been condemned Mar. 18 for carrying a hand grenade; Feinstein had been condemned Apr. 3 for his part in an attack in the Jerusalem railroad station Oct. 30, 1946. Authorities at the same time commuted to life imprisonment the death sentence of Daniel Mordecai Azulai, 20, condemned with Feinstein for the Oct. 30 attack. A few hours before their scheduled executions Apr. 22, Barazani and Feinstein blew themselves up with grenades smuggled within hollowed-out oranges to them inside Jerusalem's Central Prison.

Terrorists also used explosive devices in 5 attacks within 7 days after Apr. 17: on a British army field hospital Apr. 18 near Nathanya, in which attack a British soldier was shot to death; on 2 policemen in Tel Aviv, who were wounded Apr. 18 by a hand grenade; on 2 British jeeps, the driver of one being wounded, in Jerusalem Apr. 21; Apr. 22 near Rehovoth against the Cairo-Haifa express train, derailed by an explosive charge—in which incident 5 British soldiers and 3 civilians were killed and 38 persons injured; and on a police station outside Tel Aviv Apr. 25, when a stolen mail truck, parked outside by Stern Group operatives, was blown up and 4 policemen were killed, 6 other policemen being wounded.

Stern Group terrorists Apr. 26 claimed responsibility for the assassination that day of Deputy Police Supt. A. E. Conquest in Haifa, shot to death in his car in the center of the city from a passing taxi.

The Jewish Agency Apr. 27 again declared itself against the terrorists. It announced the start of a new antiviolence campaign aimed particularly at the *yishuv*'s youth. A special antiterrorist supplement was published in 4 Hebrew-language newspapers.

Terrorists May 4 made a large-scale assault on Acre Prison. 100 to 150 armed men, dressed in British army uniforms, threw grenades at the prison and managed to breach the walls, through which 33 Jewish and 183 Arab prisoners escaped. The British recaptured 16 of the Arabs; the defenders killed 3 Jewish attackers, wounded and captured 9. One British constable was injured in the incident.

Terrorists May 12 shot to death 2 British detectives in central Jerusalem and escaped. 2 British army officers were killed May 15 trying to remove an explosive device from the tracks of the Acre-Haifa railroad line. A freight train was derailed near Rehovoth May 15, and a maintenance train was derailed on the Tel Aviv-Haifa line.

The British authorities took new measures to expedite the judicial process with regard to the mounting number of terrorism suspects. The mandatory government Apr. 16 abolished the right of appeal against any sentence of a British military court. The government May 15 announced that it would establish permanent summary courts in the Haifa, Lydda and Jerusalem districts to deal with charges of breaking curfew, the public posting of pamphlets, the bearing of arms and a number of minor offenses. These courts were authorized to impose 2-year prison sentences and £200 fines.

Illegal Immigrants Sent to Cyprus

From mid-Nov. 1946, until the end of May 1947 14 boats arrived in Palestine, carrying altogether more than 17,000 illegal immigrants. All 14 of the refugee boats were picked up at sea by British aircraft and destroyers and escorted to Haifa, where the passengers were transferred to a waiting vessel, which took them for internment to Cyprus. Generally, the immigrants offered resistance, which was overcome by the use of tear gas and baton charges. In some cases the military made use of firearms with fatal results. When motions for writs of *habeas corpus* were made in the Palestine courts on behalf of the refugees, the court upheld the deportations on the grounds that the landing of the refugees would be prejudicial to public security.

All of these incidents gave rise to waves of indignation throughout the Jewish community. There were street demonstrations, strikes, public protests and terrorist reactions that led to sterner official countermeasures.

The only exception from deportation to Cyprus was granted in favor of the women and children and some sick persons saved in Dec. 1946 from shipwreck on the island of Syrina near Rhodes. In Cyprus many of the refugees maintained an attitude of sullen resentment and occasionally staged hunger strikes and outbreaks that resulted in a number of casualties.

The reduction of the detainees' immigration quota to 750 a month in Dec. 1946 caused consternation in the Cyprus camps, since at this rate it would take 2 years to evacuate the inmates already there and their number kept increasing as new boats arrived.

Among the ships intercepted between February and April 1947 were:

● The caique *Ha Negev,* a 350-ton vessel with 650 Jewish immigrants, intercepted at sea and taken into Haifa harbor Feb. 9, a week after sailing from a French port with an American captain and crew.

● The *Chaim Arlosoroff,* with 1,300 immigrants aboard, which ran aground near Haifa Feb. 27. (30 passengers were injured and 11 British sailors wounded in the struggle that took place when passengers captured a British boarding party and threw some of them into the sea during the boarding attempt.)

● The steamship *Abril,* chartered by the American League For Free Palestine and carrying about 600 immigrants, brought into Haifa Mar. 9. (All passengers carried "identity certificates" issued in Paris by the "Hebrew Committee of National Liberation" and declaring the bearer's "eligibility to become a citizen of the Hebrew Republic.")

● The *Molodets,* with 900 immigrants, brought into Haifa Mar. 31 after British naval vessels spotted the ship sinking. (British sailors had to use tear gas to make many of the passengers leave the vessel for transshipment to Cyprus.)

● The *Theodor Herzl,* with 2,700 immigrants, out of a French port and flying the Honduran flag. (It was brought into Haifa Apr. 14 after a fight with British forces in which 2 Jews were killed and 20 injured.)

● The *Hasha 'ar Yishuv,* formerly the *Galata,* registered in Istanbul, brought into Haifa Apr. 23 after 12 Jews and 3 sailors were wounded when immigrant passengers challenged a British boarding party.

All immigrants from these 6 blockade-running ships were taken to Cyprus. The *Empire Rival,* carrying the immigrants toward Cyprus camps from Haifa and calling at Port Said, was reported Apr. 3 to have been damaged by a limpet mine attached by terrorists.

The Cyprus camps also became scenes of violence. A disturbance occurred at the Caraolos camp Apr. 18 when immigrants due to leave for Palestine refused to sail unless the immigration quota was increased. Inmates of the camp attempted to set fire to its installations and to break out. The guards opened fire. The 13,000 inmates of the Caraolos and Xylotymbou camps went on a hunger strike Apr. 22

The British government announced Apr. 11 that it had again asked the Italian and French governments to cooperate in stemming the traffic in illegal immigration. In a letter to French Foreign Min. Georges Bidault, British Foreign Secy. Ernest Bevin also noted that some unseaworthy vessels had been allowed to set out from French ports.

Arabs Start Political Fund

A Palestinian Arab national trust was started early in 1947 in the form of the Palestine Fund, to which all Palestine Arabs were to contribute. Its sponsors said that the fund would use contributions to finance political activities and to prevent land owned by Arabs from being purchased by Jews. The creation of the fund was announced Feb. 21, 1947. It was sponsored by the Arab Higher Committee, which said it expected to raise a total of £220,000 ($1,056,000) by taxing every Arab in Palestine 2 shillings (40¢), from wholesale imposts on entertainment, transport and the sales of tobacco, newspapers and stamps, and through generous contributions by Arab merchants, lawyers, doctors and officials.

UN COMMITTEE ON PALESTINE

Special UN Assembly Session

The British Labor government expressly refused to declare itself willing to relinquish its control over Palestine. Nevertheless, the British were maintaining more than 80,000 troops in Palestine at a cost to them of about £200 million ($960 million) since the Labor government took office. "We are not going to the United Nations to surrender the mandate," Colonial Secy. Arthur Creech Jones said. "We are ... setting out the problem and asking for their advice as to how the mandate can be administered. If the mandate cannot be administered in its present form we are asking how it can be amended."

The problem would have gone to the Security Council had there been Arab and Jewish approval of a trusteeship along the lines of provincial or federal autonomy, as recommended in the Morrison and Bevin plans. Under the pressure of events in Palestine and of opposition in Britian to Labor's policy in Palestine, the British government finally asked UN Secy. Gen. Trygve Lie Apr. 2, 1947 "to summon, as soon as possible, a special session of the General Assembly for the purpose of constituting and instructing a special committee to prepare for the consideration" of the problem of Palestine and its future political status at the next regular session.

Trygve Lie called a special session of the General Assembly Apr. 28 to discuss the British request. The Egyptian government Apr. 21 asked Lie to include on the agenda a resolution calling on the UN to declare that the British mandate over Palestine had terminated and that the country was independent. Iraq, Syria and Lebanon presented identical proposals Apr. 22. Dr. Abba Hillel Silver, U.S. chairman of the Jewish Agency, sent to Trygve Lie a letter requesting "as a matter of simple justice" that the Agency be allowed to "represent the Jewish people without a vote" at the special session. He reminded the UN that the Jewish Agency had been recognized by the League

160

of Nations as the Jewish spokesman in Palestine and that the Arab states and Britain would have the right to participate.

The first special session of the General Assembly met at Flushing Meadow Park, N.Y. Apr. 28, 1947, as scheduled. Ex-Foreign Min. Oswaldo Aranha of Brazil, elected assembly president by 45 votes to 5, disclosed that 3 Zionist agencies had asked for representation: the Jewish Agency for Palestine, the Hebrew Committee of National Liberation and Progressive Zionist District No. 95 of New York. Jewish Agency Executive members boycotted the session pending a decision on their appeal for representation.

With Egypt abstaining, a 14-member UN "General Committee" voted Apr. 29 to recommend that the Assembly formally consider the original British request for a special committee to study Palestine. The committee, headed by Aranha, comprised: (a) 7 General Assembly vice presidents—Sir Alexander Cadogan of Britain; Dr. Quo Tai-chi, China; Dr. Neftali Ponce, Ecuador; Alexandre Parodi, France; Asaf Ali, India; Andrei A. Gromyko, USSR; Warren R. Austin, U.S. (b) 6 Assembly committee heads—Lester B. Pearson of Canada; Dr. Jan Papanek, Czechoslovakia; Mahmoud Hassan Pasha, Egypt; Dr. Tiburcio Carias Jr., Honduras; Jozef Winiewicz, Poland; Herman G. Eriksson, Sweden.

All 5 Arab delegates—from Egypt, Iraq, Lebanon, Saudi Arabia and Syria—pressed for a full-dress debate on Palestine at this session, with the Indian and Soviet delegates supporting them while Herschel V. Johnson of the U.S. opposed the move. Although stating that the U.S. favored an ultimate free Palestine state, Johnson also opposed Jewish demands for representation. The Arab speakers were Hassan Pasha of Egypt, Iraqi Foreign Min. Mohammad Fadhil Jamali, Faris el-Khoury of Syria, Dr. Charles Malik of Lebanon and Saudi Arabian Foreign Min. Emir Feisal al Saud.

The Jewish Agency protested Apr. 29 that its side should be heard by the UN. The Political Action Committee for Palestine, headed by Joseph Clark Baldwin, asked for representation and criticized the Agency. The Vaad Leumi (Jewish National Council) in Jerusalem cabled the UN that only the Jewish Agency was authorized to represent the Palestinian Jewish community. The American Council for Judaism, headed by Lessing Rosenwald, announced its opposition to all Jewish groups seeking a voice, saying it regarded the U.S. delegation as its spokesman. In Detroit, the Rabbinical Council of America attacked British rule and called on the U.S. to back a free Palestine.

The General Committee Apr. 30 rejected by 8-to-1 vote the Arab plea that the question of the independence of Palestine be put on the agenda. A Polish move to act immediately on the Jewish request for representation was rejected 11 to 0. The committee voted after 7 hours of confused and bitter argument. The vote on the Arab (Egyptian) motion was: In favor— Egypt. Against—Britain, Canada, China, Ecuador, France, Honduras, Sweden, U.S. Abstaining—Brazil, Czechoslovakia, India, Poland, USSR. On the Polish motion, opposed by the U.S. and Canada, there were 3 abstentions: Czechoslovakia, Poland and USSR.

During the debates, India and Britain joined in a dramatic appeal to all UN members to use their influence in persuading both sides to stop fighting in Palestine, but Aranha ruled them out of order. Khoury of Syria also accused the U.S. of contributing to unrest in the Middle East by pressuring Britain to increase Jewish immigration to Palestine.

Arab statements that their countries were tolerant toward Jews because Jews and Arabs are both members of the Semitic race drew this Jewish Agency statement: "In Iraq, between 400 and 500 Jews were murdered in a Bagdad pogrom June 1, 1941. Jews are virtual prisoners in Iraq.... There were pogroms in Egypt and Tripoli as late as Nov. 1945. It is estimated 170 Jews were massacred.... In Syria Mar. 24, 1947 the Syrian government threatened the Syrian Jews with death unless they renounced Zionism...."

The Arabs lost another vote May 1, when the General Assembly, in plenary session, voted 24-15 against putting on the agenda the question of ending Britain's mandate and establishing an independent Palestine. Voting for that step were: Afghanistan, Argentina, Cuba, Egypt, India, Iran, Iraq, Lebanon, Saudi Arabia, Syria, Turkey, Ukraine, USSR, White Russia (Byelorussia), Yugoslavia. Against: Britain, China, France and U.S. plus 20 others. Abstaining—10, including Czechoslovakia and Poland. Absent—6. The Assembly also voted without a roll call to accept the original British request for a special commission to study Palestine and report by September.

The Arabs reiterated their arguments that the British mandate was illegal, that Jewish immigration threatened the peace and that Palestine should be made an Arab state. The U.S. delegation was reported shifting toward support of the Jewish plea for representation on the ground that only the Arab side had been presented by that date. Rajai Bey Husseini, relative of the ex-grand mufti of Jerusalem, arrived in New York May 1. His coming completed the Arab Higher Committee Palestinian Arab delegation unofficially attending the sessions.

The General Committee May 2, defeating a Polish resolution on the matter, voted 8-3 to bar the Jewish Agency from arguing its case before the full General Assembly. It then adopted, 11-0, a U.S. resolution to let the Agency and other interested parties be heard before the Assembly's 55-nation Political & Security Committee. On the 8-3 vote against the Polish resolution, the 3 in favor were Czechoslovakia, Poland and the USSR; the majority were Britain, Canada, China, Egypt, France, India, Sweden and the U.S.; abstaining were Brazil, Ecuador and Honduras. On the 2d vote Czechoslovakia, Poland and the USSR abstained.

Soviet Delegate Gromyko, in urging that the full Assembly hear the Jewish Agency, argued that "such a half-and-half solution is not just." U.S. Delegate Warren Austin and Secy. Gen. Trygve Lie pointed out that the UN was an organization of 55 states but that Assembly committees could hear non-state groups. Austin's resolution to refer the matter to the Political & Security Committee was then adopted. Lester Pearson of Canada, who headed the Political Committee, declared, however, that he would oppose debate on anything but the appointment of an inquiry committee and that he favored barring Palestine's Jews and Arabs from his committee hearings.

For more than 6 hours May 3 arguments resounded in the Assembly on whether the Zionists should be heard at the plenary session. Austin led the opposition against such a procedure on constitutional grounds while Gromyko said it would only be fair to hear the Jews because the Arabs had already been heard.

In plenary session, the Assembly May 5 voted, 39-8, against a Polish-Czechoslovak resolution to give the Jewish Agency a hearing before the full Assembly. Then it voted, 44-7, in favor of a joint resolution by Argentina, Byelorussia, Chile, Uruguay and Yugoslavia directing the Assembly's Political & Security Committee to hear the Jewish Agency on the British proposal to establish an inquiry commission into the Palestine question. It left to the Political Committee the question of whether the Palestinian Arab Higher Committee and other groups would be heard.

The voting displeased both Arabs and Jews. On the first ballot the minority voting in favor consisted of Chile, South Africa and the Slav states of Byelorussia, Czechoslovakia, Poland, the USSR, Ukraine and Yugoslavia; there were 7 abstentions. On the 2d ballot the minority vote against came from Afghanistan, Egypt, Iraq, Lebanon, Saudi Arabia, Syria, Turkey; abstaining were India, Iran and Thailand, formally seated Apr. 28 as the Assembly's 55th member. Costa Rica was absent.

The Political & Security Committee, convening in Lake Success, N.Y. May 6 voted 44-0 in favor of a U.S.-Argentine resolution to give both the Arab Higher Committee and the Jewish Agency the right to be heard. A U.S. proposal to limit the debate to the point of setting up a Palestine investigating commission was defeated, 23-19. Gromyko of Russia led the fight for unlimited discussion of the Palestine question.

The Arab states abstained from voting when the final resolution was passed. (So did Turkey and France.) Egypt, Iraq, Lebanon, Saudi Arabia and Syria threatened a boycott because of the Assembly's 2d vote May 5 on the Jewish Agency. The Arab Higher Committee withdrew its application to appear before the group and demanded recognition by the entire Assembly.

The Arabs also denounced the U.S. State Department's refusal to let Rasim Khalidi, a member of the Palestine Arab Higher Committee, enter the country because of his pro-Axis war record.

Committee Hears Yishuv & Arab Views

Representing the Jewish Agency, Dr. Abba Hillel Silver (president of the Zionist Organization of America) appeared May 8, 1947 before the UN General Assembly's Political Committee. Silver said that "the Jewish people" and "the Jewish national home" were concepts basic to the Balfour Declaration and to the mandate, both of which had as goals the facilitating of the growth of the Jewish community in Palestine. He declared that the obligations of the Balfour Declaration and the mandate were no less binding on the UN than on the League of Nations.

"When we speak of a Jewish state, we do not have in mind any racial or theocratic state but one which will be based on full equality and rights for all inhabitants, without distinction of religion or race and without domination or subjugation," Rabbi Silver said. "The Balfour Declaration said that the British government viewed with favor the establishment in Palestine of a national home for the Jewish people. The mandate recognized the ground for reconstituting a Jewish national home in Palestine. These international commitments cannot now be erased. You cannot turn back the hands of history's clock. The mandatory government, which is entrusted with the obligation to safeguard the continuous growth of the Jewish national home, has, unfortunately, in recent years grievously interfered with and circumscribed it.... We are not engaged in any criticism or condemnation of the people of Great Britain. We have no quarrel with them. We have the highest regard and admiration for that people and its monumental contributions to civilization. We shall never forget that it was Britain which first gave recognition to the national aspirations of the Jewish people. It is only the unjustifiable policy which contradicts and tends to defeat the far-visioned British statesmanship of earlier years that we condemn."

Silver called on the UN to respect "those international commitments of a quarter of a century ago" and grant the Jews an independent state in which they could establish their home. He urged that immigration restrictions be relaxed in the interim. This, he said, would curb terrorism, which most Jews deplored.

As for the inquiry committee proposed by Britain, Silver urged that it visit Palestine to study developments and problems there and also to visit DP camps in Europe. In Palestine, he continued, it should determine why Jews were restricted to less than 6% of the country, why anti-Jewish laws were tolerated and why Jewish refugee ships were stopped short by the British. He added that the projected UN committee of inquiry also should inquire into the fundamental causes of the "tragic unrest and violence in the Holy Land" and into why some members of the Palestinian community had been driven to "actions which we all deplore."

Finally, it should also ask "why thousands of helpless Jewish refugees, who have been through the hells of Nazi Europe, are being driven away from the shores of the national home by the mandatory government," Silver argued. "The Jewish people were your allies in the war and joined their sacrifices to yours for the common victory. We hope that the Jewish people will be welcomed before long in the noble fellowship of the United Nations," he said.

Moshe Shertok and David Ben-Gurion testified for the Jewish Agency May 12, and Emile el-Khoury appeared for the Arab Higher Committee.

Shertok estimated that there were 630,000 Jews in Palestine in 1947 as against 50,000 in 1900, while the Arabs numbered about 1,000,000. He declared that:

● The Jews had not forced themselves on the Arabs but had settled in and built up waste regions.

● Hitler "is gone now, but not anti-Semitism," and, therefore, the Jews did not want to go back to Germany.

● In other countries Jews were treated "as 2d- or 3d-rate citizens," living in "perpetual fear of eruptions of fierce fanaticism."

● Sir Henry McMahon of Britain "himself stated that Palestine was never included in the promises made by him to the Arabs."

● If the Jews were kept in a minority in Palestine, they would never have security.

● The Arab Higher Committee was headed by a man who "was directly involved during the war in the Nazi policy of extermination of the European Jews." (The ex-grand mufti, Haj Amin el-Husseini, denying that he had ever plotted with the Nazis against the Jews, said May 13 in Cairo: "I appeal to the American nation to liberate itself from Zionist propaganda.")

Ben-Gurion, in his address, said that Britain had not only failed to solve the Palestine problem, as it had admitted, but had failed to carry out this solution agreed on by the League of Nations: "the restoration of Palestine to the Jewish people." Britain's White Paper restricting immigration "is responsible for establishing in Palestine a police state without parallel in the civilized world," he asserted. The Jews would never give up Palestine, Ben-Gurion declared.

Emile el-Khoury, in his testimony, declared that Jewish immigrants were not assimilable in Palestine and that the country had already "paid dearly for its forced contribution to the refugee problem." Haj Amin el-Husseini, ex-grand mufti of Jerusalem, had sought refuge in Germany not because he believed in Nazism but because he had despaired of Justice, Khoury maintained. The mufti was an "inveterate enemy of British policy in the Middle East," but so was Jan Christiaan Smuts an enemy of British policy, and before him George Washington, Khoury said. "The Jews are questioning the record of an Arab spiritual leader. Does that properly come from the mouth of a people who have crucified the founder of Christianity?" Khouri asked.

Khouri requested Trygve Lie's intervention against the U.S. State Department's ban on Rasim Khalidi and Dr. Khalil Budeiri, the latter an Arab Communist optician; both wanted to come to New York to speak for the Arab cause.

The Nation Associates, headed by Freda Kirchwey, charged in a memo to all 55 UN delegations that 3 members of the Palestine Arab Higher Committee's delegation ranked with the "worst of the Axis war criminals" because of their war records. It listed Khoury, Khalidi and Wasef Kamal as the 3.

Henry Cattan, 41, a Jerusalem attorney and Christian spokesman for the Arab Higher Committee, had declared May 9 that "no amount of propaganda can change the Arab character of Palestine" and asserted that the very existence of the Palestinian Arabs was threatened by the "Jewish invasion." In 1914, when the Jews comprised 6% to 7% of the population, there was no conflict, Cattan said. Conflict began he asserted, when the Zionists started to make a Jewish state out of Palestine.

British pledges of Arab independence were numerous and had preceded and followed the Balfour Declaration, Cattan said. Sir Henry McMahon, British high commissioner in Egypt, had made such a promise in 1915. After the Balfour Declaration of 1917, the British, through the "Hogarth message," had reassured the Arabs that Jewish settlement would "not jeopardize the Arabs' political and economic freedom." Other assurances had come in Feb. 1918, in June 1918, in Nov. 1918. The UN inquiry commission would have to investigate the "various pledges given to the Arabs," Cattan argued.

Cattan then charged that the League of Nations mandate to Britain violated Article 22 of the covenant guaranteeing the right of self-determination. Cattan asserted that since the League was dead, the mandate was no longer legal and that continued Jewish immigration would violate the UN Assembly resolution of Dec. 15, 1946 against forcing displaced persons on countries that did not want them. He asked for an inquiry into the British administration of Palestine and demanded that: (a) all Jewish immigration should be barred; (b) the mandate should be ended, and (c) Palestine should be made an independent Arab state. Cattan ended with a quotation from Christ: "Do unto others as ye would have them to do unto you."

Emile el-Khoury said that the Arabs would continue to resist Jewish immigration, urged an immediate cessation of immigration and warned that the Palestinian Arabs would oppose any terms of reference of the fact-finding commission that included "even the suggestion of a solution conflicting with the right of Palestine to independence as an independent whole."

Moshe Shertok, head of the Jewish Agency's Political Department, had appeared and appealed for Europe's DPs before Cattan began his testimony. David Ben-Gurion, chairman of the Jewish Agency Executive, had arrived by plane in New York from Palestine to head the Agency's UN delegation. Meantime a 5-nation subcommittee rejected 13 other applications from 12 organizations and one individual (Bishop James de Windt, patriarch of the Church of God, Faith of David, Inc.) for a hearing on the ground that they did not represent any part of the Palestine population. This was challenged by Msgr. Thomas J. McMahon, secretary of the Catholic Near

East Welfare Association, which, he said, represented the 45,400 Roman Catholics among the 130,750 Christians in Palestine.

U.S. Delegate Warren R. Austin urged the Political Committee May 7 to name a "neutral committee" of 7 countries—Canada, Czechoslovakia, Iran, the Netherlands, Peru, Sweden and Uruguay—to investigate the Palestine issue. The Big 5 would be excluded. R. Jose Arce of Argentina advocated the naming of an 11-nation committee, to include the Big 5 powers.

The Political Committee May 8-12 considered the makeup and aims of the proposed fact-finding committee. Sir Alexander Cadogan (Britain) argued May 8 that the "Big 5" should not be represented on the fact-finding committee. Herschel V. Johnson (U.S.), Dr. Quo (China) and Asaf Ali (India) also advocated that none of the permanent members of the Security Council be represented on the committee.

Gromyko opposed this latter view. He rejected U.S., British and Chinese contentions that the Big 5 should remain off the inquiry committee and said May 8 that they should shoulder their responsibility. The Soviet delegate asked the committee May 9 to make an on-the-spot investigation and also to consider independence for Palestine "without delay." U.S. deputy representative Johnson argued May 10 against Gromyko's amendment proposing that the inquiry committee consider immediate independence for Palestine.

Arab Independence Move Outvoted

All the Arab states' representatives spoke strongly in favor of independence for Palestine. Foreign Min. Mohammad Fadhil Jamali of Iraq declared May 12 that UN support of Zionist national aspirations would mean "a declaration of war by one people against another." The Turkish delegate, M. Huseyin Ragip Baydur, also supported Palestinian independence.

The UN Political & Security Committee in plenary session May 12 accepted by 29-14 vote, with 10 abstentions, a French resolution omitting any reference to independence from the version to be adopted. The 14 opposing nations were the 5 Arab states, Afghanistan, Cuba, El Salvador, Guatemala, the Philippines, Turkey, Ukraine, the USSR and Yugoslavia. The countries abstaining were Argentina, Byelorussia, Canada, Czechoslovakia, the Dominican Republic, India, Persia, Poland, Thailand and Venezuela.

The committee had first voted, 43-8, to direct the proposed inquiry committee to go wherever it wanted (meaning to European DP camps) as well as to Palestine. The Zionists wanted the DP question linked with Palestine. They also wanted a postponement of Palestinian independence until the Jews had a majority in Palestine. Russia voted for the first measure but against the French resolution. The U.S. and Britain voted for both.

Iraqi Foreign Min. Jamali declared that "supporting the national aspirations of the Jews means very clearly a declaration of war." Other Arab delegations joined him in declaring that the Arabs would resist to the end all attempts to make Palestine Jewish.

Fact-Finding Committee Formed

The UN Political & Security Committee voted, 13-11, May 13, 1947 to set up an 11-member Special Committee on Palestine (UNSCOP). It did so after barring the Big 5 from membership, over Soviet objections, by 30-3 vote. The outcome was another victory for the British-American viewpoints that the committee should be as "neutral" as possible. The countries named to the fact-finding panel were Australia, Canada, Czechoslovakia, Guatemala, India, Iran, Netherlands, Peru, Sweden, Uruguay and Yugoslavia.

In the 30-3 vote Byelorussia, the USSR and the Ukraine were in the opposition. In the 13-11 vote on the Australian resolution for a neutral committee, the U.S. voted for the measure, Britain and the USSR against; 29 nations abstained, and Liberia and Haiti were absent. The USSR and India lost on another vote when their joint amendment to instruct the inquiry committee to study the immediate independence of Palestine was defeated 26-15.

The newly created inquiry committee was instructed to report on its findings by Sept. 1 in time for the UN General Assembly session starting Sept. 16. It was also directed to consider "the religious interests in Palestine of Islam, Judaism and Christianity."

After the May 12 vote on Palestine's independence, the 5 Arab delegations had abstained on all other votes. In the end, they warned the other delegates that they were resolved to "reserve" their position regarding the entire inquiry.

Jamali May 13 again protested against the omission of any reference to Palestinian independence. In his view, he said, the dispute arose from the intention of a people to "enter and occupy a country inhabited by another people." He contended that this constituted an "aggressive invasion," and he declared that the principles of the UN Charter should be put into operation and the "invasion" stopped. Faris el-Khoury, saying that Syria favored the immediate independence of Palestine and the cessation of Jewish immigration, contended that Jewish historical claims in Palestine were unfounded; he asserted that the Arabs had "resisted the first invasion of Palestine 15 centuries before Christ."

The General Assembly May 15 approved the aims and guidelines of the Special Committee on Palestine by 46-7 vote, with Afghanistan, the 5 Arab states and Turkey opposed. Thailand abstained, and Haiti was absent. The Assembly approved the committee's makeup by 40-0 vote with 13 abstentions; the 7 countries that voted against approving the committee's guidelines were joined in abstaining by Byelorussia, Czechoslovakia, Poland, the Ukraine, the USSR and Yugoslavia.

As finally adopted, the framework of the fact-finding committee provided that: (1) It should consist of 11 members—Australia, Canada, Czechoslovakia, Guatemala, India, the Netherlands, Persia, Peru, Sweden, Uruguay, and Yugoslavia. (2) It should have "the widest powers to ascertain and record facts and to investigate all questions." (3) It should determine its own procedure. (4) It should "conduct investigations in Palestine and wherever else it may deem it useful, and receive and examine written or oral testimony from the mandatory power, from representatives of the population of Palestine, from governments, and from such organizations and individuals as it may deem necessary." (5) It should give "most careful consideration to the religious interests in Palestine of Islam, Judaism and Christianity." (6) It should prepare a report for the General Assembly and "submit such proposals as it may consider appropriate for a solution of the problem of

Palestine." (7) It should present its report to the UN Secretary General not later than Sept. 1, 1947.

Gromyko Foresees Partition

Towards the close of the special session May 14, Soviet delegate Andrei Gromyko disclosed the Soviet position on Palestine and indicated that his country was prepared to support partition for the mandated land. Gromyko maintained that:

● The Palestine question, "an acute political problem," was being considered by the General Assembly as a "direct result of the bankruptcy of the mandatory system of administration of Palestine." The very fact that Britain had submitted the question "is an admission that this administration did not solve the question of mutual relations between Arabs and Jews ... [and] has not ensured the achievement of the aims laid down when the mandate was established."

● British Foreign Secy. Ernest Bevin had admitted that the mandatory administration did "not enjoy the support of the people." The Anglo-American Committee of Inquiry's report had pointed out that Palestine was an armed camp with a tense atmosphere and with 15,000 men in police and prison administration, making Palestine "a police state".

● No Western state had been able to provide adequate assistance for the Jewish people "in defending its rights and its very existence," and this "explains the aspirations of the Jews" to establish their own state. It was an "incontestable fact that the population of Palestine consists of 2 peoples, Arabs and Jews. Each ... has its historical roots in Palestine," which has "become ... [their] native land."

● "Neither history nor conditions ... in Palestine now can justify any unilateral solution" that would establish an independent state for one of the 2 communities without consideration for the legitimate rights of the other. The legitimate interests of both the Jewish and Arab populations of Palestine can be duly safeguarded only through the establishment of an independent, dual, democratic, homogeneous Arab-Jewish state, based on equality of rights for the Jewish and the Arab populations, which might lay foundations of cooperation between the 2 peoples to their mutual interest and advantage. Only if this plan proved impossible to implement, in view of the deterioration in the relations between the Jews and the Arabs, then it would be necessary to consider the plan for the partition of Palestine into 2 independent, autonomous Arab and Jewish states.

Excerpts from Gromyko's speech:

... In consideration of the problem of Palestine ... and in the consideration of the tasks and functions of the [inquiry] committee..., one cannot fail to observe, first and foremost, the very important fact that the mandate system ... has not justified itself.... The aims proposed in the establishment of the mandate have not been achieved. The solemn declarations which accompanied the creation of the mandate system in Palestine have remained only declarations. They have not been transformed into living facts. The Anglo-American Inquiry Commission pointed out the following very interesting facts: The total number of persons employed by the police on the basis of a full working day, employed by police and in the prison administration of the country in 1945, was 15,000. These figures ... explain where considerable resources went to, which constituted such a burden on the tax-paying population. In different circumstances, these resources might have been devoted to economic and cultural interests of the country and to its development....

Is it surprising..., under these conditions which have arisen in Palestine, that liquidation of the mandate is called for both by Jews and Arabs? On this matter, Jews and Arabs are completely in agreement. Upon this question there is no divergence between them, and the United Nations must not fail to take account of this fact in considering the question of the future of Palestine.

In considering the question of the tasks of the committee which is to prepare proposals on Palestine, our attention is inevitably drawn to another important aspect of this problem.... The aspirations of an important part of the Jewish people are bound up with the question of Palestine and with the future structure of that country. It is not surprising, therefore, that both in the General Assembly and in meetings of the Political Committee of the Assembly a great deal of attention was given to this aspect of the matter. This interest is comprehensible and completely justified. The Jewish people suffered extreme misery and deprivation during the last war.... In territories where the Hitlerites were in control, the Jews suffered almost complete extinction. The total number of Jews who fell at the hands of the fascist hangmen is something in the neighborhood of 6 million. Only about $1\frac{1}{2}$ million Jews survived the war in western Europe. But these figures which give an idea of the losses suffered by the Jewish people at the hands of the fascist aggressors do not give an idea of the situation in which the great mass of Jewish people find themselves after the war.

A great many Jews who survived the war in Europe have found themselves deprived, in their countries, of their shelter and of means of earning their livelihood. Hundreds of thousands of Jews are wandering about various countries of Europe, seeking means of livelihood and seeking shelter. A great many of these are in camps for displaced persons, where they are continuing to suffer great privations.... It may be asked whether the United Nations, considering the very serious situation of hundreds of thousands of Jews who have survived the war, should not show interest in the situation of these people who have been uprooted from their countries and from their homes. The United Nations cannot and should not remain indifferent to this situation, because such an attitude would be incompatible with the high principles which are proclaimed in our Charter—the principles which envisage the defense of the rights of men.... This is the time to give help, not in words but in deeds.

... The fact that not a single western European state has been in a position to guarantee the defense of the elementary rights of the Jewish people or compensate them for the violence they have suffered at the hands of the Fascist hangmen explains the aspirations of the Jews for the creation of a state of their own. It would be unjust not to take this into account and deny the right of the Jewish people to the realization of such aspirations. It is impossible to justify the denial of this right to the Jewish people, particularly if one takes into account the experiences of this people in the 2d World War. Consequently, a study of this aspect of the question and preparation of the corresponding proposals should also be part of the important task of the committee. Among the best known of the published plans regarding the future structure of Palestine, the following must be noted: (1) creation of a single Arab-Jewish state with equal rights for Arabs and Jews; (2) one Arab state and one Jewish state; (3) creation in Palestine of an Arab state, without due regard to the rights of the Jewish population; (4) creation in Palestine of a Jewish state, without due regard to the rights of the Arab population. Each of these basic plans is accompanied by different methods to regulate relations between Arabs and Jews and settlement of a few other questions....

In analyzing the various types of plans for the future of Palestine, it is necessary first of all to ... bear in mind the incontestable fact that the population of Palestine consists of 2 peoples, Arabs and Jews. Each of these has its historical roots in Palestine. That country has become the native land of both of these people, and both of them occupy an important place in the country, economically and culturally. Neither history nor conditions which have arisen in Palestine now can justify any unilateral solution of the Palestine problem, either in favor of creation of an independent Arab state, ignoring the lawful rights of the Jewish people, or in the creation of an independent Jewish state, ignoring the lawful rights of the Arab population. Neither of these extreme solutions would bring about just settlement of this complex problem, first and foremost since they both fail to guarantee regulations of relations between Arabs and Jews, which is the most important task of all. A just settlement can be found only if account is taken, in sufficient degree, of the lawful interests of both people. These considerations are the basis upon which the Soviet Union delegation concludes that the lawful interests of both Jewish and Arab peoples in Palestine can be defended in the proper manner only by the creation of one dual, democratic Arab-Jewish state. Such a state should be founded on equal rights for the Jewish and Arab population which might constitute the foundation for cooperation between these 2 peoples in their common interests to the advantage of them both.

... This proposed solution of the problem ... has its advocates in Palestine itself. Contemporary history shows not only racial and religious discrimination unfortunately still exists in certain countries, but also offers an example of peaceful cooperation between different nationalities within the framework of a single state; cooperation in the process of which each nationality has an unlimited possibility of contributing its labor and using its talents within the framework of a single state in the general common interest of the whole people.... Settlement of the problem of Palestine by the creation of a single Arab-Jewish state with equal rights for Jews and Arabs might in this way be considered as ... the solution most deserving attention.... Such a solution ... might provide a sound basis for the peaceful coexistence and cooperation of the Arab and Jewish populations of Palestine, in the interests of both of these people, for the good of the whole population of the country and for the peace and security of the Near East. If it were found that this plan was unrealizable on account of the deterioration of relations between Jews and Arabs (it is highly important that we have the opinion of the committee on this question), then it would be necessary to consider an alternative solution, which, as the first, has its advocates in Palestine and which consists of a division of Palestine into 2 independent, separate states—one Jewish and one Arab.

... Such a solution of the question of the future of Palestine would be justified only if relations between the Jewish population and the Arab population of Palestine were, in fact, so bad that it was impossible to reconcile them and to ensure a peaceful coexistence of the 2 people in that country. Both these possible alternative plans for solution of the problem of the future of Palestine should, of course, be studied by the committee. Its task should be to study all sides and very carefully draft plans for the structure of Palestine in order to enable the committee to submit to the next session of the General Assembly well considered and fully motivated proposals which would help the United Nations find a just settlement of this problem, a settlement corresponding to the interests of the peoples of Palestine, the interests of the United Nations, and settlement in accordance with general aim—peace and international security....

Gromyko's speech was highly instrumental in influencing UN opinion. It indicated that the USSR was prepared to support partition and the creation of 2 independent states in Palestine.

Britain's Account of Its Stewardship

The British government submitted to the UN June 25, 1947 a memo on 27 years of British trusteeship in Palestine. The memo arrived a week after the UN Special Committee on Palestine had begun its fact-finding mission.

The government began by stressing that the mandate had imposed 2 basic tasks—the welfare of Palestine as a whole and the establishment of a Jewish national home—and had included explicit notice that only if each community recognized the position, needs and rights of the other could these tasks be achieved. The mandate also envisaged the 2 peoples' rapprochement and cooperation for a common aim under a progressive and liberal regime that made allowance for immigration. Moreover, the principle of Jews and Arabs ultimately sharing authority had been incorporated in the 1939 White Paper and was still observed by the mandatory administration, the memo said. But the 2 communities had, politically, economically and socially, drifted farther apart, the British held, for these reasons:

(1) Both Jews and Arabs basically feared domination by the other community and so were unwilling to compromise.

(2) There were faults in the terms of the mandate.

(3) Serious problems had been caused by the growth of the Jewish Agency.

(4) Divisions had been intensified by the use of 3 official languages (Hebrew, Arabic and English).

In the British government's view, the memo said: The Arabs, from the outset, had been "intractable," and the Jews had been "racially exclusive." The Jews' adoption of a program for a Jewish commonwealth and unrestricted immigration had ended all practical prospects of Arab-Jewish cooperation; the *yishuv's* principle of numerically equal voice (as opposed to proportionate representation) on public bodies was "artificial and unsound." Neither community recognized the extent to which its stubbornness, "impetuosity, lawlessness or violence" had slowed down the development of the country.

The memo emphasized that the mandate had foreseen no controversy serious enough to require provisions for the widely disparate Jewish and Arab outlooks, apparent as early as 1922. The mandate, in fact, tended to differentiate between the Jews and the rest of the community, the memo asserted. The concept of a Jewish national home and the prospect of Jewish immigration proceeded naturally from the mandate's preamble; the mandate itself, however, went further in stimulating separatism by setting up the Jewish Agency in a special position and by permitting communal schools and 3 different languages.

"The minds of Jewish children have been encaged, rather than freed for creative work, by an undue concentration on assertive and exclusive nationalism," the memo said. The Jewish Agency had come to rival the country's administrative system and no longer kept within the limits set out for it as a local advisory council under the mandate. It had grown to represent "Zionists throughout the world" as well as dominating all Jewish activities in Palestine. There had been no counterbalancing political development on the Arab side, the memo held.

The memo asserted that the mandatory administration had created the conditions in which a Jewish national home could be founded. It acknowledged that the Jews, "a bustling, thrusting people," had by their own initiative and outside financial aid made great progress and accomplished much. The Arabs benefited in jobs and modern comforts—although "the pace set by the Jews has made it still harder to keep a balance in the country as a whole," the memo declared.

The mandatory power had a responsibility towards the Arabs as well as toward others, the memo noted. The Arabs had exhibited "vitality and individuality" and had made great progress both in agriculture and in industry, but they had neither the money nor the powerful organizations available to the Jews. In trying to narrow the differences between the *yishuv* and Palestine's Arabs, however, the mandatory administration had been condemned by both sides.

UNSCOP Hearings

The 11-member UN Special Committee on Palestine (UNSCOP) decided at its first session, held May 26, 1947 in Lake Success, N.Y., to go to Palestine to begin its fact-finding mission and to convene there in mid-June.

Named as regular delegates to the committee May 26 were: John D. L. Hood, a counselor in the Australian External Affairs Ministry; Canadian Supreme Court Justice Ian C. Rand; Czechoslovak Amb.-to-UN Karel Lisicky; Dr. N. S. Bloom of the Dutch Foreign Ministry; Guatemalan Amb.-to-UN Jorge Garcia Granados; Lahore High Court Judge Sir Abdur Rahman of India; Iranian Delegate-to-UN Nasrullah Entezam; Peruvian Amb.-to-Vatican City Arturo Garcia

Salazar; Chief Justice Emil Sandstroem of Sweden; Uruguayan Delegate-to-UN Enrique Rodriguez Fabregat; Joze Brilej of the Yugoslav Foreign Ministry.

UN Secy. Gen. Trygve Lie disclosed May 28 that in the interest of impartiality, neither Jews nor Arabs could serve on UNSCOP's secretariat. Lie May 14 had named Dr. Victor Hoo of China, assistant UN secretary general for trusteeship affairs, to head the UNSCOP secretariat. He appointed Dr. Alfonso Garcia Robles of Mexico as Hoo's principal secretary.

UNSCOP June 2 elected Justice Sandstroem as its chairman and decided that the mandatory power, the Arab Higher Committee and the Jewish Agency might appoint liaison officers to assist its work. The members of UNSCOP emplaned from New York for Palestine June 6 and June 10. Before their arrival in Palestine, Deputy Chairman Jamal el-Husseini of the Arab Higher Committee had announced a boycott of UNSCOP by the Arab community.

(The Political Committee of the Arab League, made up of the foreign ministers of the 7 member states, met in Cairo June 8 and then advanced the argument that the UN, by failing to include any mention of Palestinian independence or self-determination in UNSCOP's field of inquiry, had departed from the principles of the UN Charter.)

UNSCOP began its sessions in Jerusalem June 16, 1947. Palestinian Arabs boycotted UNSCOP and observed a one-day strike as it began work. UNSCOP members made an 11-day, 2,000-mile tour of Palestine during which they visited Haifa, Jericho, the Dead Sea Valley, Gaza, Jaffa, Tel Aviv, the Negev and Beersheba area, Galilee, the Valley of Jezreel, Safad, Tiberias, Acre (where UNSCOP's Czechoslovak and Guatemalan members interviewed terrorists held in the prison) and Rishon-le-Zion. They stopped at several Jewish settlements— old and new communities developed by Jewish pioneers—saw Jewish villages for victims of the Nazis and a few Arab villages and visited Arab institutions and the Hebrew University in Jerusalem.

Before beginning its public hearings, UNSCOP rejected requests by the Stern Group and Irgun Zvai Leumi for permission to testify. UNSCOP also blocked a move by the Irgun to turn the hearings into a forum for its extremist views. The Irgun had sent UNSCOP a special memo demanding a Jewish state on both sides (*shtei gedot*) of the Jordan (embracing Palestine and Transjordan), had called for the end of "British occupation rule in Erez Yisrael" (the land of Israel) and had demanded the transfer of power to a "Hebrew provisional government."

Jewish Agency Views

Moshe Shertok and David Ben-Gurion of the Jewish Agency presented their organization's positions in statements made before UNSCOP during the early days of the hearings.

Shertok, in his statement June 17, 1947, dwelt on agricultural and landholding features. He said:

- Palestine owed its existence as a distinct country to the facts that it was the birthplace of the Jewish people and that, in Palestine, the Jewish people had been able to make their contribution to the cultural and spiritual treasury of mankind.
- Palestine had never been so small in area as it was then; it had extended on both sides of the Jordan before World War I and further north, east and west as well.
- It was the deliberate aim of the Jews in Palestine to create their own economy in order to be able to live a fully independent Jewish life.
- The Negev, which comprised 40% of the country's area, was mostly Arab populated and arable. The northern section of the Negev contained good soil and was capable of very extensive agricultural development. In this zone there were only 17 Jewish settlements, mostly established in recent years. (Shertok described the 5 distinct geographical zones of Palestine, giving for each zone the number of Jewish agricultural settlements.)
- Officially, however, the country had a different system of zones, based on whether and to what extent Jews were free or not free to acquire land in specified areas. In 63% of the country's area the Jews were completely barred from buying land. In 32% every transaction between Jew and non-Jew required special governmental permission. In only 5% of Palestine were Jews free to buy land. The restrictions were in inverse ratio to Jewish landholdings. Where they had bought a large proportion of the land they could buy the remainder; where they had bought very little they were completely prohibited from buying anything.

● Every *dunum* of land owned by Jews in Palestine had had to be bought and reclaimed at their own expense. They had received no help from the mandatory administration. Even in regard to state domain, in spite of the very express provision of the mandate to place suitable land at the disposal of Jews, they had obtained practically nothing. They had received some entirely uncultivable land for individual and housing purposes but nothing for agriculture.

● Jews possessed just over 6% of the land of Palestine. About 40% to 45% of this was nationally owned (by the Jewish National Fund). The rest was privately owned or held as concessions.

● Jewish agricultural settlements had not resulted in the creation of a class of landless Arabs. Where land had been bought from absentee landlords, Arab tenants, when removed, were in every case resettled elsewhere. Not one Arab village had disappeared. It was not easy to find an instance in the history of colonization where largescale settlement had been conducted with so much respect for the interests of the existing population.

The next agency representative, David Ben-Gurion, July 4 described the character of the Jewish people and their inextricable bond with Palestine, persisting through centuries of exile. He cited historical instances, from antiquity to the 20th century, to show that the Jews could successfully form a nation in Palestine with plenty of room for a large population. Ben-Gurion castigated the British, who had ignored the recommendations of their own commissions and who had decided that the Jews would remain a permanent minority, not to exceed ⅓ of the population, according to the 1939 White Paper policy. He said:

● "Jewish misery may vary from time to time. It may become more or less acute, but it never ceases. Jewish insecurity originates in 3 fundamental disabilities of Jews throughout the world: they are deprived of statehood; they are homeless, and they are in a minority position everywhere. Unless and until these 3 disabilities are completely and lastingly remedied, there is no hope for the Jewish people, nor can there be justice in the world."

- With Hitler destroyed, "Palestine is now the only place in the civilized world where racial discrimination still exists in law. Even if there were no national home, we should not acquiesce in such discrimination."
- The 1939 White Paper, "in closing the gates of Palestine to Jews in the hour of the greatest peril, is responsible for the death of tens of thousands, perhaps of hundreds of thousands of Jews who could have been saved from the gas chambers had Palestine been open to them."
- "Hundreds of thousands of the ... [surviving Jews of Europe] are still in camps, in that same Germany, surrounded by the murderers of their people, surrounded by the same hatred as under Hitler. In a Gallup Poll recently taken by the American military authorities in the American Zone of Germany, 60% of the Germans approached approved of the massacre of the Jews by Hitler, 14% condemned the murders, 26% were 'neutral.' The Jews do not want to stay where they are. They want to regain their human dignity, their homeland. They want a reunion with their kin in Palestine after having lost their dearest relatives. To them, the countries of their birth are a graveyard of their people. They do not wish to return there and they cannot. They want to go back to their national home."
- "It does not matter so much what name is given to the [future] regime [in Palestine], whether you call it mandate, international trusteeship, Palestine state, national state, Arab state or Jewish state. Neither does it matter very much what the formal constitution would be." "The most crucial question is immigration."
- The British military repressive measures in Palestine were, as Winston Churchill had said, a "squalid war against the Jews." "If there are any complaints against the government, it is not that they have done too much for the population but that they have done almost nothing for the national home and very little for the inhabitants of the country."
- "The [British] memo [of June 25, 1946] makes a great point of the disparity between Jews and Arabs in Palestine. A disparity there is, in mentality and social outlook, in public spirit, in dynamic power and in many other things. There is also a disparity between people living in the 20th century and those living in the 15th or some even in the 7th century. But in stressing the point of disparity, the memorandum is rather one-

sided; it brings it up as an accusation against Jews and gives it as a reason for curbing their progress. Now, if a disparity between Jews and Arabs is a defect which ought to be remedied by the administration, then the government should mention all the disparities between Jews and Arabs and try to remedy them all."

● On the subject of disparities, there was "the disparity in numbers. There are some 600,000 Jews in Palestine and some 1,100,000 Arabs. There are no reliable figures in this respect. There is an even greater disparity than that. The Arabs own 94% of the land, the Jews only 6%. The Arabs have 7 states, the Jews none. The Arabs have vast underdeveloped territories— Iraq alone is 3 times as large as England with less than 4 million people. The Jews have only a tiny beginning of a national home and even that is begrudged them by the Palestine administration. The most glaring disparity perhaps is that the Arabs have no problem of homelessness and immigration, while for the Jews homelessness is the root cause of all their sufferings for centuries past. Some of these disparities were summed up by the Permanent Mandates Commission of the League of Nations in 1939 when they said: 'It should be remembered that the collective sufferings of Arabs and Jews are not comparable, since vast spaces in the Near East, formerly the abode of numerous populations and the home of a brilliant civilization, are open to the former, whereas the world is increasingly being closed to settlement by the latter.'"

● The Zionist line was to realize the maximum potentialities of Palestine, to "afford full opportunities for the Jewish people to rehabilitate themselves, while raising the standard of the Arabs to the same level, and in this way to create a living example for the whole Middle East, where Jews and Arabs will cooperate and work together as free and equal partners."

● "And now I put the question to you: Who is prepared and able to guarantee that what happened to us in Europe will not happen again? Can human conscience, and we believe that there is a human conscience, free itself of all responsibility for that catastrophe? There is only one safeguard: a homeland and statehood! A homeland, where a Jew can return freely as of right. Statehood, where he can be master of his own destiny. These 2 things are possible here, and here only. The Jewish people cannot give up, cannot renounce these 2 fundamental rights, whatever may happen."

"The problem of Jewish-Arab relations," Ben-Gurion said, "is not merely the problem of Jews and Arabs in Palestine. It is the problem of the relations of the Jewish and Arab peoples as a whole. Their national aspirations in that broader sense are not only compatible but complementary. Nobody can seriously claim that a Jewish Palestine could in any way endanger or harm the independence or unity of the Arab race. The area of western Palestine is less than 1% of the vast territory occupied by the Arab states in the Near East, excluding Egypt. The number of Arabs in this country is less than 3% of the number of Arabs who have gained their political independence. The Arabs in Palestine, even if they were a minority, would still be a part of that large Arab majority in the Middle East. The existence of Arab states to the north, east, and south of Palestine is an automatic guarantee, not only of the civil, religious and political rights of the Arabs in Palestine, but also of their national aspirations. ... Only by establishing Palestine as a Jewish state can the true objectives be accomplished: immigration and statehood for the Jews, economic development and social progress for the Arabs."

Ben-Gurion appeared before UNSCOP in Jerusalem again July 7 and suggested that the UN assume temporary supervision of Palestine—by force if necessary—while the *yishuv* built a Jewish state there. If partition were decided on, the Jews could take care of themselves. Ben-Gurion was sharply cross-examined by UNSCOP member Sir Abdur Rahman, an Indian Moslem, who feared an Arab-Jewish war if any of the *yishuv's* demands were granted.

Other Agency representatives appearing before UNSCOP were Rabbi Yehuda Fishman (who July 5 described the historic ties between Jews and Palestine; on being questioned July 9 by Rahman as to when God had promised the Promised Land to the Jews, Fishman replied: "about 4,000 years ago"); David Horowitz (who dealt July 5 with the country's economic absorptive capacity), and Jewish Agency Treasurer Eliezar Kaplan (who July 6 gave data relating to Jewish colonization and to industrial and agricultural development). They argued that Britain was exploiting Palestine for its own benefit and that the country could hold 2 to 3 times its current population with proper irrigation and industrial development.

Weizmann Urges Partition

Jewish Agency Pres. Chaim Weizmann, troubled by failing vision, July 8 asserted his belief that partition was the only solution for the Palestinian problem.

For any partition plan to work, Weizmann said, 2 requirements were essential: (1) the area of the Jewish state should be so drawn that water and electrical power resources would be sufficiently available to develop the land effectively and allow for the absorption of largescale immigration, and (2) such an area ought to consist of Galilee, the coastal plain, the Negev and the Jewish area of Jerusalem. Such a state could absorb another 1½ million people, Weizmann asserted.

Weizmann revealed his meetings with leaders of Syria, Lebanon and Palestine since 1917 in search of peace settlements. His understanding with King Feisal of Iraq would have led to a permanent settlement and recognition of the future Jewish state had not Britain intervened and betrayed Feisal, Weizmann held. He asserted that Jewish attempts to win Arab friendship had "never stopped and will not stop until we begin to understand each other. One of the most important prerequisites for such friendship is to establish a definite, clear and equal status between the Jews and the Arabs."

Weizmann described his role in early Zionist history in the 20th century, and the 2 main purposes—as he saw them—of the British mandate. One was a sort of restitution to the Jewish people for their contribution to civilization, the other was utilitarian—the needs of victory in World War I.

Zionists had predicted that the position of Jews would be changed only with statehood, Weizmann said, and the fate of the 6 million Jews killed in Europe and of those in the displaced persons' camps was "proof that the situation demands speedy remedy." He had warned the Anglo-American Committee that time was of the essence: "We have lost so much blood, we cannot afford to lose any more. For us it is a question of survival: it brooks no delay."

Weizmann defined a national home as the construction by a people of a country. The *yishuv's* instrument for this goal was the Jewish Agency, "which had the function of a body which would conduct the colonization, immigration, improvement of the land and do all the work which a government usually does, without really being a government." "If we are able to acquire land, if we are able to bring in Jewish immigration, whether it is a large immigration or not, whether it will correspond to the needs which are inherent in the position of the Jews or not, eventually, in the fullness of time, in God's own time it will become a Jewish state," he asserted.

Weizmann called British policy doomed, saying: "The mandate was born out of hope. The White Paper [of 1939] was born out of fear—the fear which was brought into the world by Hitler, by Nazism, by all this darkness which has covered the bright horizon of Jews before the war. This fear has found expression in a great many forms, particularly in the form of the White Paper. This fear was a result of the appeasement policy: appeasement of Germany; appeasement of the Arabs. The British nation has paid dearly for this appeasement policy."

Jews could not stay in other countries and build them up, Weizmann asserted. The experience in Germany had shown this. Only a short while ago a conspiracy had been discovered in France, and one of the projects of the proposed coup was a detailed program of how to exterminate the French Jews on the pattern set by Hitler and the Nazis.

As for the objection that geographical exigencies restricted Jewish immigration, Weizmann countered: "There is no question about it that when Palestine was promised ... [in Nov. 1917], at that time by 'Palestine' was understood 'Palestine and Transjordan.' Then Transjordan was cut off. As you know, the size of Transjordan is much greater than that of Palestine—more than 3 times. ... And here is a sort of irony. First you amputate Palestine. You cut off a country which is 3 or 4 or 5 times the size of Palestine, and then you turn round on poor Zionists and tell them: you are a small country; you cannot bring any population there; you must displace others, and we cannot allow that, and so on. ... You cannot throw it in our face that we are trying to bring a population into a small country. In fact, what we have been trying to do since that time is, by ingenuity and scientific development, to increase the size of the country, and as you cannot increase it materially, or geographically, we have tried to increase it in such a way that we are trying to make 2 blades of grass grow where one blade has grown before; in fact, to make 4 tomatoes grow where one has been growing before, by intensifying—sometimes over-intensifying—and utilizing every little knot and every nook and cranny in Palestine and making it produce human sustenance. That has been our business since Palestine has been amputated. But it has been done, and I am not harking back to it, and I even realize that today in order to have peace in this country, stability in the Middle East—and the Middle East is important not only for Jews and Arabs, but also for the whole of the civilized world—we have great responsibility not to disturb the peace in this part of the world."

Weizmann returned to his argument for partition: "I think I am speaking the mind of a great many Jews ... [in saying that the *yishuv* favors] ... a form of partition which would satisfy the just demands of both the Jews and the Arabs. We realize that we cannot have the whole of Palestine." Partition had "2 great advantages. It is final, and it helps to dispel some of the fears of our Arab friends. I am not saying that you would dispel easily all fears. Fear is not a matter of logic. It is a matter of emotion, and emotional reaction cannot be dispelled by logical performance. But at any rate we can do all we can in order to help in future to mitigate their fear. If it is final the Arabs will know and the Jews will know that they cannot encroach upon each other's domain. To us it means something else. It means equality of status with our Arab neighbors: the most important requisite for good relations between us and them. As long as they consider us inferior in political status, they will not be anxious to make peace with us. Therefore, it is a desirable solution, although it represents, as I have already pointed out, a new and great sacrifice on the part of the Jewish people. It cannot be whittled down, it cannot be bargained down, and the part of Palestine which would remain after partition must be something in which Jews could live and into which we could bring a million and a half people in a compara-tively short time. It must not be a place for graves only, or graveyards, or, as you sometimes see on very full trams, 'standing room only.'"

After the Jewish Agency had concluded its case, UNSCOP Delegate Jorge Granados stated July 9 that British emergency regulations under which Palestine had become a police state were contrary to the mandate and therefore illegal. UNSCOP voted, 6-3 (Guatemala, Uruguay and Yugoslavia in the minority), not to visit Cyprus, where 17,000 Jewish immigrants were interned.

The commission also heard representatives of the Vaad Leumi (the Jewish National Council for Palestine), the Agudath Israel organization, the General Federation of Jewish Labor (Histadrut—the trade union branch of the Zionist movement in Palestine), the Communist Party of Palestine (which called for an independent binational state), the Ihud organization (whose chief spokesman, Dr. Judah Magnes, rector of the Hebrew University of Jerusalem, also favored a binational state with political parity between Jews and Arabs) and representatives of the ancient Jewish community of Jerusalem (generally anti-Zionist).

The Rt. Rev. W. H. Stewart, the Anglican bishop of Jerusalem, and the Rev. W. Clark-Kerr, moderator of the Church of Scotland Presbytery of Jerusalem, argued July 11 for a unitary state with cultural and religious cooperation between the Moslem, Jewish and Christian communities.

Sir Henry Gurney, chief secretary of the mandatory government of Palestine, and other mandatory officials presented a supplementary memo to UNSCOP in Jerusalem July 20 to answer what mandatory authorities considered to be "misleading points and omissions" in the Jewish Agency's evidence. Gurney's memo said:

● "During the 11 years since 1935, when the last attempt to establish a legislature was frustrated, each side (Arab and Jewish) has in turn freely resorted to violence and declined even to discuss with the other any possible reconciliation of their differences. Since the beginning of 1945, the Jews ... have supported by an organized campaign of lawlessness, murder, and sabotage their contention that ... nothing should be allowed to stand in the way of a Jewish state and of free Jewish immigration to Palestine.... The Jewish community in Palestine still publicly refuses its help to the administration in suppressing terrorism, on the ground that the administration's policy is

opposed to Jewish interests. The result has been to give active encouragement to dissidents and freer scope to their activities."
● Palestine was not a "police state," nor was Haganah a purely defensive body but one used in 1946 for terroristic purposes. The Jewish Agency had shared in and organized terrorism; the right of any community "to use force as a means of gaining its political ends was not admitted in the British Commonwealth," however. "The fact that a national home could never have been established without expenditure of British resources and British lives apparently requires to be restated.... Had it not been for the defense of Palestine undertaken by the mandatory power during the war of 1939-45, the national home would have disappeared."
● The Arab disturbances of 1936-9 had resulted in the loss of 4,000 lives and cost £1 million ($4.8 million) worth of damage, and the Jewish postwar disturbances had taken 270 lives and cost £1½ million ($7.2 million).

UNSCOP ended its Jerusalem hearings July 20 after 13 open and 18 closed sessions and left for Beirut, Lebanon, where it remained for 4 days. UNSCOP members flew July 24 to Amman, Transjordan. There Premier Samir Pasha el Rifai reiterated most of the arguments given to the full committee July 21-22 in Beirut by Lebanese Foreign Min. Hamid Bey Frangie and Iraqi Foreign Min. Mohammad Fadhil Jamali, who spoke for the other 6 Arab League members.

Basically, the Arab views were: (1) Palestine belonged to the Arabs; (2) the Arabs never accepted the "ambiguous" Balfour Declaration; (3) the Jews were imperialistic invaders whose immigration "must be stopped forthwith"; (4) the ban on Jews' buying land must be retained; (5) Palestine should get unpartitioned independence under an Arab majority—which would not persecute the *yishuv* minority, no matter what the Zionists argued; (6) the plight of European refugees did not involve Palestine; (7) the Arabs would justly resist with force any unfavorable decision.

Chairman Emil Sandstroem of Sweden asked: "In your opinion, would the Jews have possibilities of developing freely in a Palestinian Arab state? Developing the question further: would they have the right of an educational system of their own; and further, what would happen to Jewish industry?" Lebanese Foreign Min. Frangie replied: "Our answer to the first part of this question is in the affirmative. In answer to the 2d part, the constitution of the independent state of Palestine will provide for the right of religious bodies and other societies and individuals to maintain, in addition to educational establishments administered by public authority, private schools and universities, subject to the compulsory teaching of Arabic in the schools and to government control for the purpose of maintaining educational standards and preventing subversive teaching, with the object of creating common allegiance without discrimination among the citizens of the states. In answer to the 3d part of the question, Palestinian-Jewish industry will be treated as any other Palestinian industry and will be subject to the same laws."

Iraqi Foreign Min. Jamali declared: "Were it not for Zionism, the atmosphere in the Arab world between the members of the various sects and religions would be very harmonious and peaceful. We, in Iraq, before that Nazi *coup d'etat,* never had any conflict between Jews and non-Jews. We consider Moslems, Christians and Jews as Arabs. We consider them all Arabs, all Iraqis. To us, Jews are only people who have a different faith, but they are part of us. We have nothing against them. They have lived, and they live today more prosperously than other sects and religions in Baghdad. There are great men in economics, finance and commerce in Iraq. So, the atmosphere is most cordial, were it not for Zionism."

In an oblique charge that Jews were an imperialist implantation, Frangie also said: "A Jewish state, however small, would constitute a danger for the Arab world both from the interior and the exterior. From the interior it would create friction, exert a certain economic pressure and would gradually infiltrate in order to create disorder. From the exterior, a Jewish state would constitute a bridgehead against the Arab world. Such is the collective answer of the delegations of the Arab states. I would like to add some words myself. I think that the question of creation of a Jewish state cannot be taken without 2 other connected problems: that is, the question of immigration and that of foreign subsidies. A Jewish state would, of course, be master of the immigration into Palestine. It might decide that immigration would be without limits, and the economic argument, which would be that it is impossible for a very large number of people to live in a very small territory, would become void if the Jewish state can still reckon with foreign financial support. Therefore, with the doors of the country wide open to immigration, and financial support from outside, the Jewish state would become extremely populated. Therefore, it might not be one million, but 2, 3, 4 million, since it would not depend on its own economy or its own production. As soon as it goes beyond a certain limit in numbers, ... it becomes a bridgehead against the Arab world. This is what we absolutely want to avoid. A Jewish state would not be accepted by the Jews if they had to put an end to immigration. Further, if they go on obtaining subsidies, this very highly populated country, enjoying foreign financial support, would certainly constitute a military danger for the Arab world."

Most of the UNSCOP members left July 24 for Geneva. UNSCOP set up a subcommittee July 30 under the chairmanship of the Australian delegate, John D. L. Hood, to visit refugee and displaced persons' camps in Germany and Austria. During the next 3 weeks the subcommittee visited Munich, Salzburg, Vienna, Berlin, Hamburg and Hanover before returning to Geneva Aug. 20.

UNSCOP Findings

UNSCOP published its findings Aug. 31 and submitted to the 2d General Assembly Sept. 26 a majority report in which it described the mandate as unworkable. UNSCOP recommended unanimously that the mandate be ended, that the mandatory authorities be made directly responsible to the UN and that Palestine be declared independent. (Most UNSCOP members also recommended that the land be partitioned between Jews and Arabs.)

Surveying the land's peoples and where they lived, UNSCOP found "no clear territorial separation of Jews and Arabs by large contiguous areas." It said: "Jews are more than 40% of the total population in the districts of Jaffa (which includes Tel Aviv), Haifa and Jerusalem. In the northern inland areas of Tiberias and Beisan, they are between 25% and 34% of the total population. In the inland northern districts of Safad and Nazareth and the coastal districts of Tulkarm and Ramle, Jews form between 10% and 25% of the total population, while in the central districts and the districts south of Jerusalem they constitute not more than 5% of the total. Thus, though the main concentration of Jewish population is on the coastal plain, the Jerusalem area and the northern uplands, there is a considerable concentration of Arabs, even in these areas, since these are the most populous parts of the country."

As for how these people lived, UNSCOP discovered that: "Although the total population of Palestine is less than 2 million, its economic life presents the complex phenomenon of 2 distinctive economies—one Jewish and one Arab—closely involved with one another and yet in essential features separate. Apart from certain parts of the country which are predominantly Jewish and others which are predominantly Arab in population, this 'economic separateness' of the 2 communities does not correspond to any clear territorial divisions."

Arab agriculture was reported to be "based to a considerable extent on cereal production, and tend[ed] to be subsistence farming. Only about 20% to 25% of Arab agricultural production (excluding citrus) is marketed," UNSCOP found. "Jewish agriculture, on the other hand, is largely intensive and cash-crop farming. About 75% of Jewish agricultural production is sold on the market. It is marketed mainly through Jewish marketing organizations to Jewish retailers. The occupational structure of the Jewish population is similar to that of some homogeneous industrialized communities, while that of the Arabs corresponds more nearly to a subsistence type of agricultural society."

UNSCOP described the *yishuv* as "a highly organized and closely-knit society which, partly on a basis of communal effort, has created a national life distinctive enough to merit the [British] Royal Commission's title of a state within a state. Proud of its own achievements in self-government and cultural life, ... [the *yishuv*] is sensitive to any apparent lack of appreciation of what it regards as its just and reasonable needs. Its initiative, purposefulness and self-confidence react strongly against a situation in which it finds itself under an 'alien bureaucracy.' Its memories of the Arab rising of 1936-39, and more recent anti-Jewish pogroms in Middle Eastern countries, coupled with the immediate background of Hitlerism, keep it constantly vigilant and preoccupied with securing adequate defense for the national home."

UNSCOP described the atmosphere that it found in Palestine as one of "profound tension": "In many respects the country is living under a semimilitary regime. In the streets of Jerusalem and other key areas barbed wire defenses, roadblocks, machine-gun [emplacements] ... and constant armored car patrols are routine measures. In areas of doubtful security, administration officials and the military forces live within strictly policed security zones and work within fortified and closely-guarded buildings. Freedom of personal movement is liable to severe restriction and the curfew and martial law have become a not uncommon experience. The primary purpose of the Palestine government, in the circumstances of recurring terrorist attacks, is to maintain what it regards as the essential conditions of public security. Increasing resort has been had to special security measures provided for in the defense emergency regulations. Under these regulations, a person may be detained for an unlimited period, or placed under police supervision for one year, by order of an area military commander; and he may be deported or excluded from Palestine by order of the high commissioner. Where there are 'reasons to believe that there are grounds which would justify ... detention ... or deportation,' any person may be arrested without warrant by any member of his majesty's forces or any police officer and detained for not more than 7 days, pending further decision by the military commander. The regulations concerning military courts prohibit a form of judicial appeal from or questioning of a sentence or decision of a military court. Under the regulations, widespread arrests have been made; and as of July 12, 1947, 820 persons were being held in detention on security grounds, including 291 in Kenya under Kenya's 1947 ordinance dealing with the control of detained persons. The detainees were all Jews with the exception of 4 Arabs. In addition to these, 17,873 illegal immigrants were under detention."

The committee was given this description of the administration's attitude toward the maintenance of public security under current circumstances: "The right of any community to use force as a means of gaining its political ends is not admitted in the British Commonwealth. Since the beginning of 1945 the Jews have implicitly claimed this right and have supported by an organized campaign of lawlessness, murder and sabotage their contention that, whatever other interests might be concerned, nothing should be allowed to stand in the way of a Jewish state and free Jewish immigration into Palestine. It is true that large numbers of Jews do not today attempt to defend the crimes that have been committed in the name of these political aspirations.... Nevertheless, the Jewish community of Palestine still publicly refuses its help to the administration in suppressing terrorism, on the ground that the administration's policy is opposed to Jewish interests. The converse of this attitude is clear, and its result, however much the Jewish leaders themselves may not wish it, has been to give active encouragement to the dissidents and freer scope to their activities."

The committee took note of the *yishuv's* persistent attempts to smuggle Jewish immigrants into Palestine despite the administration's preventive measures. UNSCOP also noted "the far-reaching support that such attempts received from the Jewish community in Palestine and abroad." UNSCOP viewed the "unremitting struggle to admit further Jews into Palestine, irrespective of the quota permitted by the administration, as a measure of the rift that has developed between the Jewish Agency and the Jewish community, on the one hand, and the administration on the other." Until the current state of tension ran its course, UNSCOP held, there was "little practicable basis ... for the discharge by the Jewish Agency of its function under the mandate of 'advising and cooperating' with the administration in matters affecting the interests of the Jewish community."

UNSCOP turned next to Palestine's Arabs. "As far as the Arab community is concerned," UNSCOP said, "the committee has had less opportunity of ascertaining its attitude in detail in view of the boycott on association with the committee pronounced by the [Palestinian] Arab Higher Committee. During the hearings of representatives of the Arab states at Beirut, however, the Arab assessment of the present situation of unrest in Palestine was stated thus: Zionism ... does not content itself with mere propaganda in favor of the fulfillment of its expansionist projects at the expense of the Arab countries. Its plan involves recourse to terrorism, both in Palestine and in other countries. It is known that a secret army has been formed with a view to creating an atmosphere of tension and unrest by making attempts on the lives of representatives of the

governing authority and by destroying public buildings....
This aggressive attitude, resulting from the mandatory power's
weakness in dealing with them, will not fail to give rise in turn
to the creation of similar organizations by the Arabs. The
responsibility for the disturbances which might result
therefrom throughout the Middle East will rest solely with the
Zionist organizations, as having been the first to use these violent tactics. It was declared [by an Arab spokesman] at the same
[UNSCOP] meeting that 'against a state established by
violence, the Arab states will be obliged to use violence; that is a
legitimate right of self-defense.' "

The commission noted that "Arab resistance to Jewish
political demands in Palestine has in part taken the form of an
economic boycott of Jewish goods, decided on by a resolution
of the Council of the Arab League in Dec. 1945. Representatives of the Arab states stressed in evidence to the committee
that the boycott would prove effective [because of] ... the
dependence of Jewish industry on the market of Arab countries.
Within Palestine, though it would be difficult to estimate its
present effectiveness, the boycott is regarded by the Arab
leaders as an important means of furthering their political
aims. During the Arab conference in Haifa in July 1947, Jamal
el-Husseini spoke of the necessity of 'strengthening the boycott
in order to pull down Zionist existence,' and warned Arab
merchants who did not observe the boycott that they would be
regarded as 'traitors,' since 'the nation cannot keep patient over
humiliation.' "

UNSCOP summarized the basic contentions of the Arab
and Jewish claims separately, with a brief appraisal of each
claim:

The Jewish case —UNSCOP found the *yishuv* to be openly
seeking "the establishment of a Jewish state in Palestine and
Jewish immigration into Palestine both before and after the
creation of the Jewish state, subject only to the limitations
imposed by the economic absorptive capacity of that state. In
the Jewish case, the issues of the Jewish state and unrestricted
immigration are inextricably interwoven. On the other hand,
the Jewish state is needed in order to assure a refuge for the
Jewish immigrants ... clamoring to come to Palestine from the
displaced persons camps and from other places in Europe,
North Africa and the Near East, where their present plight is

difficult. On the other hand, a Jewish state would have urgent need of Jewish immigrants in order to affect the present great numerical preponderance of Arabs over Jews in Palestine. The Jewish case frankly recognizes the difficulty involved in creating at the present time a Jewish state in all of Palestine in which Jews would, in fact, be only a minority, or in part of Palestine in which, at best, they could immediately have only a slight preponderance. Thus, the Jewish case lays great stress on the right of Jewish immigration, for political as well as humanitarian reasons. Special emphasis is therefore placed on the right of Jews to 'return' to Palestine."

UNSCOP noted that "the establishment of the Jewish home and state will, it is claimed, do no political injustice to the Arabs, since the Arabs have never established a government in Palestine."

In its appraisal of the Jewish case, UNSCOP noted that the British mandate had been made responsible for placing the country under such political, administrative and economic conditions as would assure (a) the establishment of a Jewish national home, as laid down in the preamble, and (b) the development of self-governing institutions. UNSCOP also noted that "both the Balfour Declaration and the mandate involved international commitments to the Jewish people as a whole." "It was obvious that these commitments were not limited only to the Jewish population of Palestine, since at the time there were only some 80,000 Jews there," it found. "This would imply that all Jews in the world who wish to go to Palestine would have the right to do so."

UNSCOP reached this conclusion: "The Jewish assurance that no political injustice would be done to the Arabs by the creation of a Jewish state in Palestine, since the Arabs have never established a government there, gains some support from the fact that not since 63 BC, when Pompey stormed Jerusalem, has Palestine been an independent state. On the other hand, the fact remains that today in Palestine there are over 1,200,000 Arabs, 2/3 of the population, who oppose a Jewish state and who are intent on establishing an independent Arab state. Any solution assuring the continued development of the Jewish national home in Palestine would necessarily involve continued Jewish immigration, the postponement of independence and also administration by a 3d party, at least until the Jewish

people become a majority there. Such a solution would have to
be enforced, in view of the opposition of the Arab population.
Many Jews contend that, if given the opportunity, the Jews
alone could defend a Jewish state. Even this, however,
envisages the possibility of a violent struggle with the Arabs."

The Arab case—UNSCOP reported that "the Arab case
seeks the immediate creation of an independent Palestine west
of the Jordan as an Arab state. It rests on a number of claims
and contentions ... summarized below:

"The Arabs emphasize the fact of an actual Arab numerical majority, in the ratio of 2 to one in the present population of
Palestine. They postulate the 'natural' right of the Arab
majority to remain in undisputed possession of the country,
since they are and have been for many centuries in possession of
the land. This claim of a 'natural' right is based on the contention that the Arab connection with Palestine has continued
uninterruptedly from early historical times, since the term
'Arab' is to be interpreted as connoting not only the invaders
from the Arabian Peninsula in the 7th century, but also the
indigenous population which intermarried with the invaders
and acquired their speech, customs and modes of thought in
becoming permanently Arabized.

"The Arabs further stress the natural desire of the Arab
community to safeguard its national existence from foreign in-
truders, in order that it may pursue without interference its
own political, economic and cultural development.

"The Arabs also claim 'acquired' rights, based on the general promises and pledges officially made to the Arab people in
the course of the First World War, including, in particular, the
McMahon-Husein correspondence of 1915-1916 and the Anglo-
French Declaration of 1918. The 'Hogarth Message,' the Basset
letter, and the 'Declaration to the 7'* are regarded as further
support for the Arab claim to an independent Palestine."

---

* The *McMahon-Husein Correspondence of 1915-6* was an exchange of letters
between Sharif Husein of Mecca and the British high commissioner in Cairo,
Sir Henry McMahon, representing the British government's effort to induce
the sharif, a vassal of the Turks, to join the Allied side. The British agreed, in
this correspondence, that in the event of an Allied victory an independent Arab
state or confederation of states would be established in certain (unspecified)
areas liberated from Turkish rule.

The *Anglo-French Declaration of 1918* was issued Nov. 7 in Palestine,
Syria and Iraq in the form of an official communique from the Egyptian

In its appraisal of the Arab case, UNSCOP came to the view that "the Arabs of Palestine consider themselves as having a 'natural' right to that country, although they have not been in possession of it as a sovereign nation." "The Arab population, despite the strenuous efforts of Jews to acquire land in Palestine, at present remains in possession of approximately 85% of the land," UNSCOP found. "The provisions of the land transfer regulations of 1940, which gave effect to the 1939 White Paper policy, have severely restricted the Jewish efforts to acquire new land."

Expeditionary Force staff headquarters. It said that the goal envisaged by France and Britain was the complete and final liberation of the peoples oppressed by the Turks and the setting up of national governments and administrations deriving their authority from the choice of the indigenous populations. France and Britain promised to further the establishment of indigenous governments in Syria and Mesopotamia and in those (unspecified) territories they had still not liberated.

The *Hogarth Message* of May 1916 was a note sent by D. C. Hogarth, director of the (British) Arab Bureau in Cairo (the British Foreign Office's principal policy instrument in the Middle East) to the Foreign Office, expressing the hope that the Sykes-Picot Agreement of 1916 (a secret understanding between Britain and France dividing the Middle East into British and French spheres of influence with an international area in Palestine) would be regarded as a purely opportunistic measure because it did not promise a final solution of the Near East question.

The *Basset Letter* of Feb. 8, 1918 was a communication from the British government, signed by Lt. Col. J. R. Basset, acting British agent in Jedda, to King Husein of the Hejaz (Mecca), reaffirming the former British pledge regarding the liberation of the Arab peoples from Turkish rule.

The Declaration to the 7 was the British reply to a memorial submitted (anonymously) to the British Foreign Office through the (British) Arab Bureau in Cairo by 7 Arab leaders living in Egypt (Rafiq al-Azm, Shaikh Kamel al-Qassabi, Mukhtar al-Sulh, Abdul-Rahman Shahbandar, Khaled al-Hakim, Fauzi al-Bakri and Hasan Himadeh) requesting specifics on British intentions regarding (1) territories free and independent before the outbreak of World War I; (2) territories liberated from Turkish rule by the action of the Arabs themselves; (3) those liberated by the Allies, and (4) those still under Turkish rule. In this declaration, read to the 7 in Cairo June 16, 1918, Britain promised to recognize the complete and sovereign independence of the Arabs inhabiting territories under conditions (1) and (2) and, with regard to (3), to stand by its proclamations made on the capture of Baghdad and Jerusalem, which defined British policy towards the inhabitants of the region and declared that their future government would be based on the principle of the consent of the governed.

UNSCOP noted that "the desire of the Arab people of Palestine to safeguard their national existence is a very natural desire. However, Palestinian nationalism, as distinct from Arab nationalism, is itself a relatively new phenomenon, which appeared only after the division of the 'Arab rectangle' by the settlement of the First World War. The national home policy and the vigorous policy of immigration pursued by the Jewish leadership has sharpened the Arab fear of danger from the intruding Jewish population. With regard to the promises and pledges made to the Arabs as inducement for their support of the Allies in the First World War, it is to be noted that apparently there is no unequivocal agreement as to whether Palestine was included within the territory pledged to independence by the McMahon-Husein correspondence. In this connection, since the question of interpretation was raised Great Britain has consistently denied that Palestine was among the territories to which independence was pledged."

UNSCOP's Recommendations

During its deliberations in Geneva, UNSCOP held informal meetings as a means of appraising comprehensively the numerous aspects of the Palestine problem. During these discussions, these recommendations were approved unanimously:

(1) "The mandate for Palestine shall be terminated at the earliest practicable date."

(2) "Independence shall be granted in Palestine at the earliest practicable date."

(3) "There shall be a transitional period preceding the grant of independence in Palestine which shall be as short as possible, consistent with the achievement of the preparations and conditions essential to independence."

(4) "During the transitional period the authority entrusted with the task of administering Palestine and preparing it for independence shall be responsible to the United Nations."

(5) "In whatever solution may be adopted for Palestine, the (a) the sacred character of the Holy Places shall be preserved and access to the Holy Places for purposes of worship and pilgrimage shall be ensured in accordance with existing rights, in recognition of the proper interest of millions of

Christians, Jews and Moslems abroad as well as [of] the residents of Palestine in the care of sites and buildings associated with the origin and history of their faiths; (b) existing rights in Palestine of the several religious communities shall be neither impaired nor denied, in view of the fact that their maintenance is essential for religious peace in Palestine under conditions of independence; (c) an adequate system shall be devised to settle impartially disputes involving religious rights as an essential factor in maintaining religious peace, taking into account the fact that during the mandate such disputes have been settled by the government itself, which acted as an arbiter and enjoyed the necessary authority and power to enforce its decisions; (d) specific stipulations concerning Holy Places, religious buildings or sites and the rights of religious communities shall be inserted in the constitution or constitutions of any independent Palestinian state or states which may be created."

(6) "The General Assembly [shall] undertake immediately the initiation and execution of an international arrangement whereby the problem of the distressed European Jews, of whom approximately 250,000 are in assembly centers, will be dealt with as a matter of extreme urgency for the alleviation of their plight and of the Palestine problem."

(7) "In view of the fact that independence is to be granted in Palestine on the recommendation and under the auspices of the United Nations, it is a proper and an important concern of the United Nations that the constitution or other fundamental law as well as the political structure of the new state or states shall be basically democratic, *i.e.,* representative, in character, and that this shall be a prior condition to the grant of independence. In this regard, the constitution or other fundamental law of the new state or states shall include specific guarantees respecting (a) human rights and fundamental freedoms, including freedom of worship and conscience, speech, press and assemblage, the rights of organized labor, freedom of movement, freedom from arbitrary searches and seizures, and rights of personal property; and (b) full protection for the rights and interests of minorities, including the protection of the linguistic, religious and ethnic rights of the peoples and respect for their cultures, and full equality of all citizens with regard to political, civil and religious matters."

(8) "It shall be required, as a prior condition to independence, to incorporate in the future constitutional provisions applying to Palestine those basic principles of the Charter of the United Nations whereby a state shall (a) undertake to settle all international disputes in which it may be involved by peaceful means in such a manner that international peace and security, and justice, are not endangered; and (b) accept the obligation to refrain in its international relations from the threat or use of force against the territorial integrity or political independence of any state, or in any manner inconsistent with the purposes of the United Nations."

(9) "In appraising the various proposals for the solution of the Palestine question, it shall be accepted as a cardinal principle that the preservation of the economic unity of Palestine as a whole is indispensable to the life and development of the country and its peoples."

(10) "States whose nationals have in the past enjoyed in Palestine the privileges and immunities of foreigners, including the benefits of consular jurisdiction and protection as formerly enjoyed by capitulation or usage in the Ottoman Empire, [shall] be invited by the United Nations to renounce any right pertaining to them to the reestablishment of such privileges and immunities in an independent Palestine."

(11) "The General Assembly shall call on the peoples of Palestine to extend their fullest cooperation to the United Nations in its effort to devise and put into effect an equitable and workable means of settling the difficult situation prevailing there, and to this end, in the interest of peace, good order, and lawfulness, to exert every effort to bring to an early end the acts of violence which have for too long beset that country."

Each recommendation was accompanied by a detailed explanatory comment. Finally, UNSCOP submitted another piece of advice. "Recommendation 12" on "the Jewish problem in general" was not unanimous but was approved by a substantial majority (Guatemala and Uruguay dissented and Australia recorded no opinion). UNSCOP's 8 other members recommended that "in the appraisal of the Palestine question, it shall be accepted as incontrovertible that any solution for Palestine cannot be considered as a solution of the Jewish problem in general."

Majority Recommends Partition

The committee set up 2 small working groups to explore partition proposals. One was a working group on constitutional matters, the other a working group on boundaries. The partition plan was subsequently favored by 7 committee members, representing Canada, Czechoslovakia, Guatemala, the Netherlands, Peru, Sweden and Uruguay.

The "Plan of Partition with Economic Union" consisted of these 3 parts: partition with economic union; boundaries; the city of Jerusalem.

The plan's basic premises were that:

"(1) ... The claims to Palestine of the Arabs and Jews, both possessing validity, are irreconcilable, and that among all of the solutions advanced, partition will provide the most realistic and practicable settlement, and is the most likely to afford a workable basis for meeting in part the claims and national aspirations of both parties.

"(2) ... Both of these peoples have their historic roots in Palestine, and ... both make vital contributions to the economic and cultural life of the country.

"(3) The basic conflict in Palestine is a clash of 2 intense nationalisms.

"(4) Only by means of partition can these conflicting national aspirations find substantial expression.

"(5) The partition solution provides that finality which is a most urgent need in the solution.

"(6) Partition is based on a realistic appraisal of the actual Arab-Jewish relations in Palestine.

"(7) Partition is the only means available by which political and economic responsibility can be placed squarely on both Arabs and Jews.

"(8) Jewish immigration is the central issue in Palestine today and is the one factor, above all others, that rules out the necessary cooperation between the Arab and Jewish communities in a single state. The creation of a Jewish state under a partition scheme is the only hope of removing this issue from the arena of conflict."

Under partition, Palestine was to reorganize (within 2 years) into an independent Arab state, an independent Jewish state and the city of Jerusalem. During the transitional period, under UN supervision and by agreement with Britain, 150,000 Jewish immigrants at a uniform monthly rate were to be admitted into the borders of the proposed Jewish state, 30,000 of whom were to be admitted on humanitarian grounds. Should the transitional period continue for more than 2 years, immigration would be allowed at the rate of 60,000 per year. Restrictions on the transfer of land, instituted in 1939, would be lifted in the area of the proposed Jewish state.

Some economic unity between the 2 states was also recommended. This was to take the form of (a) a customs union, common currency and common management and operation of the railroads, interstate highways, postal and communications services and port facilities of Haifa and Jaffa, surplus revenues from all of which—after from 5% to 10% thereof went to the city of Jerusalem—would be shared equally; and (b) economic cooperation and collaboration in land reclamation, irrigation and soil conservation under a Joint Economic Board.

Provision was also made for liberty of transit and visiting on behalf of all residents and citizens of each state in the other state in Palestine and in the city of Jerusalem and for the preservation of, and free access to, the Holy Places and religious buildings.

The primary objectives of UNSCOP's majority plan were political division and economic unity. The plan divided the 2 states:

Arab state—Western Galilee would be bounded on the west by the Mediterranean and in the north by the frontier of Lebanon from Ras en Naqura to Qadas; on the east the boundary starting from Qadas would pass southwards, west of Safad to the southwestern corner of the Safad subdistrict; thence it would follow the western boundary of the Tiberias subdistrict to a point just east of Mount Tabor; thence southwards to the point of intersection southeast of Afula. The southwestern boundary of Western Galilee would take a line from this point, passing south of Nazareth and Shafr Amr, but north of Beit Lahm, to the coast just south of Acre.

The boundary of the hill country of Samaria and Judea starting on the Jordan River southeast of Beisan would follow the northern boundary of the Samaria district westwards to the point of intersection southeast of Afula, thence again westwards to Lajjun, thence in a southwestern direction, passing just west of Tulkarm, east of Qalqilia and west of Majdal Yaba, thence bulging westwards towards Rishon-le-Zion so as to include Lydda and Ramle in the Arab state, thence turning again eastwards to a point west of Latrun, thereafter following the northern side of the Latrun-Majdal road to the 2d point of intersection, thence southeastwards to a point on the Hebron subdistrict boundary south of Qubeiba, thence following the southern boundary of the Hebron subdistrict to the Dead Sea.

The Arab section of the coastal plain would run from a point a few miles north of Isdud to the Egyptian frontier, extending inland approximately 8 kilometers.

Jewish state—Eastern Galilee, the northeastern sector of the proposed Jewish state, would have frontiers with Lebanon in the north and west and with Syria and Transjordan on the east and would include the whole of the Huleh basin, Lake Tiberias and the whole of the Beisan subdistrict. From Beisan the Jewish state would extend northwest following the boundary described with respect to the Arab state.

The Jewish sector on the coastal plain would extend from a point south of Acre to just north of Isdud in the Gaza subdistrict and include the towns of Haifa, Tel Aviv and Jaffa. The eastern frontier of the Jewish state would follow the boundary described in regard to the Arab state.

The Beersheba area would include the whole of the Beersheba subdistrict, including the Negev and the eastern part of the Gaza subdistrict south of the point of intersection. The northern boundary of this area, from the point of intersection, would run southeastwards to a point on the Hebron subdistrict boundary south of Qubeiba, and thence follow the southern boundary of the Hebron subdistrict to the Dead Sea.

The majority recommendation called for the administration of Jerusalem, Bethlehem and some surrounding villages as a demilitarized area within the economic union of Palestine by the UN under a permanent trusteeship agreement. In the 2-year probationary period from Sept. 1, 1947 until the completion of the partition arrangements, Britain, either alone or jointly with one or more members of the UN, would administer Palestine under UN auspices.

Minority Recommendation: A Federal State

A minority of UNSCOP members opposed partition as impracticable, unworkable and pro-Zionist. The representatives of India, Iran and Yugoslavia argued that "the well-being of the country and its peoples as a whole" outweighed Jewish aspirations for a separate state. They proposed the development of the mandate, after a 3-year transitional UN-administration period, into an independent federal union comprising Arab and Jewish nation-states with Jerusalem as the common federal capital. The transitional government would be entrusted to an authority to be decided on by the UN General Assembly.

The area of the proposed Arab state would be greater than in the majority plan. It would include the port of Jaffa, the city of Beersheba and a strip of territory along the Egyptian border from the Mediterranean Sea to the Gulf of Aqaba. The Arab and the Jewish states would each be divided into 2 parts, neither of which would be contiguous. The southern part of the Jewish state would consist of parts of the Hebron and Beersheba sub-districts. The northern part would consist of a coastal area from Acre to Tel Aviv, the Plain of Esdraelon and the valleys of eastern Galilee.

Jewish immigration into the Jewish state would be permitted for 3 years—but not in such numbers as would exceed its absorptive capacity, and with due regard for the rights of the population already there and for their expected natural increase.

The jurisdiction of the state governments, under the minority plan, would cover interstate migration, education, taxation for local purposes, the right of residence and settlement, commercial licenses, grazing rights, punishment of crime, social institutions and services, public housing, public health, local roads, agriculture and local industries. Immigration, currency, interstate communications and transportation and matters of external relations and defense were to be under a federal government. Its legislature would be bicameral, with equal representation in one house and proportional representation in the other. Laws would be enacted by a majority in both houses. In case of a government deadlock in both houses, an issue in dispute was to be submitted to an arbitral body consisting of 5 people, including not fewer than 2 Arabs and 2 Jews.

The federal union would have a constitution containing guarantees of equal rights for all minorities in the 2 states, safeguards against discriminatory federal or state legislation and assurances of freedom of access to all holy places in Palestine. There would be a federal court of final appeal on all constitutional matters, with its minimum of 4 Arab and 3 Jewish members to be elected by both houses of the federal legislature. The legislature also would elect a federal head of state and deputy head of state, each identifiable as coming from the other of the country's 2 major communities.

Terrorism Continues

Incidents of terrorism continued in Palestine in spite of the UN's efforts to hasten a political solution. The violence greatly increased the strain already put on the authorities and the population. An unusual instance in mid-May 1947—the slaying of a Jew in the village of Fajja by an Arab gang—occasioned the first armed clash in 8 years between Palestinian Arabs and Jews. One Jew and one Arab were killed and 7 Arabs were wounded when an armed unit, believed to be of Haganah, attacked the village.

Jewish terrorists resumed operations after a military court in Jerusalem June 16 condemned 3 Jewish terrorists to be hanged for their part in the May 4 raid on Acre Prison. The Irgun Zvai Leumi was foiled May 18 by Zev Weber, a Haganah member, in an attempt to destroy the British military headquarters in Tel Aviv; Weber was killed trying to defuse detonators in a tunnel beneath a building opposite the headquarters.

Authorities in Jerusalem June 20 reported the escape of Maj. Roy Farran, a British army officer with the Palestine police, just after he had been received from the custody of Syrian authorities. Farran had been charged in the disappearance May 6 of Alexander Rubowitz, 17, an alleged member of the Stern Group. Terrorists, reportedly from the Stern Group, killed 3 British soldiers in Tel Aviv and one in

Haifa and wounded another in Haifa June 29. Both attacks had been made from autos and reportedly were in "reprisal" for Rubowitz' disappearance into a car in Jerusalem. Farran the same day surrendered voluntarily to Palestine authorities. Stern Group terrorists were blamed for another attack June 29 in which 4 British soldiers were wounded on a beach at Herzlia.

UNSCOP June 29 voted, 9-0, to condemn the outbreaks of terrorism as being in "flagrant disregard" of the UN General Assembly's May 15 appeal for an interim truce while UNSCOP gathered data in Palestine. After an appeal from relatives of the 3 condemned Jewish terrorists, UNSCOP June 22 adopted, 9-1 (Australia opposed), a resolution asking UN Secy. Gen. Trygve Lie to inform the British government of UNSCOP's opinion that the executions would have "possibly unfavorable repercussions." The mandatory government June 23 termed UNSCOP's resolution improper while the matter was still under judicial appeal. The British government July 1 rejected the appeal.

Lt. Gen. G. H. A. MacMillan, British military commander in Palestine, July 8 confirmed the death sentences pronounced June 16 on Irgun operatives Meyer Nakar, 21, Jacob Weiss, 23, and Absalom Habib, 20. The Irgun July 9 broadcast a warning that "we shall make our arrows drunk with the blood of the hangman" if the 3 were executed. Irgun members July 12 kidnaped 2 British army intelligence sergeants—Mervyn Paice, 43, of Bristol and Clifford Martin, 20, of Coventry—as they left a restaurant in the seaside town of Nathanya with a Jewish clerk, who was beaten unconscious. More than 5,000 troops and police began an intensive search for the 2 sergeants, and Nathanya was placed under military control.

British authorities July 29 executed Nakar, Weiss and Habib in Jerusalem. The bodies of Sgts. Paice and Martin were discovered July 31 hanging in a eucalyptus grove near Nathanya; they reportedly had been dead for at least one day before their bodies were found. The British officer in command of the search party suffered severe wounds from an explosive device wired to one of the dead men. In a note pinned to the other, and signed by an Irgun "tribunal," was written:

"2 British spies held in captivity since July 12 have been tried, after the completion of investigations into their criminal anti-Hebrew activities, on the following charges: illegal entry into the Hebrew homeland; membership in a British criminal terrorist organization known as the army of occupation, responsible for torture, murder, deportation and denying the Hebrew people the right to live; illegal possession of arms; anti-Jewish spying while in civilian clothes; premeditated hostile designs against the underground. Found guilty of these charges, they have been sentenced to hang and their appeal for clemency dismissed. This is not a reprisal for the execution of the 3 Jews but a routine judicial fact."

The Jewish Agency and the Vaad Leumi July 31 called a joint meeting and issued an appeal to "the Palestine Jewish community and the whole Jewish people to stand at our side in fighting this ghastly evil of terrorism." The 2 groups condemned the 2 sergeants' executioners as "a set of criminals ... impervious to the voice of conscience" and offered their "heartfelt sympathy to the relatives of the innocent victims of this horrible deed"—asking them "not to identify the Jewish people with the perpetrators of this foul murder."

Some British troops in armored cars drove into Tel Aviv the evening of July 31 and opened fire in several districts of the city. 5 Jews were killed—2 by a grenade thrown into a restaurant—and several injured before order was restored and military police took the soldiers into custody. The British later reported that none of the weapons mounted on the armored cars had been fired.

In other terrorist attacks during July: a British soldier was killed and 2 other soldiers wounded July 20 in a truck explosion near Nathanya; a British policeman and a Jewish civilian were shot and killed July 20 in Haifa; a Jewish boy of 10 was killed July 21 by a mine that exploded beneath a truck in Haifa; 6 Jews were wounded and one of them was captured July 21-22 in attacks on authorities in Jerusalem.

Terrorist outbreaks continued into August. One Jewish terrorist was killed and 2 suspected terrorists taken prisoner Aug. 1 in an attack on a British army barracks in Jerusalem. Terrorists held up the Barclays Bank branch in Haifa Aug. 4, killed a Jewish bank official and escaped with £1,300 (about $6,240).

Striking at dawn Aug. 5, British security forces arrested 35 leading Zionists in Palestine and sent them to the Latrun detention camp in an attempt to wipe out the Irgun leadership. In reprisal, Irgun terrorists blew up the headquarters building of the mandatory Labor Department in Jerusalem, and 3 British police constables perished in the explosion.

Those arrested in the British raid included Mayor Israel Rokach of Tel Aviv, holder of the honor of Commander of the British Empire—who suffered a heart attack after being placed under house arrest—Mayor Oved Ben Ami of Nathanya and Mayor Abraham Krinitzki of Ramat Gan. All 3 had signed the *yishuv*'s resolution of July 31 pledging cooperation with the British against the terrorists. Rokach and Krinitzki were released Sept. 11.

Acts of terrorism recurred continually in the 3 months before the announcement Nov. 16 of the first stage of Britain's withdrawal from Palestine. Among developments reported:

● The Cairo-Haifa express was derailed and its Jewish engineer killed Aug. 9.

● At least 23 persons perished in communal disorders that broke out Aug. 11 in the border area between Arab Jaffa and Jewish Tel Aviv and continued for 4 days: Arab terrorists Aug. 11 attacked a Jewish cafe near Tel Aviv, stabbing 3 Jewish men, one Jewish woman and one Arab to death and wounding 8 other persons. One Arab was stabbed to death during retaliatory attacks by both sides Aug. 13. One Jew and 4 Arabs died in further clashes Aug. 14. A Haganah group Aug. 15 attacked an Arab house in an orange grove between Tel Aviv and Petah Tiqva, killed 4 Arabs with gunfire and then blew up the house; 4 Arab children and their 4 parents died inside. In a Kol Yisrael broadcast that day, Haganah identified the house as the headquarters of an Arab gang.

● Sami Taha, secretary-general of the Arab Labor Federation and a prominent Arab moderate, was assassinated in Haifa Sept. 12 by armed men who fired from a passing auto and sped away. Taha had clashed with the ex-grand mufti of Jerusalem and with other Palestinian Arab groups on Arab policy in Palestine and had been attacked in Arab-language newspapers for his moderate opinions.

• Jewish terrorists raided the Barclays Bank branch in Tel Aviv Sept. 26 and escaped with £45,000 (about $216,000) after killing 4 British policemen in the street outside.

• The Irgun took responsibility for blowing up the mandatory police headquarters in Haifa Sept. 29 and said that the terrorist act was in retaliation for the deportation of Jewish immigrants to Germany and Cyprus. 4 British and 4 Arab policemen and 2 Arab civilians were killed and 51 persons, including Jewish civilians, were injured in the blast.

• Authorities took measures Oct. 14 to protect foreign consulates in Jerusalem after an explosion Oct. 13 in the garden of the U.S. general consulate slightly injured 2 women employes. (An attempt had been made Sept. 27 on the Swedish consulate.) The attacks were believed made by Arabs in protest against support given by the U.S., Sweden, Czechoslovakia and Poland (whose consulates also were threatened) to UN proposals for Palestine's partition.

• Members of the Stern Group Nov. 3 raided a police station in Tel Aviv, shot to death a Jewish policeman, seriously wounded a British policeman and released 2 Jewish prisoners. Terrorists in Jerusalem Nov. 3 shot a Jewish detective to death.

• Jewish terrorists Nov. 12 shot 2 British police officers to death and wounded another seated at a sidewalk cafe in Haifa. Elsewhere, British troops and police surprised a group of young Jews receiving instructions in the use of weapons from Stern Group operatives at a farm near Raanana outside Tel Aviv. 2 of the young men and 3 young women died in the gun battle that ensued.

• Terrorists attacked a cafe filled with British troops on King George Avenue, Jerusalem, Nov. 13. 7 soldiers were killed there and a policeman was killed from ambush outside. In a shooting in Haifa, gunmen killed 2 British civilians and wounded 2 others.

• 4 British soldiers were killed from ambush by terrorists Nov. 14—2 in Jerusalem and 2 in Tel Aviv. Terrorists wounded a British police sergeant in an attack on a Jerusalem barracks.

• Armed terrorists shot 5 Arabs to death and seriously wounded another Nov. 15 in an attack on an Arab settlement at Raanana near Tel Aviv.

● Stern Group terrorists Nov. 20 executed 4 Arabs near
Raanana in reprisal for the deaths of the 5 Jewish youths in the
gunfight near there Nov. 12. Arabs retaliated by wounding 5
Jews on a bus near Tel Aviv Nov. 20. Unknown terrorists Nov.
22 killed an Arab in Haifa.

Illegal Immigration Attempts

Palestine immigration authorities continued, with the help
of British naval forces, to thwart until mid-Nov. 1947 all
known efforts of Jewish refugees to enter the country illegally.
The most publicized of these attempts was that involving the
1,814-ton American vessel *President Warfield,* renamed *Exodus
1947* after being put into Haganah hands.

The ship arrived without any passengers Apr. 24 at the
Italian port of Spezia across the Gulf of Genoa from southern
France. After Italian authorities prevented any Jewish immigrants from going aboard, *Exodus* took on 4,554 immigrants
at the French Mediterranean port of Cette and proceeded July
11 ostensibly to Colombia but actually to Palestine. The *Exodus*
was overtaken July 18 by British vessels and boarded after a 3-
hour fight in which 2 immigrants and the *Exodus'* first mate,
William Bernstein, 24, of New York, were killed, more than 30
persons injured and the *Exodus* and the British vessels
damaged.

The *Exodus* reached Haifa July 19, and its remaining
passengers were put aboard 3 British prison ships—the *Ocean
Valour,* the *Ocean Vigour* and the *Runnymede Park*—for
transshipment to Cyprus. The *Exodus'* surviving crew and
captain, Bernard Marks, 25, also an American, were arrested.
It was reported later that British Foreign Secy. Ernest Bevin
had said he would "make an example of this ship."

The Palestinian government announced officially July 21
that the *Exodus'* 4,529 healthy passengers were being sent not
to Cyprus but back to France. As a precaution, the mandatory
authorities first placed Jerusalem's 90,000 Jews under nightly
house arrest. Haganah in retaliation July 23 sank the British
transport *Empire Lifeguard* as it was discharging 300
immigrants being admitted to Palestine under the monthly
quota from Cyprus. The British refloated the ship.

When the 3 British prison ships reached Port-de-Bouc west of Marseilles July 29, the immigrants refused to debark and only a few, who were ill, were put ashore. The French government informed the refugees that all who chose to enter France would be welcome. The French National Assembly July 30 resolved to ask Britain to solve the "tragic affair" urgently and humanely and congratulated Premier Paul Ramadier for refusing to force the Jews ashore. French groups began sending food and medicine aboard.

Despite British attempts to frighten the refugees off the ships with stories that they would be shipped "far away," only 82 debarked from the steaming holds. Finally, the British gave the refugees until 6 p.m. Aug. 22 to leave the ships or sail for Germany, "the only territory under British jurisdiction outside Cyprus where such a large number of people can be adequately housed and fed at short notice." The refugees still aboard rejected the British ultimatum, and the ships set sail for Hamburg 20 minutes after the deadline had passed. The 3 ships discharged the refugees—many of them forcibly—at the port of Hamburg Sept. 8 and 9. They were interned at Poppendorf camp near Luebeck, where they asserted to British interrogators that they were from "Palestine."

U.S. State Secy. George C. Marshall disclosed Sept. 10 in Washington that the U.S. had urged Britain to reconsider sending the refugees to Germany but that Britain had replied that there were no facilities for housing them elsewhere. The British Foreign Office later acknowledged, however, that the refugees could have been accommodated at Cyprus.

Attempts to land illegal immigrants were made from time to time during the fall of 1947 by several ships.

2 vessels, the *Bruna* and *Louisiana,* were intercepted by the British navy off Haifa July 28 and boarded without incident. The immigrants (some 1,200) were shipped to Cyprus. A converted tank-landing craft, the *Farida,* was intercepted Sept. 27 off Haifa with 470 persons from central Europe aboard. The vessel was brought into port after a scuffle in which one immigrant offering resistance to the boarding party was shot to death and several others were wounded. 2 more ships, the *Northlands* and *Paducah* (each from a Rumanian port and flying the Panamanian flag), were boarded off Haifa Oct. 2, and the 3,850 immigrants aboard were sent to Cyprus. Another

vessel, the schooner *Kadimah,* was brought into Haifa Nov. 16 with some 500 men, women and children aboard.

A small launch, the *Aliyah,* was found the same day, however, on the shore between Acre and the Lebanese border. It was surmised that an estimated 150-200 immigrants aboard had reached Jewish settlements in Galilee.

Arab Discontent

The UN General Assembly's political committee recognized the Arab Higher Committee May 8, 1947 as the sole political spokesman for the Arab community in Palestine. This development followed assurances by Sir Alexander Cadogan, Britain's UN delegate, that the group was representative of the Palestinian Arab people's views. Higher Committee leaders thereupon described the Arab people of Palestine as increasingly dissatisfied with UN measures taken in regard to Palestine.

Jewish liaison personnel and journalists accompanying UNSCOP after mid-June were not permitted to visit certain Arab establishments or municipalities. Arab communities in Haifa, Jaffa and Jerusalem held mass demonstrations in mid-June, and the ex-grand mufti, in a message to his followers, declared that "Zionists must not have an inch of this country." Deputy Chairman Jamal el-Husseini of the Higher Committee warned July 6 that revolt would be inevitable unless the Palestinian Arab struggle for independence succeeded and the UN gave the Arabs justice. In mid-August there occurred the week-long series of clashes in the Jaffa-Tel Aviv area.

UN DEBATE: THE PARTITION RESOLUTION

Views Aired Before Session

Arab and Jewish reactions to UNSCOP's recommendations were aired before the opening Sept. 16 of the UN General Assembly's 2d regular session.

Arab League Secy. Gen. Abdul Rahman Azzam Pasha charged in New York Sept. 1 that UNSCOP was displaying a pro-Zionist bias. He served notice that favorable General Assembly action on either the majority or the minority recommendations would lead to war in the Middle East that would probably develop into a world conflict. The Arab Higher Committee Sept. 8 in a statement from UN headquarters called both plans absurd, impracticable and unjust. It warned the UN that "not a single Jew will be allowed to migrate to Palestine" and that the "Arabs will fight to the last man to defend their country, to defend its integrity and to preserve it as an Arab country." The Zionist Inner General Council Sept. 3, meeting in Zurich, Switzerland, expressed satisfaction with the partition proposal but reserved judgment until after the General Assembly had made its decision.

Meanwhile, the Arabs registered a gain in voting strength with the admission Aug. 18 of Yemen and Pakistan to the UN.

The General Assembly, anticipating a stormy debate, agreed in plenary session Sept. 23 to the UN Secretariat's suggestion to refer the Palestine question to a special committee consisting of all the UN member-states. The General Assembly adopted this course of action by 29-11 vote, with 6 abstentions; the Arab states strongly opposed it. Gen. Nuri Pasha as-Said, ex-premier of Iraq, declared that the matter was of such a serious nature that it should be studied at the top level—*i.e.,* by the Political & Security Committee—instead of by an *ad hoc* committee. The new *ad hoc* Palestine Committee held 14 meetings within 24 days and heard representatives of both the Arab Higher Committee and the Jewish Agency.

Britain Asks for Mandate's End

British Colonial Secy. Arthur Creech Jones told the UN's *ad hoc* committee Sept. 26 that Britain had decided to relinquish its mandate over Palestine at an early but unspecified future date. The British would leave Palestine accordingly, regardless of whether the UN solved the Palestine problem, Creech Jones said. Britain would not undertake to impose any settlement not agreeable to both Jews and Arabs, he added. He declined to indorse UNSCOP's proposals.

Creech Jones added his hope that "the UN may have more success than Britain ... in persuading the 2 peoples to cooperate in attaining their independence." "If, however, no basis of consent for settlement can be found, ... any recommendations made by the General Assembly should be accompanied by a clear definition of the means by which they are to be carried out," he said.

Lt. Gen. Sir Alan Cunningham, the high commissioner for Palestine, in a statement to the foreign press in Jerusalem Oct. 8, reinforced Creech Jones' warning by stressing that British evacuation would take place even if the Arabs and Jews failed to reach prior agreement on the independence of Palestine and even if the departure of Britain involved economic chaos and possibly bloodshed.

Deputy Chairman Jamal el-Husseini of the Arab Higher Committee put the Palestinian Arab case before the *ad hoc* committee Sept. 29. The Arabs would oppose "to the last drop of their blood" any scheme for partitioning Palestine, he said. Husseini rejected both the majority and minority reports of UNSCOP; the Higher Committee's basic position comprised "3 nos"—no partition, no further Jewish immigration and no Jewish state—he said. The "one and only course" open to the Palestinian Arabs was the establishment of an independent democratic Arab state covering Palestine entirely, he added.

"The Arabs of Palestine are solidly determined to oppose with all the means at their disposal any scheme that provides for the dissection, segregation or partition of their tiny country, or that gives to a minority, on the ground of creed, special and preferential rights or status," Husseini asserted. "They will oppose such schemes with the same zeal and with the same sacrifice as any other people would do under the same circumstances. We are alive to the fact that if they so desire the big powers could, by brute force, crush such opposition." Husseini continued: "The Arab communities in the Middle East are a homogeneous whole. It would be illogical for the United Nations to try to weaken this homogeneity by introducing an alien body such as a Jewish state. If such a political monstrosity were carried out, no sane person could expect to see peace prevail in that part of the world. It would become a new Balkans." The Zionist movement was "an invasion" of Palestine, a land "not theirs by birthright." The UN, whose *"raison d'etre* ... is to assist self-defense against aggression," was duty-bound to uphold the Palestinian Arabs' cause, which the Arabs would not forsake—even if it came to bloodshed.

Husseini stressed that Palestine could not physically absorb into its area, about that of Vermont or Wales, any more people. He said: Even without immigration, the natural rate of increase alone would double the population within 20 years, making a density of 400 persons per square mile—even though more than half the land was uncultivable. On the other hand, both Uganda and Birobidzhan (the capital of the Jewish autonomous area of the Habarovsk territory in Soviet Siberia) welcomed Jewish settlement. The Zionists coveted "the strategic position of Palestine that neither Uganda nor Birobidzhan possesses."

Dr. Abba Hillel Silver appeared before the *ad hoc* committee Oct. 2 as American section chairman of the Jewish Agency executive and said that the Agency "most reluctantly" accepted the UNSCOP plan for partition as "one of the sacrifices aimed at finding a way out of the present intolerable impasse." He characterized the proposed area of the projected Jewish state, however, as constituting a "serious attenuation" of Jewish rights.

In accepting UNSCOP's partition proposals, Silver took it as understood that the Jewish state "must have in its own hands those instruments of economic and financial control necessary to carry out large-scale immigration and related economic development." Silver said that the *yishuv* was ready for immediate independence and proposed that its underground army, Haganah, be authorized to help keep order if the UN should decree a transitional period under recommendations outlined by UNSCOP.

In a gesture of reconciliation toward the Palestinian Arabs, Hillel said: "Sincerely and without reservation, we offer peace and friendship.... If it is met with the same spirit, rich and abundant blessings will redound to all. If not, we shall be compelled to ... defend our rights to the utmost."

A general debate on UNSCOP's recommendations opened Oct. 4 in the *ad hoc* committee. Camille Chamoun of Lebanon called the partition scheme an injustice to the Arabs and contrary to the spirit of the UN Charter. Iraqi Foreign Min. Mohammad Fadhil Jamali accused the U.S. of sending American "men, money, arms and ships to Palestine for terrorism and illegal immigration." He appealed to the U.S. government to close "schools" allegedly set up in the U.S. for instructing Zionists in "terrorism and warfare."

Jamali also made a philosophical distinction between the religion of Jews and the political philosophy of Zionism—one of a long series of such distinctions made by Arab leaders: "Judaism is a world religion but Zionism is a political movement of an aggressive and virulent nature which has nothing to do with Palestine except in its aim to penetrate the Middle East, using Palestine as the gate. Zionism is one of those 'isms' which has a good deal of fanaticism and chauvinism. Practically it follows the same methods of propaganda and of aggression and penetration as those of the Nazis. Zionists are invoking the principle that historical relation with a country gives the right to possession. This cannot stand universal application and acceptance. To accept it universally would mean chaos, disturbance, and struggle all over the world. Palestine for the Palestinians, and the Palestinians alone, is the only right approach to the solution of the problem of Palestine."

Panama and Uruguay favored partition, Pakistan opposed it. Poland urged that the UN encourage immediate Jewish mass immigration into Palestine. Egypt termed the Arabs "implacably opposed" to Zionism. Czechoslovakia appealed to both sides to achieve an equitable compromise—as did El Salvador and Colombia.

Czechoslovak Foreign Min. Jan Masaryk described UNSCOP's report as coming "nearer [than previous efforts such as the Morrison and Bevin plans] to giving at least partial satisfaction to both parties' natural claims and to the possibility of their being realized." In a personal aside, he added: "I confess without any feeling of shame but, rather, with a slight feeling of pride, that I helped many Jews get to Palestine. I know nothing about pipelines [an allusion to Anglo-Arabian oil interests that feared their rights of way would be jeopardized by the acceptance of any of UNSCOP's recommendations], but one pipeline I have watched with horror all my life. It is the pipeline through which for centuries Jewish blood has flowed sporadically, but with a horrible incessant stream from 1933 to 1945. I am not thinking of the Jews living in comfort and security. I am thinking of the ghetto Jews, of the gas-chamber Jews who are still in concentration camps and whose only crime is that they happen to be members of an old and proud race."

Faris el-Khoury of Syria said that the Jews had been "aggressors and marauders" when they invaded Palestine in biblical times. "The Jews are not a race," he held, "and only a small portion of them can claim to be the children of Israel or even Semites. There are European Jews, Slavs and others. The Arabs of Palestine will not give up their homeland to aliens from the 4 corners of the world." Khoury assailed U.S. support for the partition plan as a move to win Jewish votes in the next Presidential election.

Dr. Jorge Granados of Guatemala, a member of UNSCOP, proposed that during the transitional period, after the British withdrawal, Palestine be policed by an international force supplied by the smaller powers; he also urged that the Arab port of Jaffa be transferred to the Arab states. He attacked the ex-grand mufti of Jerusalem, whom he called a man "at once amazing and abominable" and whom he accused of helping to organize the pro-German revolt in Iraq in 1941. Granados also criticized the British administration in Palestine. He charged that "certain officials in the British administration have adopted towards the whole Jewish community a hostile attitude akin to anti-Semitism."

Mrs. Vijaya Lakshmi Pandit of India said that since Palestine was predominantly Arab, the problem could be solved only through the establishment of an Arab state, with full democratic rights for the Jewish minority.

American support for partition was expressed Oct. 11 by Rep.-to-UN Herschel V. Johnson, who said that the U.S. government supported the basic principles of the UNSCOP majority report. Certain modifications to that report were necessary, however, Johnson said. He held that Jaffa should be in the Arab state, not in the Jewish state. He reported that the U.S. was willing to participate in a UN program aimed at reaching a workable political settlement in Palestine, a solution that "might require the establishment of a special constabulary or police force recruited on a volunteer basis by the United Nations."

Soviet Delegate Semen K. Tsarapkin Oct. 13 voiced approval of the UNSCOP majority report favoring partition and economic cooperation. Tsarapkin held that both the Arabs and the Jews had the right to self-determination. He said: "The creation of a Jewish state is an urgent problem. ... The plan proposed by the minority has its advantages inasmuch as it is based on the idea of a single Arab-Jewish state. But under present circumstances, when relations between Arabs and Jews have reached such a pitch of tension that conciliation has become impossible, the minority proposal apparently cannot be put into practice." Tsarapkin advocated the establishment of a special committee to deal with border disputes.

Canada, South Africa and New Zealand also approved partition. Saudi Arabia opposed it. Argentina held that the only legal solution was the free determination of the future of Palestine by the inhabitants of the country.

Concluding Arguments

Jamal el-Husseini, deputy chairman of the Arab Higher Committee, made a final presentation of the Palestinian Arabs' case Oct. 18; Moshe Shertok and Chaim Weizmann did the same for the *yishuv*.

Husseini contended that Rabbi Silver, "the spokesman for the Jewish Agency, glided over the important fact that the eastern Jews, known as the Sephardim, may be the descendants of Israel [but that] the Ashkenazim, the east European Yiddish-speaking Jews who created the Zionist movement, have no ethnic connection with Israel and, subsequently, with Palestine. The Ashkenazim, who are on the whole the sponsors and supporters of the Zionist movement, had neither historic nor ethnic connection with either the Holy Land or the Israelites, who were residents of that country 2,000 years or more ago." Husseini asserted that the Ashkenazi Jews originally were "Khazars—a people of Turkish origin whose life and history are interwoven with the very beginnings of the history of the Jews of Russia." He tried to identify the 2 by citing the *Jewish Encyclopaedia's* definition of the Khazars. "They want to repatriate the descendants of the Khazars to a land in which the Khazars never set foot," he maintained. Husseini also said:

• "The Arab inhabitants of Palestine are those people who have clung to its soil. They are mostly Arabs by blood. They speak Arabic, and they have the same traditions and culture as those Arabs who achieved the Arab conquest of Palestine.... Now a new horde is invading Palestine under the name of Zionists, with the intention of uprooting its Arab inhabitants in order to take their place."

• The Arabs cultivated citrus fruits and dug the first artesian wells before the advent of Jewish immigrants. The Arabs owned 52% of the citrus groves and more than 90% of the olive groves. Not the Zionists but the Supreme Moslem Council had brought about the reclamation of most of Palestine's swamp lands. On the whole, despite lack of funds (which made Arab-worked land look less attractive than Jewish-worked land), the Arab agricultural achievements were economically sound.

• "The Zionists secured the best lands in Palestine, mainly from non-Palestinian absentee landlords, when no legislation existed for the protection of tenants or small farmers. Under the British mandate we have witnessed the forcible eviction of Arab tenants who lived on those lands for generations. We have seen not a few of them die on the land before they were forced to quit."

• "None of these lands were deserts which were brought to blossom by the hands of Zionists. The Plain of Sharon, the Valley of Jezreel and the Plain of Esdraelon have always been under cultivation and were never desert."

Husseini discussed the political aspirations of his countrymen: "The question for us, after all, is not one of bread and butter. It is one of much higher issues. It is with our liberties, our freedom, our independence, our national existence, and the future of our children that we are concerned. These cannot be measured by, or bartered for, pounds or dollars."

"The right of self-determination in Palestine is our right, and we shall stick to it as long as it is the basis of the UN Charter.... With the antagonism of the 70 million Arabs of the Arab world and hundreds of millions of people of the Orient who support the Arabs' just and lawful defense of their own country against the Jewish invasion, a small Jewish state of one million people in the heart of this Arab world can have no chance of survival. If it is to survive by permanent foreign support it is bound to become a running sore that will continue to affect adversely the international relations of many countries in the Middle East.... If it is thought that the Arab of Palestine, as a little child who is forced by his mother to take a bitter pill, will object a little, kick a little, and then give way to a melting candy in his mouth, may I solemnly declare that this is a dangerously fallacious illusion."

Husseini dismissed, as irrelevant, Rabbi Silver's claim on the Jews' behalf to "Palestine as their home for many years before the Balfour Declaration." "Many people may be physically or morally homeless and may covet the homes of others, but neither homelessness nor love can give a right to possess the homes of others," he said. "We all know that the Jews are greatly divided on Zionism.... One of the greatest Jews of modern times, the late Henry Morgenthau [U.S. ambassador to Turkey 1913-6], denounced Zionism in the following terms: 'Zionism is the most stupendous fallacy in Jewish history. It is wrong in principle, impossible of realization, unsound in its economics, fantastic in its politics and sterile in its spiritual ideals.'"

Moshe Shertok spoke for the Jewish Agency. He pointed out that the Agency found itself at a serious disadvantage in relation to its Arab counterpart since it alone represented the Jewish people at the UN while the Palestinian Arabs had all the Arab states to speak for them. The Arabs, he charged, had released an inexhaustible barrage of political attack and factual misrepresentation. The 2 focal points of the issue were, "first, that Palestine is the only country in which the Jewish people can hope to attain a secure home and a national status on equal footing with other independent nations; and, 2d, that the Arabs of Palestine are not a people in themselves but a fraction of a much larger unit, amply secure in the possession of vast areas and in enjoyment of full-fledged sovereignty and independence."

"The purpose of the mandates for Syria and Iraq was to prepare the countries for independence; the primary purpose of the Palestine mandate was to promote the establishment of the Jewish national home," Shertok declared. In an attack on Sir Mohammed Zafrulla Khan, the Pakistani delegate, who had spoken against Jewish immigration and partition, Shertok said that such Arab leaders as King Hussein of Hejaz and his son the Emir Feisal had indorsed Jewish settlement in Palestine, recognizing the country as the Jewish homeland.* Out of the 57 members of the UN, 47 had been members of the League of Nations—with Egypt and Iraq among them—and all, including the 2 Arab states, had indorsed the Palestine mandate, Shertok noted.

Most of the independent Arab states owed their independence to their alliance with Britain during World War I, Shertok continued. "The pledge to grant the Arabs independence in large areas and the setting aside of Palestine for the Jewish people were organic parts of the same war settlements." In World War II "the only community in the Middle East which really fought in the war and which had its heart in the fighting were the Jews of Palestine." This war aid was rewarded "by a regime in Palestine which inflicted untold suffering on the Jewish survivors of the European tragedy." "We claim the application of a [UN] Charter principle to the case of the Jewish people," he said—apparently referring to the determination "to establish conditions under which justice and respect for the obligations arising from treaties and other sources of international law can be maintained."

---

* Hussein wrote in *Al Qibla* (Mecca) Mar. 23, 1918: "We saw the Jews ... streaming to Palestine from Russia, Germany, Austria, Spain, America.... The cause of causes could not escape those who had the gift of deeper insight; they knew that the country was for its original sons, for all their differences, a sacred and beloved homeland." Feisal and Chaim Weizmann Jan. 3, 1919 had concluded an agreement indorsing the Balfour Declaration and recognizing Palestine as a separate Jewish entity with which the projected Arab state would maintain diplomatic relations provided that Arab demands in other territories were met by Britain and France.

Responding to Arab accusations that no Jewish race existed, Shertok said that "Hitler and the [ex-]mufti [of Jerusalem] were not in the least bothered about the origin of the Jews whose doom they decreed."

The "racial land law which prevents Arabs from selling to us and [Jews] from buying land in most parts of Palestine" vitiated against both Jewish and Arab development, Shertok claimed. Placing the Negev—45% of the area of Palestine, with less than 5% of its population—in the Jewish state would benefit both Jews and Arabs alike, he held. "That Palestine will continue to be inhabited by Jews and Arabs we regard as a decree of history," Shertok added. "The Jewish Agency has already stated that it regards the area proposed for the Jewish state in the majority report, with certain modifications, ... as constituting the indispensable minimum."

Jewish Agency Chairman Chaim Weizmann began his address Oct. 18 with an argument against the Arab contention that Jews were not a nation. He said: "I was rather somewhat amazed to learn that I am not a Jew, that I am a Khazar, a Tartar, a Turk—anything but a Jew. I feel like a Jew, I suffer like a Jew, and I am still a Jew in spite of the previous speaker's argument."

Weizmann said: He had consistently advocated partition as representing the only practical compromise. He had accepted for the Jews settlement "in $\frac{1}{8}$ of the area in which the national home was to be established by international consent." Partition was the "inevitable ... consummation of the mandate." Yet the "main justification, the main necessity for a Jewish state" arose from the facts. A community of 700,000 confronted another group at "a different stage of development" but numerically superior. It had either to be independent or to remain a minority, under Arab rule. The latter alternative had been rejected by past commissions and tribunals. "The idea that a national home can ever be equated with a minority position in an Arab state deserves no further consideration at all; it would burst out of such an unnatural framework."

Weizmann, rebuking the equation of Zionism with Nazism made by the representatives of Syria and Iraq, said: "Of course I do not dispute the right of those 2 gentlemen to speak with some authority and intimacy on the nature of Nazism. I cannot rival their contacts in that field."

Weizmann concluded with a scriptural quotation: "The Lord shall set his hand again the 2d time to recover the remnants of his people. And he shall set up an ensign for the nations and shall assemble the outcast of Israel and gather together the depressed of Judah from the 4 corners of the earth."

The *ad hoc* committee Oct. 23 assigned the task of modifying UNSCOP's majority proposal in the light of objections raised in the debate to a subcommittee of 10 supporters of partition under the chairmanship of Polish Representative Pruszynski. The other countries represented were the U.S., the Soviet Union, Czechoslovakia, Guatemala, Haiti, Peru, South Africa, Uruguay and Venezuela. A 2d subcommittee, chaired by Sir Mohammed Zafrulla Khan of Pakistan and comprising 6 Arab states (Transjordan not being a UN member) and Afghanistan, Pakistan and Colombia, was charged with the task of formulating a plan for a unitary Palestine state out of UNSCOP's minority report and the proposals submitted by Saudi Arabia, Iraq and Syria. A 3d subcommittee, on conciliation, failed to reduce the areas of disagreement.

U.S. Representative Herschel Johnson suggested at a closed-door session of the first subcommittee Oct. 31 that the new Arab and Jewish states become independent by June 1, 1948, should the General Assembly approve the partition of Palestine. He proposed that Britain continue to be responsible in the interim period for law and order. He recommended further that a 3-man UN mission go to Palestine, in the event of a favorable decision on partition, to help advise the 2 new countries in collaboration with the British authorities. Johnson also suggested that both Jews and Arabs form "shadow" governments in the interim period with power to recruit and arm their own security forces.

Big 2 Agree on Partition

UN diplomacy helped in the achievement during the first part of November of a Soviet-American agreement on the implementation of the partition plan.

Semen Tsarapkin presented the Soviet proposals. The Kremlin recommended to the UN *ad hoc* committee the termination of the mandate by Jan. 1, 1948 and the assumption by the Security Council thereafter of responsibility for order during a transitional period of no longer than one year. The Kremlin also urged that all British troops be withdrawn from Palestine within 3 to 4 months after the termination of the mandate and proposed that the new UN Palestine Committee (headed by Dr. Herbert Evatt of Australia) demarcate the borders of the Arab and Jewish states and appoint provisional councils of government for both states. These provisional councils, under the Security Council's direction and with the approval of the *ad hoc* committee, would organize elections for constituent assemblies that would set up democratic central and local governments. The provisional councils also would set up armed militias of citizens capable of maintaining internal order and preventing border clashes. Finally, each militia would have its own chief of staff; both chiefs would be under the political control of the Security Council during the transition period.

The *ad hoc* committee set up a working group of representatives of the U.S., the USSR, Canada and Guatemala in an effort to draw up a draft for general acceptance. These countries had put forward their own plans for implementing the partition decision. Apart from the U.S. plan and the Soviet plans, already outlined, there were a Guatemalan plan for an international police force (excluding the big powers) to implement partition and Canadian proposals presented Nov. 8 by Lester Pearson.

Ottawa recommended that Britain hand over the mandate to the UN by Jan. 1, 1948 but continue to administer Palestine until the Arab and Jewish states were ready to set up their own governments. Canada further suggested 3 optional ways under which partition could be supervised: (1) a full committee comprising all 11 members of the Security Council, (2) a smaller committee of the Council, or (3) an *ad hoc* committee of the General Assembly that would answer to the Council.

This 8-point agreement was reached Nov. 10 by Washington and the Kremlin after closed Soviet-U.S. discussions in New York:

(1) The mandate would terminate May 1, 1948, and all British forces would be withdrawn by that date.

(2) The independent Arab and Jewish states would come into existence July 1, 1948, or such earlier date after May 1, 1948, as might be recommended by the UN *ad hoc* Palestine Committee and approved by the Security Council.

(3) A commission consisting of 3 to 5 representatives of the powers favoring partition would be appointed by the General Assembly.

(4) This commission would implement measures recommended by the General Assembly.

(5) The commission would help Britain terminate its functions under the mandate.

(6) The commission would be responsible for Palestine's administration from the termination of the mandate until the new states had been set up.

(7) The commission would act under the Security Council's authority and guidance and follow recommendations and instructions from the Council and the General Assembly.

(8) The commission would submit monthly progress reports to the Security Council.

British Delegate-to-UN Sir Alexander Cadogan issued a statement Nov. 13 on his government's behalf. He said:

There are 2 aspects of the withdrawal, the military and the civil. On the military side every effort is being made to reduce to a minimum the period required for the operation. It is not possible to foresee exactly how long it will take to withdraw from Palestine not only the troops but their very substantial supplies and equipment. I am authorized to state, however, that our authorities have been directed to plan for the evacuation to be completed by Aug. 1, 1948. So long as British troops remain in any part of Palestine, they must of course maintain law and order in the areas of which they are still in occupation. I am instructed, however, to make it clear that British troops would not be available as the instrument for the enforcement of a settlement in Palestine against either Arabs or Jews.

The fact that it would be impracticable to withdraw the last military contingents from Palestine before next summer does not imply that we shall continue to maintain a civil administration in Palestine throughout the intervening period. On the contrary, we reserve the right to lay down the mandate and bring our civil administration to an end at any time after it has become evident that no settlement acceptable to both Jews and Arabs has been reached by the Assembly. In that event there would be an interval between the termination of the mandate and the withdrawal of the last British troops. During that interval his majesty's government would no longer maintain a civil administration in Palestine, and would confine themselves to preserving order in areas still controlled by their remaining forces. It follows that if a UN commission were at work in Palestine, taking preparatory steps for a settlement which would require enforcement, it must not expect British authorities either to exercise administrative responsibility or to maintain law and order except in the limited areas in which they would remain in occupation during the process of withdrawal.

Yishuv Waives Jaffa

The UN's *ad hoc* Palestine Committee, acting on the proposal by U.S. Representative Herschel Johnson, agreed Nov. 12 that Jaffa, originally assigned to the Jewish state, would be included in the Arab state, since its population was almost wholly Arab. Moshe Shertok raised no objection and promised freedom of transit between Jaffa (which would form an Arab enclave in the Jewish state) and the Arab state proper.

Working Group's Proposals

The 4-Power Working Group agreed Nov. 17 on a method of carrying out the partition of Palestine. It left the status of Jerusalem and a final decision on the Negev for later consideration, however. The working group, comprising Canada, Guatemala, the USSR and the U.S., submitted these 12 proposals to the *ad hoc* committee Nov. 18:

(1) The mandate would terminate at a date—not later than Aug. 1, 1948—to be agreed on by the *ad hoc* committee and Britain.

(2) Britain would advise the commission as far in advance as possible of its intention to evacuate its forces progressively from each area of Palestine.

(3) Independent Arab and Jewish states would come into existence not later than Oct. 1, 1948; special provision would be made for Jerusalem.

(4) There would be a transitional period between adoption by the General Assembly of recommendations on the question of Palestine and the establishment of the 2 independent states.

(5) The General Assembly would appoint a commission consisting of Guatemala, Iceland, Norway, Poland and Uruguay.

(6) The commission would administer Palestine during the transitional period in conformity with the recommendations of the General Assembly under the guidance of the Security Council. The commission would have power to regulate and legislate as required for the sake of order in Palestine.

(7) The commission would choose and establish in each state a provisional council of government after consultation with democratic parties and other public organizations in the Arab and Jewish states. The commission would supervise the activities of both Arab and Jewish provisional councils.

(8) Subject to these recommendations, the provisional councils would have full authority in the areas under their control, including authority over immigration and land regulation, during the remainder of the transitional period.

(9) The provisional councils would have full responsibility for the administration of Palestine between the termination of the mandate (no later than Aug. 1, 1948) and the establishment of the 2 independent states (by Oct. 1, 1948).

(10) The provisional councils, under the UN commission's supervision, would organize the administrative systems of central and local governments.

(11) The provisional councils would recruit within the shortest time possible from the residents of their states armed militias of numbers sufficient to maintain internal order and prevent border clashes.

(12) The provisional councils would hold elections to a constituent assembly not later than 2 months after the British withdrawal. Arab and Jewish residents of Jerusalem who signify their intention of becoming citizens of either state would be entitled to vote.

To meet British objections, the recommendations were redrafted. The redraft, accompanied by a critique of "British policy, which has not been entirely helpful and which has made the work of our committee difficult," was approved Nov. 24 by the U.S. delegate.

The *ad hoc* committee's 2d subcommittee set up Oct. 23 submitted its proposals Nov. 19 on the basis of UNSCOP's minority report. The committee, headed by Sir Mohammed Zafrulla Khan of Pakistan, contended that the UN had no legal right to partition Palestine and recommended the establishment of a unitary Palestinian state as follows:

● A provisional Palestinian government would come into existence at the earliest possible date. Britain thereupon would begin to remove its forces and take no longer than a year to do so.

● The provisional government would suspend all immigration during this period and continue to enforce the existing land purchase regulations.

● The UN should come to some international agreement on the general problem of displaced Jews.

● The UN and all powers concerned should consult the International Court of Justice at The Hague on controversial issues involved in the mandate's execution. These included the Balfour Declaration.

● After a sufficient interval, Palestine should become a unitary sovereign state with a democratic constitution.

The *ad hoc* committee Nov. 24 rejected the 2d subcommittee's proposals, by 29-12 vote, with 14 abstentions and in the absence of Paraguay and the Philippines. Cuba joined the UN's 11 Moslem states in supporting the 2d subcommittee's proposals. The USSR and the U.S. voted against them, and India and Yugoslavia were among those states abstaining. The committee Nov. 25 approved its first subcommittee's partition plan by 25-13 vote, with 17 abstentions and the same 2 countries' delegates absent. The USSR and the U.S. voted in favor; Thailand joined those opposed, and Britain and France were among those abstaining.

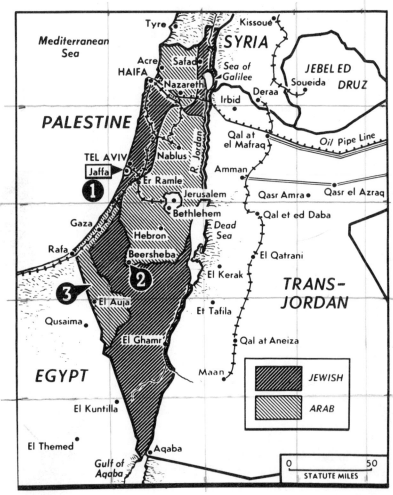

Wide World

Partition plan recommended by UN Special Committee on Palestine Nov. 25, 1947 and accepted by UN General Assembly vote Nov. 29. Under the plan, Jaffa (1) was to become an Arab enclave in the proposed Jewish state. Beersheba (2) in the Negev would also be Arab, as would a large Negev area (3) along the Egyptian frontier.

The final decision rested with the General Assembly, where a ⅔ majority of those voting was required to pass a resolution such as that favoring partition. The result of the voting in the *ad hoc* committee was that the supporters of partition were short of votes. It became known Nov. 27 that the Siamese delegate, who had voted against the partition resolution, had been dismissed by his government. On the same day the Philippines delegate, who had abstained in the committee, was reported to be wavering in favor of partition. Matters crystallized when 7 delegates who abstained Nov. 25 committed themselves; Belgium, France, Haiti, Liberia, Luxemburg, the Netherlands and New Zealand came out in favor of partition. It also became known that the representative of China would continue to abstain and that the Greek delegate, who had previously abstained, would vote against the resolution.

General Assembly Votes for Partition

The General Assembly, meeting in plenary session, voted Nov. 29, 1967 to partition Palestine into 2 independent states, Arab and Jewish. The voting had been originally scheduled for Nov. 27, but the French delegate called for a 24-hour delay in order to attempt a last-minute reconciliation of the conflicting standpoints. None took place.

Following the vote, the 6 Arab delegations (Egypt, Iraq, Lebanon, Saudi Arabia, Syria and Yemen) walked out of the Assembly. Faris el-Khouri of Syria declared that the UN had been "murdered."

The Assembly vote was: *For partition, 33*—Australia, Belgium, Bolivia, Brazil, Byelorussia, Canada, Costa Rica, Czechoslovakia, Denmark, Dominican Republic, Ecuador, France, Guatemala, Haiti, Iceland, Liberia, Luxemburg, the Netherlands, New Zealand, Nicaragua, Norway, Panama, Paraguay, Peru, Philippines, Poland, South Africa, the Soviet Union, Sweden, Ukraine, United States, Uruguay and Venezuela. *Against partition, 13*—Afghanistan, Cuba, Egypt, Greece, India, Iraq, Lebanon, Pakistan, Persia, Saudi Arabia, Syria, Turkey and Yemen. *Abstaining, 10*—Argentina, Chile, China, Colombia, El Salvador, Ethiopia, Honduras, Mexico, the United Kingdom and Yugoslavia. *Absent* —Thailand.

The General Assembly also appointed a 5-man UN commission, made up of representatives of Bolivia, Czechoslovakia, Denmark, Panama and the Philippines, to go to Palestine under the authority of the Security Council to take over the country's administration from the British and, after Britain's withdrawal, to transfer power to the Arab and Jewish provisional governments.

The UN Trusteeship Council Dec. 2 set up a 6-man subcommittee of delegates from Australia, China, France, Great Britain, Mexico and the U.S. to draw up plans for the internationalization of the city of Jerusalem. The council named as chairman Benjamin O. Gerig, professor of government at Haverford College, Pa. Dr. Ralph Bunche, 43, director of the UN Secretariat's Trusteeship Division, was appointed Dec. 3 as permanent head of the UN personnel to accompany the UN Commission to Palestine.

The partition resolution designated these areas for the 2 states in Palestine:

Jewish state in Palestine—The new Jewish state would have 3 areas:

● Eastern Galilee (with Safad and Tiberias as its most important towns), which would lie west of Jordan and include all but the eastern shore of Lake Tiberias and the greater part of the Valley of Jezreel.

● The industrialized Mediterranean coastal strip, which ran east from Tulkarm to Haifa across the Plain of Esdraelon in the north and around Rehovoth in the south; it included Tel Aviv and the coastal Plain of Sharon.

● The Negev desert region, which ran to the Gulf of Aqaba, excluding the Gaza Strip.

Palestinian Arab state—The state for the Arabs of Palestine, then expected to be the 8th independent Arab nation in the Middle East, also would consist of 3 areas:

● Western Galilee, which would include the town of Nazareth, the port of Acre and the Mediterranean seaboard south of the Lebanese border.

● Central Palestine, from the Jordan River and the Dead Sea to the Jewish border in the coastal sector, which would make up the greater part; its chief towns: Hebron, Jericho, Nablus, Lydda, Ramleh and Beersheba; on the Mediterranean the port of Jaffa, next to Tel Aviv, would form an Arab enclave in the Jewish state.

● In southern Palestine, a great part of the Negev along the Egyptian border plus the Gaza Strip.

Jewish & Arab Reactions

The UN's decision to create a Jewish state was greeted with dancing and singing in the streets of Tel Aviv and Jerusalem and with rejoicing by Jews in New York, Belgrade and Vienna, in the displaced persons' camps in Germany and in the detention camps in Cyprus. Tens of thousands of Jews sang or listened to the new national anthem (*Hatikvah — The Promise*) and saw the blue-and-white banner with the *Mogen David* (Shield of David), symbol of the new state, fly from buildings throughout the Jewish areas of Palestine.

The Palestinian Arab Higher Committee Nov. 30 passed a resolution in Jerusalem rejecting the UN decision to partition the country. It ordered a 3-day general strike by all Arabs throughout Palestine starting Dec. 2 and called on all Palestinian Arabs to boycott Jewish stores, businesses and places of employment. The Higher Committee also resolved to adopt "necessary preliminary measures for carrying out a non-cooperation policy in preparation for declaring a state of emergency in Palestine." Dr. Hussein Khalidi, secretary of the Arab Higher Committee, called the UN's decision of Nov. 29 tantamount to a "declaration of war."

The partition decision evoked angry protests everywhere in the Arab world. There were violent anti-American, anti-Soviet and anti-UN demonstrations in Aden, Egypt, Iraq, Jordan and Lebanon, and vandals burnt down synagogues and Jewish homes in Aleppo, Syria.

BIRTH OF THE JEWISH STATE

An assembly of *yishuv* representatives in Tel Aviv proclaimed the creation of the state of Israel May 14, 1948 just a few hours before Britain's 25-year mandate ended. The British mandate expired at midnight. The new country was the 3d Jewish state in history to be established in Palestine.

The Vaad Leumi, assembled in Tel Aviv, issued the following proclamation May 14, 1948 to announce the creation of the new state of Israel:

THE PROCLAMATION OF INDEPENDENCE

IN THE LAND OF ISRAEL the Jewish people came into being. In this Land was shaped their spiritual, religious and national character. Here they lived in sovereign independence. Here they created a culture of national and universal import, and gave to the world the eternal Book of Books.

Exiled by force, still the Jewish people kept faith with their Land in all the countries of their dispersion, steadfast in their prayer and hope to return and here revive their political freedom.

Fired by this attachment of history and tradition, the Jews in every generation strove to renew their roots in the ancient Homeland, and in recent generations they came home in their multitudes.

Veteran pioneers and defenders, and newcomers braving blockade, they made the wilderness bloom, revived their Hebrew tongue, and built villages and towns. They founded a thriving society, master of its own economy and culture, pursuing peace but able to defend itself, bringing the blessing of progress to all the inhabitants of the Land, dedicated to the attainment of sovereign independence.

In 1897 the First Zionist Congress met at the call of Theodor Herzl, seer of the vision of the Jewish State, and gave public voice to the right of the Jewish people to national restoration in their Land.

232

This right was acknowledged in the Balfour Declaration on 2 November 1917 and confirmed in the Mandate of the League of Nations, which accorded international validity to the historical connection between the Jewish people and the Land of Israel, and to their right to re-establish their National Home.

The holocaust that in our time destroyed millions of Jews in Europe again proved beyond doubt the compelling need to solve the problem of Jewish homelessness and dependence by the renewal of the Jewish State in the Land of Israel, which would open wide the gates of the Homeland to every Jew and endow the Jewish people with the status of a nation with equality of rights within the family of nations.

Despite every hardship, hindrance and peril, the remnant that survived the grim Nazi slaughter in Europe, together with Jews from other countries, pressed on with their exodus to the Land of Israel and continued to assert their right to a life of dignity, freedom and honest toil in the Homeland of their people.

In the Second World War, the Jewish community in the Land of Israel played its full part in the struggle of the nations championing freedom and peace against the Nazi forces of evil. Its war effort and the lives of its soldiers won it the right to be numbered among the founding peoples of the United Nations.

On 29 November 1947 the General Assembly of the United Nations adopted a resolution calling for the establishment of a Jewish State in the Land of Israel, and required the inhabitants themselves to take all measures necessary on their part to carry out the resolution. This recognition by the United Nations of the right of the Jewish people to establish their own State is irrevocable.

It is the natural right of the Jewish people, like any other people, to control their own destiny in their sovereign State.

ACCORDINGLY WE, the members of the National Council, representing the Jewish people in the Land of Israel and the Zionist Movement, have assembled on the day of the termination of the British Mandate for Palestine, and, by virtue of our natural and historic right and of the resolution of the General Assembly of the United Nations, do hereby proclaim the establishment of a Jewish State in the Land of Israel—the State of Israel.

WE RESOLVE that, from the moment the Mandate ends, at midnight on the Sabbath, the sixth of Iyar 5708, the fifteenth day of May 1948, until the establishment of the duly elected authorities of the State in accordance with a Constitution to be adopted by the Elected Constituent Assembly not later than 1 October 1948, the National Council shall act as the Provisional Council of State, and its executive arm, the National Administration, shall constitute the Provisional Government of the Jewish State, and the name of that State shall be Israel.

THE STATE OF ISRAEL will be open to Jewish immigration and the ingathering of exiles. It will devote itself to developing the Land for the good of all its inhabitants.

It will rest upon foundations of liberty, justice and peace as envisioned by the Prophets of Israel. It will maintain complete equality of social and political rights for all its citizens, without distinction of creed, race or sex. It will guarantee freedom of religion and conscience, of language, education and culture. It will safeguard the Holy Places of all religions. It will be loyal to the principles of the United Nations Charter.

THE STATE OF ISRAEL will be prepared to cooperate with the organs and representatives of the United Nations in carrying out the General Assembly resolution of 29 November 1947, and will work for the establishment of the economic union of the whole Land of Israel.

WE APPEAL to the United Nations to assist the Jewish people in the building of their State, and to admit the State of Israel into the family of nations.

EVEN AMIDST the violent attacks launched against us for months past, we call upon the sons of the Arab people dwelling in Israel to keep the peace and to play their part in building the State on the basis of full and equal citizenship and due representation in all its institutions, provisional and permanent.

WE EXTEND the hand of peace and good-neighbourliness to all the States around us and to their peoples, and we call upon them to cooperate in mutual helpfulness with the independent Jewish nation in its Land. The State of Israel is prepared to make its contribution in a concerted effort for the advancement of the entire Middle East.

WE CALL upon the Jewish people throughout the Diaspora to join forces with us in immigration and construction, and to be at our right hand in the great endeavour to fulfil the age-old longing for the redemption of Israel.

WITH TRUST IN THE ROCK OF ISRAEL, we set our hands in witness to this Proclamation, at this session of the Provisional Council of State, on the soil of the Homeland, in the city of Tel Aviv, this Sabbath eve, the fifth day of Iyar, 5708, the fourteenth day of May, nineteen hundred and forty-eight.

Arabs Attack

7 Arab states already had declared war against the new state May 13 in Damascus. As the mandate officially expired, Israel was at once invaded by Egypt from the south, the Transjordanian Arab Legion from the east and Lebanese and Syrian troops from the north. The other 3 belligerents, Iraq, Saudi Arabia and Yemen, assumed a war footing.

Just 7 months after the partition resolution was passed, the last British troops left Haifa June 30, 1948.

INDEX

Note: Arab names beginning with the prefixes *al-*, *el-*, *as-*, etc. are indexed alphabetically as though the name started with the letter following the *al-* or *el-*, etc. For example, Khaled al-Hakim is indexed thus: HAKIM, Khaled al-.